Melville

Melville

by

Edward H. Rosenberry

Professor of English
University of Delaware

Routledge & Kegan Paul
London, Henley and Boston

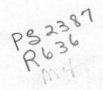

First published in 1979
by Routledge & Kegan Paul Ltd
39 Store Street,
London WC1E 7DD,
Broadway House,
Newtown Road,
Henley-on-Thames,
Oxon RG9 1EN and
9 Park Street,
Boston, Mass. 02108, USA
Set in Compugraphic Garamond
and printed in Great Britain by
Ebenezer Baylis and Son, Limited
The Trinity Press,
Worcester, and London

British Library Cataloguing in Publication Data

Rosenberry, Edward Hoffman
Melville.
1. Melville, Herman – Criticism and interpretation
813'.3   PS2387   78–40838

ISBN 0–7100–8989–9

To Elizabeth

Contents

Illustrations

Preface

Herman Melville, once the forgotten man of American letters, now enjoys a rare celebrity shared only by those few writers in every language who have not only enriched a culture but also enlarged the mythology of a people. Since the resurgence of interest in his work in the 1920s, no American author has received more critical attention or proved more resistant to historical consensus. Even his masterpiece, *Moby-Dick*, for all its classic status, remains an interpretive adventure for every reader. Fifty years of intensive study seem only to have heightened the challenge to students of Melville's life and works to offer new versions of Ariadne's thread to readers yet to follow his labyrinthine ways.

The present effort aims, if not to make the crooked straight, at least to make the rough places plain. The author and the books he wrote are seen against their background of time and place and then described in such a way as to define possibility without foreclosing response. The account of Melville's work is essentially chronological, with the exception of *The Confidence-Man* and *Billy Budd*, which are treated out of their precise historical sequence in order to place them in an artistic context better suited to illustrating the range of Melville's literary accomplishment. This range is suggested in the chapter headings, which group the writings in generic categories.

To facilitate reading of the text I have dispensed with footnotes. Wherever necessary, quotations from Melville's writings are identified parenthetically in the text. Dated biographical and epistolary materials are readily traced in the day-dated *Melville Log*, ed. Jay Layda (New York, 1951) or *The Letters of Herman Melville*, ed. Merrell R. Davis and Richard H. Gilman (New Haven, 1960). The remaining background of authority and reference for each chapter is assembled in the Bibliographical Notes at the end of the book.

No amount of documentation can fully demonstrate the debt of an undertaking like this to all who have written on Melville during the half century of his revival. And no footnote has been devised to acknowledge what a teacher owes to his students or a scholar to his colleagues. However, special thanks are due to John A. Munroe and the late Ernest J. Moyne, who gave valuable advice on the historical parts of my manuscript.

Chronology

1819   HM born, New York City, August 1.
1830   Family moves to Albany, New York.
1832   Father dies bankrupt.
1837   HM teaches school, Pittsfield, Massachusetts.
1839   HM sails as crew member on packet *St Lawrence*, New York–Liverpool.
1840   HM visits uncle Thomas Melvill, Galena, Illinois.
1841   HM sails on whaling ship *Acushnet* out of Fairhaven, January 3; cruises around Cape Horn and through Galapagos Islands.
1842   HM deserts ship in Marquesas, July 9; signs on *Lucy Ann*, August 9; leaves ship at Tahiti, September 24; signs on whaler *Charles and Henry*, November.
1843   HM arrives Sandwich Islands (Hawaii), April; signs on frigate *United States* as ordinary seaman, August 17.
1844   HM discharged from navy at Port of Boston, October 14.
1846   *Typee* published (London: Murray, February; New York: Wiley and Putnam, March).
1847   *Omoo* published (London: Murray, March; New York: Harper's, May). HM marries Elizabeth Shaw, August 4.
1849   Son Malcolm born, February. *Mardi* published (London: Bentley, March; New York: Harper's, April). *Redburn* published (London: September; New York: November). HM visits England and Europe, October to January.
1850   *White-Jacket* published (London: January; New York: March). HM moves to Pittsfield; meets Hawthorne, August 5; publishes 'Hawthorne and His Mosses,' August 17 and 24; purchases 'Arrowhead,' September. Hawthorne's *The Scarlet Letter* published.

1851   Son Stanwix born, October. *Moby-Dick* published (London: October, as *The Whale*; New York: November). Hawthorne publishes *The House of the Seven Gables* and moves from Lenox.

1852   *Pierre* published (New York: August; London: November). Hawthorne's *The Blithedale Romance* published.

1853   Daughter Elizabeth born, May. HM begins writing stories for magazines.

1854   *Israel Potter* published serially.

1855   Daughter Frances born, March. *Israel Potter* published (New York: March; London: May).

1856   *The Piazza Tales* published. HM sails for Europe and the Middle East, October; visits Hawthorne in Liverpool *en route*.

1857   *The Confidence-Man* published (New York and London: April). HM returns from travels, May.

1858–60 HM makes three lecture tours.

1863   Family moves from Pittsfield to New York, October.

1864   Hawthorne dies.

1866   *Battle-Pieces and Aspects of the War* published, August. HM appointed Customs Inspector No. 75, Port of New York, December.

1867   Son Malcolm dies of self-inflicted wound, September.

1876   *Clarel* published, June.

1885   HM retires from Customs post, December.

1886   Son Stanwix dies, February.

1888   *John Marr and Other Sailors* privately printed. HM begins work on *Billy Budd*.

1891   *Timoleon* privately printed. HM dies, September 28.

1

The Time of Melville

Sometime in the course of Herman Melville's obscure middle years, when the best work of his youth was finished and seemingly forgotten, he read Matthew Arnold's 'The Function of Criticism at the Present Time' and underlined the observation that 'for the creation of a master-work of literature two powers must concur, the power of the man and the power of the moment.' In another essay in the same volume he also marked a quotation from Wordsworth's *Prelude* describing 'a mind for-ever/Voyaging through strange seas of Thought, alone.' During the long years of neglect and misunderstanding which he had to endure, Mel-ville's appreciation of the loneliness implicit in any great effort of imagination was no doubt sharpened to some poignancy, but as a working author he knew well enough that the creative intellect, as Arnold insisted, 'must find itself amidst the order of ideas.' Writing of Hawthorne at the height of his own powers, Melville had acknowledged both aspects of the artist's life: 'Great genuises are part of the times; they themselves are the times.'

Because he called himself 'a pondering man' and confessed to being a notorious miner of old books, commentators who revived interest in Melville following the First World War described him as 'mariner and mystic' or 'sailor, philosopher, and poet.' He was all of these things; but he was first a New Yorker and a citizen of the United States throughout a lifetime that nearly spanned the nineteenth century. The matrix of his experience was the nation of which he was a part during the era of its most explosive growth, its most traumatic episode, and its most decisive molding of the communal character. Melville's books have frequently been interpreted as an allegory of his inner life; they are no less an allegory of the nation's life, moving collectively – often singly – from youth to age, from innocence to experience, from comedy to tragedy. The insular idyll of *Typee* and *Omoo*, mirroring the infancy of a culture, expands to the dream-world of *Mardi*, projecting possibilities to a global horizon and beyond. The dream then sharpens to painful reality in the circumstantial adventures of *Redburn* and *White-Jacket*; and the mightiest confrontation in American literature, the sinking of the *Pequod* by the great white whale, climaxes *Moby-Dick*, written in the year of the last fateful maneuvers of North and South before their irreconcilable hostility threatened to sink the ship of state. In *Pierre*, a tale of bitterness and frustration, a remembered pastoral peace succumbs to dark urban forebodings, more fully realized in the Wall Street tragedy of 'Bartleby' and the bleak Dickensian decline of *Israel Potter*. Following the symbolic portrayal of a world divided by slavery in 'Benito Cereno,' the Civil War itself is directly chronicled in *Battle-Pieces*, and the cynical hypocrisies of Reconstruction together with the materialism of the 'Gilded Age' are sardonically prophesied in *The Confidence-Man*. Finally, it is the spiritual testing, the agonizing self-appraisal of an older and sadder America that is reflected in the penitential verses of *Clarel* and in *Billy Budd*'s enigmatic parable of the wrenching national dilemma of freedom and restraint. If historians have tended to place Melville with Whitman among America's most nationalistic writers, it is because he not only pictured the face of his world but also saw behind it the root problem of mediating somehow between – as historian Francis Parkman put it – 'two vicious extremes, democracy and absolute authority.'

The paradoxical tendency of American romantic writers to be at once nationalistic and introspective is partly explained, perhaps partly conditioned, by the predominantly inward character of national development in the century following the achievement of independence. Once her footing with Britain was established in 1812 and her international posture defined by the Monroe Doctrine a decade later, the United States settled in to a long period of internal growth and change largely unaffected by fateful concerns outside her own borders, or beyond her nearest neighbors, until caught up in the global upheavals of the twentieth century. A vigorous and unbroken expansion of trade in every ocean steadily enhanced the American position among the nations. As rising power kept aggression at bay, the nearly empty land slowly filled with Europe's overflow, and the frontier retreated like a battle-line across the continent. Growth was the first principle of the new nation, but it was a principle according to nature, not a plan.

Few Americans in those first heady decades of the nineteenth century saw anything but gain in the conquest of the wilderness, the exploitation of resources, and the multiplication and enlargement of cities. The closing of the western frontier, an accomplished fact by the time of Melville's death in 1891, seemed as remote as interplanetary flight to any who bothered to contemplate such hypothetical matters at the time of his birth in 1819. In that year the legendary Daniel Boone, whose frontier had been the forests of Kentucky, was still living, the White House was still commonly referred to as 'the Palace,' the first steam-powered ship crossed the Atlantic, and William Ellery Channing, spokes-man for a religion of optimism, delivered a liberating blast against the gloomy and confining faith of the pilgrim fathers. The federal govern-ment was in the hands of its fifth president, but all of Monroe's prede-cessors except Washington himself were still alive. Eight new states had joined the original thirteen, making a total which would be more than doubled when Melville died. (He pictured thirty in *Mardi* in 1849, and by the next year California had outmoded his fable.) At the time of his birth such eastern states as Kentucky, Tennessee, and Mississippi were regarded as western, and the Mississippi River was the absolute outpost of progress. Within the seven decades of his lifetime a national popula-tion of nine million increased exactly sevenfold; the European immigra-tion that was to contribute so much to the character as well as the size of the United States quadrupled in the 1830s, tripled in the next decade, and doubled again in the 1850s to pass the one million mark. The port of New York, at the Melville family doorstep, saw the bulk of this influx, especially as fed by the great Erie Canal, which made numberless jobs in the building, and which after its opening in 1825 formed the main artery of commerce to inland markets until superseded by the railroads in mid-century.

When James Fenimore Cooper began his great chronicle of the frontier in the 'Leatherstocking Tales,' he could look back toward the winning of independence in 1783, only shortly before his own birth, and observe with accuracy that a mere forty years had elapsed 'since this whole territory was a wilderness.' In its four decades of statehood, he noted in *The Pioneers* (1822), New York's population

has spread itself over five degrees of latitude and seven of longitude, and has swelled to the powerful number of nearly a million and a half, who are maintained in abundance, and can look forward to ages before the evil day must arrive when their possessions will become unequal to their wants.

Although Cooper himself did not live to see this general optimism over-shadowed by events, the drama of Melville's older America was to be

3

much concerned with the closing of that hypothetical gap. While the euphoria lasted, it was fed as with dry tinder by seemingly limitless quantities of space and money. Predictably, most of the money was generated by the space, in land development, transportation, and merchandise; and the space in turn became farms and towns and new states as the money poured in. A few unlucky merchants like Melville's father, who died a bankrupt in the importing business, faced ruin in the speculative jungle of the young republic, but the great majority of enterprising citizens justified the rising myth of open opportunity in a new country, and many made fortunes sufficient to found permanent commercial dynasties.

The frontier, popularly pictured as a line of trees darkening westward at the edge of the last clearing, in fact extended both east and west, over sea as well as land, and possessed a dynamic character only partially to be understood in terms of geography. In its landward thrust it moved at first toward the opening of arteries without which isolated farms and mines and trading posts could never coalesce into a nation, or the conquest of the western plains and mountains be contemplated. By 1819 the essential arteries were defined. Linking north and south was the great Mississippi River, cutting 2,000 miles through the heart of the country and needing only the steamboat, newly invented, to realize its potential as the greatest inland waterway in the world. Linking east with west would be, at its completion, the Erie Canal, providing cheap barge service over 350 miles from the Great Lakes to Albany at the head of the navigable Hudson River above New York.

The history of post-Civil War America has been in part the history of increasing speed and efficiency of transportation, starting with the railroads, but each gain has seen a concomitant loss in the cultural forms that accrue to any activity that people share together over sufficient periods of time. The society of the rivers and canals was American society in slow motion: 'one cosmopolitan and confident tide,' as Melville pictured it in *The Confidence-Man*: 'Natives of all sorts, and foreigners; men of business and men of pleasure; parlor men and backwoodsmen; farm-hunters and fame-hunters; . . . gold-hunters, buffalo-hunters, bee-hunters, . . . and still keener hunters after all these hunters.' Together with the rivermen immortalized by Mark Twain, the bargemen and 'canawlers' who gave this shifting society its distinctive flavor were a colorful lot, brawling, boasting, inventing feats and language as outrageous as anything spawned in the camaraderie of the north woods or the western mining camps. Some of this wild and rootless breed, along with fresh-water sailors from the Great Lakes, found their way to the higher adventure of the Atlantic whaling fleet or merchant marine.

Steelkilt, the quarrelsome crewman of the *Town-Ho* in *Moby-Dick*, was one of these wandering adventurers, and Herman Melville himself was typical of the countless impecunious city boys and farm boys who gravitated to that other frontier in the booming years of America's maritime supremacy. Young Melville sampled both of its major enterprises: the freight and passenger service between New York and Liverpool, and the whale fishery in the Pacific out of a Massachusetts port. In its commercial development the United States has had some of the character of an island, trading principally with the ports of Europe and Asia, with the added disadvantage of having her coasts virtually inaccessible to each other. Even under the most urgent motivation in the nation's history, the Gold Rush of 1849, the 3,000-mile overland journey to California was fraught with such epic difficulty that many eastern fortune-hunters booked passage around Cape Horn in a 15,000-mile voyage that might run a month longer than a trip to China. But the enormous challenges of isolation could only be a spur and not a deterrent to the 'Yankee enterprise' on which the young nation prided itself. It was a driving force based partly on the Puritan work ethic which from the earliest settlement has been the mainspring of progress in the New World, but owing something of its energy as well to a piratical love of adventure which in its very condition of running across the Puritan warp has added color and variety to the essential toughness of the national fabric. Benjamin Franklin, the quintessential American of the formative years, stayed on land and built his success on a model later popularized by Horatio Alger; but he showed the romantic strain, even in a pragmatic nature, when he recalled in his Autobiography the 'strong inclination for the Sea' that heightened his boyish disgust for candle-making in his father's shop: 'My dislike to the Trade continuing, my Father was under Apprehensions that if he did not find one for me more agreeable, I should break away and get to Sea, as his son Josiah had done to his great vexation.'

Many a family tree in the springtime of the republic grew sailors along with merchants and magistrates, and flourished equally – as the title of one of Cooper's popular novels had it – *Afloat and Ashore*. The appeal of that tale was broadened and its story balanced by portraying two young heroes who start by running away to sea and end, one as a ship master and one as a lawyer. The most gifted recreator of the American past, Nathaniel Hawthorne, symbolizes in his own descent this divided heritage: his great-great-grandfather was a judge, whose fame is forever linked with the witchcraft trials over which he presided in Salem in 1692; his father, a sea captain who left Hawthorne's mother one of the hundreds of widows forming a substantial stratum of Salem society. Salem in the nineteenth century was not the leader in fishing that Gloucester was, or the leader in whaling that Nantucket and New Bedford were, or the 'hub of the universe' that the China trade made of Boston before the Civil War; however, Salem was a microcosm of these activities and remained at least the center of the Sumatra pepper trade until 1844, when Hawthorne arrived at the Custom House there in time to chronicle the port's decline. A decade earlier the picture of prospering Salem preserved by English visitor Harriet Martineau may be taken as representative of the culture of seafaring America and the character of the men who were formed by it:

Salem, Mass, is a remarkable place. This 'city of peace' will be better known hereafter for its commerce than for its witch tragedy. It has a population of fourteen thousand and more wealth in proportion to its population than perhaps any town in the world. Its commerce is speculative but vast and successful. It is a frequent circumstance that a ship goes out without a cargo for a voyage around the world. In such a case the captain puts his elder children to school, takes his wife and younger children and starts for some semi-barbarous place where he procures some odd kind of cargo which he exchanges with advantage for another somewhere else; and so goes trafficking around the world, bringing home a freight of the highest value.

These enterprising merchants of Salem are hoping to appropriate a large share of the whale fishery and their ships are penetrating the northern ice. They speak of Fayal and the Azores as if they were close at hand. The fruits of the Mediterranean are on every table. They have a large acquaintance at Cairo. They know Napoleon's grave at St Helena, and have wild tales to tell of Mozambique and Madagascar, and stores of ivory to show from there. They speak of the power of the king of Muscat, and are sensible of the riches of the southeast coast of Arabia. Anybody will give you anecdotes from Canton and descriptions of the Society and Sandwich Islands. They often slip up the western coast of their two continents, bringing furs from the back regions of their own wide land, glance up at the Andes on their return; double Cape

Horn, touch at the ports of Brazil and Guiana, look about them in the West Indies, feeling almost at home there, and land some fair morning in Salem and walk home as if they had done nothing remarkable.

It was a common saying among later generations of Americans that 'there are better ships nowadays, but no better men.' The reason there were better ships, of course, is that they were designed and built by visionary craftsmen like Donald McKay, whose masterpieces in wood and canvas were the envy of the seafaring nations. Certainly the judgment applied with equal force to the sailors it was intended to praise and to the imaginative entrepreneurs who sent them around the globe – men like Frederick Tudor, who made a fortune peddling ice to a world that didn't know what it was. Samuel Eliot Morison, noting the shipment of palm-leaf hats to the Sandwich Islands, has remarked that 'Yankee merchants would carry coals to Newcastle, if Newcastle wanted them!' The early years of the nineteenth century were properly thought of as a golden age, though it was soon enough to slip into a gilded one, and even the golden days were shadowed by an illicit but profitable slave trade, comparable only to the narcotics trade in our own time, and by a number of intrinsic evils in the symbiotic relationship between those who owned and commanded the ships and those who worked them with their hands.

Two of democracy's major faults, in the geological sense of that term, showed themselves with a laboratory clarity and persistence in America's vigorous maritime life. The more subtle and irremediable of these was economic. The maritime world demonstrated at least as well as any other that money is power, and that 'to everyone that hath shall be given, . . . but from him that hath not shall be taken away even that which he hath.' For owners and investors, and close behind them the masters of their ships, the profits accruing to such high-risk capital were enormous, often 100 per cent, sometimes 200 per cent, 300 per cent or more. One major firm in the China trade, N. L. & G. Griswold, were popularly referred to by their initials as 'No Loss, Great Gain.' By the iron law of uncontrolled capital such returns created goods and jobs and a great deal of self-perpetuating wealth to keep the cycle going; by the same law it accomplished these effects with the minimum benefit to the men in the forecastle, who served their perilous time before the mast with little but exercise, bad food, and an occasional orgy to look forward to. On whaling ships a semblance of democracy was imparted to the process by the *lay* system, whereby each man contracted for a set share (lay) of the profit of a voyage; but the appearance of proportional sharing only made the actual exploitation more cynical, and the inequity was often compounded to the verge of slavery by the levying of hidden charges that could bring a man home from a three-year voyage in debt to his employer. The 'company store' syndrome in mines and factories was to repeat this oppressive pattern in countless American communities throughout the century.

The assumptions that so deeply divided the seaman from his masters revealed themselves not only in how he was paid but in how he was treated. The structure of command aboard even a badly disciplined ship presupposed, then as now, a total and unquestioning obedience to the will of one man, however mistaken one might believe (or know) him to be. It is of course axiomatic that this must be so if emergencies are to be met and objectives achieved. 'Though an army be all volunteers, martial law must prevail,' Melville wrote in *Mardi*; and his context extends the principle to civil government itself, which in order to function at all must act by delegated authority. What was too often lacking in the maritime society was moral accountability, of the sort that can derive only from enlightened social legislation, rapid and dependable communications, and, above all, the humanity on the part of those in authority to remember that, as Burns insisted in another divided society, 'a man's a man for a' that.' The isolation of sailing ships was an ideal medium for the corruptions to which absolute power is prone, and from which there may be no redress but mutiny. In the wake of revolutions asserting the rights of man on two continents, these little floating monarchies were still free to tyrannize their populace with starvation wages, sweatshop conditions, sometimes (in the navy, until 1850) the threat of flogging, and, universally, contempt or condescension. The life afloat focussed the real and potential ills of society as with a burning glass.

It is hard to see, in retrospect, what drew free Americans to the cramped and fetid forecastles of whaling ships, where they knew they must live confined for years with meager subsistence and negligible expectations. They knew that their days and months would pass, like a soldier's, in unpredictable alternation between periods of dead inactivity, punctuated perhaps by a 'scrimshaw' or whalebone-carving project for a waiting wife or mother, and sudden paroxysms of activity so violent as to threaten life, limb, and even the ship itself. Yet streams of men of every race and condition signed on for such voyages, impelled by desperation, or lured by the excitement of hunting the biggest game alive, or simply

8

responding in a peculiarly American way to the almost mystical challenge of a reckless trade, an open horizon, and the sea itself. If thousands of them sought temporary respite by 'jumping ship' in the South Seas, they generally returned in some other bottom, confirmed in a fraternity of unique craftsmanship, shared risk, and an unmistakable pride in their product, which was (as Melville liked to point out) 'the light of the world.' The aristocracy of this brotherhood were the Nantucket men, who scorned any prey less than the great sperm whale, yielding the finest oil and wax, and who so impressed St Jean de Crèvecoeur with their exemplary industry and independence that he devoted nearly half of his *Letters from an American Farmer* to drawing their collective portrait as a New World model in answer to his master question, 'What Is an American?' But change and decay are the order of the world: just as Nantucket's sand bar eventually silted up her harbor, so the oil that had lighted and lubricated the nation gave way to petroleum, whalebone vanished along with the more stringent formalities of ladies' fashions, and the challenge and beauty of sail retreated before the efficiency of steam.

The average American, of course, did not – and does not – look upon change as decay, but as progress and development. The notion that Old is Bad and New is Good is a popular prejudice which Americans have frequently seemed to erect into a principle. This principle and its corollary, More is Better, are among the putative products of the frontier, whether on sea or land. Conservation and restraint are not easily learned in the presence of plenty, and America in its first century was a veritable cornucopia, not merely of promises, but of gifts ripe for the taking. It is not surprising that in an undeveloped continent and its open waters every settler and explorer grasped what he could reach, and the federal government more ponderously followed suit. No activities are closer to the heart of the national myth or more deeply ingrained in the national character than 'moving West' and 'staking a claim.' From time to time some race of the multitudes, such as the Gold Rush to California in 1849 or the Homesteaders' land rush into Oklahoma in 1889, has raised this process to a public spectacle; but as long as a frontier remained every young man in need of a fresh start was urged to 'Go West' to make his fortune. When this sort of adventuring was practiced on a national scale it was known as 'Manifest Destiny,' even or especially if it involved political and military persuasion, as in the acquisition of Texas and California from Mexico. The whalers, competing for their free-for-all catch in international waters, had a telling image for the law of expansion: every whale

9

in the ocean was either a 'fast-fish' or a 'loose-fish,' depending on whether it was at the moment in the physical possession of someone from whom it could not conveniently be stolen or wrested.

To the extent that expansion and aggrandizement are expressions of simple greed, they bespeak in American history only a universal human failing for which democracy has no cure. The unremitting tug-of-war between slave states and free states throughout the first half of the nineteenth century insured the exercise of primitive motives in much of the political development of the country, and the prospect of speculative fortunes accounts for much of the rest. Still, a thread of idealism runs through the process, unifying it on some sturdier principle and offering to redeem it for the nation's anthems and statues. American patriotism, though often enough a mask for self-interest, had its well-spring in a dream of the pilgrim fathers, for whom political philosophy was a consideration secondary to the overriding obligation to establish a New Jerusalem in the west as witness to a divine plan for the regeneration of mankind. Spokesmen for the public conscience therefore stressed, as a characteristic tract of 1841 phrased it, 'God's Hand in America.' The secular symbols fell into place behind the biblical, headed by the patriarchal figure of George Washington, later joined by 'Father Abraham,' and, prominently enshrined beneath the eagle and the flag, the Declaration of Independence as the national Decalogue. The date of its enunciation assumed a sacred importance, and the deaths of two former presidents on July 4, 1826, was as impressive to the nation as a comet in the sky. Historians like George Bancroft and poets like Walt Whitman interpreted the democratic faith to and for the country with dignity and fervor, and gave a note of credibility to overblown conceptions of a 'Promised Land' and a 'Chosen People.'

The Virgilian motto on the Great Seal of the United States, *Novus Ordo Seclorum*, makes clear that the founding fathers believed in earnest that they had created something new under the sun. For this belief the most revealing formulation was that of Ralph Waldo Emerson, a spokesman of oracular standing, who divided the forces of society into 'the Party of the Past' and 'the Party of the Future.' However vital the heritage that linked Americans to their past, there was never the slightest doubt that the United States saw itself, in the era of its greatest expansion, as the Party of the Future. That this youthful conviction, confirmed by success, should have expressed itself in ostentatious self-praise and invidious comparisons with the Old World is hardly surprising. Even tempered by biblical imagery, the pride of chauvinism

10

pictured the nation in such popular verse as that of Mrs L. H. Sigourney as 'a lonely ark, that rid'st / A tossing deluge, dark with history's wrecks,' while abroad 'A mighty wind / Doth shake the palaces of ancient time.' 'There is dry rot in all the main timbers of the Old World,' a Yankee skipper told Shelley and Trelawney in Leghorn in 1822, 'and none of you will do any good until you are docked, refitted, and annexed to the New.' To the American the world was a coin with two faces. On its back side he saw what Senator Stephen A. Douglas described in 1851: 'Europe is antiquated, decrepit, tottering on the verge of dissolution. It is a vast graveyard.' But turn the coin, and, as a Dickens American announces to Martin Chuzzlewit, fresh from London: 'You will see the sun shine *here*!' As late as 1884 the English poet James Thomson wrote in *A Voice from the Nile*, 'I think we must forgive the Americans a good deal of vulgarity and arrogance for some generations yet.'

Steadfast Dodge, one of Fenimore Cooper's solemn clowns, gave it as his opinion in *Home As Found* that 'God never intended an American to kneel.' Cooper's novel, published in 1838, anatomizes the national era to which President Andrew Jackson (1829–37) gave his name, and it provides for the Age of Jackson the kind of corrosive caricature that the post-war years of Grant (1869–77) were to receive in Mark Twain's *The Gilded Age*. Exercising a cosmopolitan perspective he despaired of finding in his myopic countrymen, Cooper prefaced his tale with the statement that

> the American nation is a great nation, in some particulars the greatest the world ever saw . . . ; but we are also equally ready to concede, that it is very far behind the most polished nations in various essentials, and chiefly that it is lamentably in arrears to its own avowed principles.

It remained for better writers than Cooper to penetrate the moral wilderness to which he only alludes, but his crude and caustic novel catches perfectly the provinciality of manners which was the face of Jacksonian America and at least an index of its heart. At heart Americans may have viewed themselves with a normal mixture of modesty and pride, but naïve or defensive expressions of those impulses turned them into subservience and pretension. Among Cooper's cartoon figures are both 'old' and 'young' Americans: 'the first distrusting everything native, . . . the second distrusting nothing, and least of all, itself.' Apart from ignoring challenge, which seems never to have been an American option, these

11

extremes are responses to be expected to such taunts from the British establishment as Sidney Smith's notorious query of 1820, 'Who reads an American book?' Writing in 1845, the year Herman Melville began his literary career, Cooper remarked in a footnote to *Satanstoe* that

> the American who could write a book – a real, live book – forty years since, was a sort of prodigy. . . . It is now the fashion to extol everything American, and from submitting to a degree that was almost abject, to the feeling of colonial dependency, the country is filled, today, with the most profound provincial self-admiration.

The 'young' American voices which Cooper scouted as most given to this callow puffery were in fact formally organized for that purpose under that very banner. Calling themselves 'Young America,' a lively group of minor literary talents banded together in New York in the late 1830s and 1840s to promote the native and the national in literature. They were activated in part by Jacksonian political liberalism, in part by the sort of cultural evangelism that found its most durable spokesmen in Emerson and Whitman. All were ardent Democrats – as opposed to Whigs – and they clustered in the pages of the *United States Magazine and Democratic Review*, edited by John L. O'Sullivan, originator of the slogan 'Manifest Destiny.' Predictably, their program of cultural advancement was too narrowly partisan and too shallowly gifted to have any broad or lasting effect. However, they attracted greater talents, among them Poe, Hawthorne, and Melville; and the general stir gave even genius a useful sense of national identity as it raised American artistic productivity to the urgency of an issue. Along with the patriotism that underlay the stridencies of Young America was a practical consideration as well: until international copyright laws were enacted in 1891, the year of Melville's death, to protect writers on both sides of the Atlantic, American authors labored under a competitive disadvantage to English authors, who could be reprinted in the United States without royalty payments. Although English authors could complain of piracy with equal justice, at least they were being published. The situation from the American point of view was fairly summarized by Evert Duyckinck, editor of the *Literary World* and a leader of the Young America group:

> It was felt that American authors were oppressed and driven out of the market by the state of the trade; the strong feeling of nationality in the Press was aroused; and it was determined, however unconsciously, that all the geese that should be produced this side of the Atlantic should be called swans.

This surge of nationalism in American letters, prompted as it was by an impulse to break away from conservative and traditional influences, took on a strong populist cast. Democracy was to be the master theme of the national literature, and the new breed of author was to be a 'man of the people.' The model for this new culture was political rather than literary. In the autumn of 1828 Andrew Jackson had been elected president in a water-shed campaign that had swept out of office John Quincy Adams, last of the line drawn from the New England or Virginia aristocracy, and that had installed in the highest office a Tennessee backwoodsman whose heroic exploits had earned him the sobriquet 'Old Hickory.' As the first of a legendary line of 'log cabin' presidents, Jackson dramatized and made institutional the myth of the untutored genius in American public life who drew his strength from nature and a congenital kinship with the common man. Both sources ran deep in national history and popular philosophy. The common man, that ubiquitous denominator of democratic society, was born in the revolutions that ushered in the nineteenth century and was raised for a time to the eminence of respect traditionally occupied by the privileged and the learned. The Nature to which he owed his unmediated powers was the conception of romantic philosophers and poets – Rousseau and Wordsworth, to head the list – in whose appealing scheme of values both wisdom and virtue are intuitive and the cultivated arts a mark of decadence if not of corruption. It is one of the ironies of the Jacksonian era that the anti-intellectualism inherent in populist politics should have received the unintentional endorsement of the many artists and intellectuals who supported the Democratic party, or at least defended the liberal ideals it represented to their minds.

Among the major writers of the day the coalition was more apparent than real, an accident of history which for a fruitful moment caused equalitarian theorists and practicing politicians to adopt the same compass course. Washington Irving's public career coincided in part with Jackson's administration, but the governmental positions he held, in London and Madrid, were diplomatic posts more suggestive of his essential Toryism than of any commitment to the new Democracy. Andrew Jackson, on his part, showed as little interest in Irving's patrician talents when in later years he recalled the dean of American letters as someone named 'Erwin' who was 'only fit to write a book and scarcely that.' Emerson's fundamental sympathy with equalitarian politics, abstract at best, was baffled by his blind admiration for the principal Whig ornament, Daniel Webster, and an equal and opposite

13

distaste for the uncultivated Jackson, whom he saw as 'a most unfit man
. . . doing the worst things.' Even more than Emerson, Henry Thoreau
espoused a purely hypothetical democracy, radical in its interpretation of
individual liberty and positively subversive in its contempt for governmental institutions. If the Transcendentalists stayed aloof from politics,
Cooper plunged into the maelstrom of partisan controversy and lost all
theoretical perspective in the heat of his personal embroilment, which
carried him unhappily from ardent liberalism to reactionary disillusionment. Bryant and Whitman were strong links between a Democratic
government and the reading public, but mainly as editors of leading
metropolitan newspapers rather than as poets. Bryant's verse was simply
apolitical, and Whitman's for all its social fervor, was largely incomprehensible to the very populace it celebrated. Hawthorne was a life-long
Democrat, even holding minor offices under several administrations, but
his only overt political act was to write a campaign biography for
Franklin Pierce, a personal friend who chanced to become president.
Whatever Jacksonian bias may be arguable in *The House of the Seven
Gables* was a substratum too subtle to qualify as advocacy. Melville, like
Hawthorne, was drawn by personal friendship – in his case with
Duyckinck and the Young America group in New York – into a fleeting
episode of hack writing for the Democratic party, after which he spent
the rest of his life uttering criticisms of all politicians, usually from a
disengaged symbolic distance.

To men of letters, who felt commitments of culture as well as commitments of conscience, the changing America that emerged in the Jackson
years posed troubling contradictions and conflicts of sympathy. The arts
in the nineteenth century, though decreasingly elitist, were by no means
proletarian, and the nation's intellectuals remained invincibly middle-
class. The erosion of cultivated manners in public life, of gentlemanly
standards of courtesy and moderation in social intercourse, was a matter
of dismay to lovers of civility, who watched the halls of Congress turning
into what more than one observer called a 'bear-garden,' given over to
noisy quarrels and the expectoration of tobacco juice. On the other hand,
there could be no better evidence than vulgarity that government in a
free society was no longer the exclusive preserve of the well-bred. If the
Jacksonian 'spoils' system of rotating public office encouraged a good
deal of unseemly and sometimes dishonest scrambling for preferment, it
also prevented the entrenchment of more insidious kinds of privilege and
gave to federal government a popular responsiveness which has been in
the main a strength rather than a weakness of democracy. A not incon-

siderable by-product has been the participation in public life of men like Irving, Hawthorne, Melville and Lowell, whose occasional presence in office has served in some measure as historic counterpoise to the downward leveling that always threatens popular government with mediocrity. In the final analysis, the great matters of conscience in the United States, the abolition of crimes against the helpless parts of society – such crimes as the flogging of seamen and the continued enslavement of African blacks – the resolution of such issues on humanitarian principles was aided by an orderly diffusion of responsibility which is profoundly different from the post-revolutionary rule-by-rabble which most Americans observed in Europe with detestation and fear.

The resolution of the greatest national issue of all engaged the minds and hearts of all Americans and was quite as traumatic as any revolution. In the words of Abraham Lincoln, who presided over the resolution, that issue was whether a nation 'conceived in liberty and dedicated to the proposition that all men are created equal . . . can long endure.' The survival of the union itself was brought to test when the vital and irreconcilable interests of two carefully balanced sections of the country reached the flash-point of hostility in the spring of 1861. From its founding, the republic most obsessed of all modern nations with the dream of a perfect society had been morally crippled by the one social institution most incompatible with that ideal: involuntary servitude. In the North, principle and interest combined to put an early end to slavery; but in the South the equally early industrialization of agriculture resulting from the development of the cotton gin made slavery indispensable to the plantation system and swept Southerners past the point of no return in defending what their chief apologist, John C. Calhoun, called their 'peculiar institution.'

Rarely in human history have moral and political considerations been so hopelessly confused as in the mounting sectional feud that beset the United States and darkened their collective future in the four decades leading to the Civil War. Of the debating of right and wrong there is no end; from the start the issue was joined as a power struggle between those who would legislate morality for the nation and those who would insist on the right of self-determination. The nation had expanded state by state across the continent, with each addition carefully contrived to preserve the unstable balance between free soil and slave. The beginning of this deadly game in the so-called Missouri Compromise of 1820 alarmed Thomas Jefferson like 'a firebell in the night.' The last great compromise thirty years later, admitting California at the cost of a

stringent Fugitive Slave Law, confirmed the militance of both Abolition-
ists and Secessionists and brought disgrace upon its northern architect,
the 'god-like' Daniel Webster. Outrage fed on outrage. John Brown, the
messianic agitator who undertook to foment armed rebellion at Harper's
Ferry, Virginia, in 1859, crystallized the fanaticism of both sides. Thereafter the man of the South and the man of the North each confronted his
adversary with what one southern writer called 'inveterate monomania,'

> which presents to his diseased mind all objects under one image.
> He is haunted by a spectre, whose shadowy form darkens and
> discolors all his perceptions, and this phantom he pursues with the
> reckless speed of a wild huntsman, trampling on every obstacle to
> his headlong course.

In this posture the nation passed through the 'sad arch,' as Melville
called it, 'between contrasted eras,' and entered on the tragic phase of its
history. Four bloody years of mutual destruction, culminating in the
catastrophe of Lincoln's assassination, spelled the end of innocence in
America. The elemental grief of personal loss for millions of Americans
prefigured the more enduring anguish of a people finally bereft of the
consolations of universal optimism. Even the tonic of Emancipation and
the catharsis of peace in 1865 were swallowed up in the shabby corruptions of Reconstruction. Union had been preserved and the future of the
nation was secure, but what future it was secure for was no longer
discernible in any common vision. The simple goals of an untested
idealism appeared, in the murky aftermath of holocaust, like dreams of
childhood, altogether insubstantial, delusive, perhaps absurd, before
such powerful confirmations of the essential evil in even the best of
human enterprises. All of the faults that had had an air of rawness, of
youthful insensitivity or undisciplined energy, in the United States
depicted by Cooper in the pre-war years, after the bruising disillusionments of war took on a look of settled vice, hardened self-interest, and
mean hypocrisy. The nation's greatest loss may have been that
intangible asset Harriet Martineau and other observers thought they
detected in the early years of the century: 'a sweet temper diffused like
sunshine over the land.'

Long before the war, however, the cause of America's threatened
moral subversion had been plain to her radical idealists. Thoreau saw
around him 'a nation of speculators, stockholders, and money-changers.'
Emerson complained that 'Things are in the saddle/And ride mankind.'
Even a pragmatic critic like Cooper took alarm at the voracity with

which 'all principles are swallowed up in the absorbing desire for gain.' But Cooper rationalized the fevered materialism of his contemporaries as an 'infatuation,' an 'exhilarating intoxication,' and hence 'a disease too violent to last.' By the time James Russell Lowell came to write his centennial ode, nearly forty years after Cooper's *Home As Found*, the ferment had lapsed into 'inert prosperity,' a 'bovine comfort in the sense alone.' The voice of history, Lowell thought in 1876,

> Denounces as degenerate,
> Unfaithful guardians of a noble fate.

Longfellow too fought off despair in visions of tragedy, and the aging Whitman, reassessing his indomitable America in *Democratic Vistas* in 1871, exhumed an old Calvinist term in bemoaning the 'depravity' of a commercial culture suffering from 'hollowness at heart.' In the same year the nation's most mordant critic, Mark Twain, published in the New York *Tribune* a 'Revised catechism' for the post-war era:

> What is the chief end of man? – to get rich. In what way? – dishonestly if we can; honestly if we must. Who is God, the one only and true? Money is God, Gold and greenbacks and stock – father, son, and the ghost of same – three persons in one; these are the true and only God, mighty and supreme; and William Tweed is his prophet.

'Boss' Tweed, who headed the Tammany gang in control of New York politics for a decade and fattened himself with an estimated $100,000,000 of city funds, fulfilled a more ancient prophecy by dying in jail; but, immortalized by the cartoons of Thomas Nast, he became for generations of Americans a folk figure embodying the inflated rapacity of the power brokers in an unregulated democracy. Tweed, together with a whole rogue's gallery of pious scoundrels and the fools they battened on, sat to Twain and his collaborator, Charles Dudley Warner, for definitive portraits in *The Gilded Age* (1873). In their midst, still clinging to a threadbare innocence, stands Colonel Sellers, Twain's impecunious and irrepressible promoter, for whom life is promises and everything glitters. He is the ghost, now sunk to comedy, of optimism and confidence, those fundamental virtues of America's Golden Age. The irony implicit in Sellers's grand and empty hopes constitutes Twain's comment on the fraudulence of the age: a materialism built on wishful speculation and unsecured credit not only worships false gods but betrays the trust which

17

holds society together. 'I feel,' says the novel's heroine, 'as if I were living in a house of cards.'

What America had to learn in the nineteenth century was what its best minds had always known: that a vision of possibility is subject to all the distortions to which its human medium is prone. The discovery of the century was that both opportunity and wisdom have limits, and that what several generations of gloomy theologians had once posited about the nature of man was not, after all, so far from the truth. Against the heady assurances of revolutionary politics and transcendental philosophy had to be reckoned an inherited and existentially reinforced sense of moral inadequacy. This was the theme that engaged the greatest writers of the age, stamping their pages with that special quality of romantic imagination which Melville saw in Hawthorne with a 'shock of recognition,' and termed 'the power of blackness.' Ironically, it is Emerson, chief prophet of the mystical optimism that gave American romanticism its characteristic and deceptive flavor, who spoke most clearly for the tragic vision that lies at its heart:

> Let us honestly state the facts. Our America has a bad name for superficialness. Great men, great nations, have not been boasters and buffoons, but perceivers of the terror of life, and have manned themselves to face it.

2

Melville in His Time

In the summer of 1851 Herman Melville, then a successful novelist of thirty-two, wrote a long, excited letter to his friend Nathaniel Hawthorne about a new book which he was just finishing – he called it only his 'Whale' – and which he would in fact dedicate to the great romancer who had influenced its conception more than any other living force. The letter speaks in every line of an artist who has made his most strenuous effort and who stands for one unique moment at a pinnacle from which he can survey his life with almost preternatural clarity of perspective. A brief passage in that letter constitutes an autobiography of exceptional compression and penetration:

> My development has been all within a few years past. I am like
> one of those seeds taken out of the Egyptian Pyramids, which, after
> being three thousand years a seed and nothing but a seed, being
> planted in English soil, it developed itself, grew to greenness, and
> then fell to mould. So I. Until I was twenty-five, I had no
> development at all. From my twenty-fifth year I date my life. Three
> weeks have scarcely passed, at any time between then and now,
> that I have not unfolded within myself. But I feel that I am now
> come to the inmost leaf of the bulb, and that shortly the flower
> must fall to the mould.

The time of Herman Melville's unfolding began on October 14, 1844, two and a half months after his twenty-fifth birthday, when he stepped ashore at Boston harbor from a long and devious series of cruises through the oceans of the world. From these voyages, in the course of the next six years, he would draw the stories that were to make him famous. That day in Boston, therefore, by his own formulation, invites a look backward to the seed-time, and then forward to the flowering and subsequent decline – if that is the word for the sort of 'mould' into which

19

he may be said to have fallen after the publication of *Moby-Dick*.

In the most literal sense, the seed from which Herman Melville sprang was, on both sides of the family, of a character already more venerable than most blood lines in the young republic could claim to be. On his mother's side, by the early decades of the eighteenth century, the Gansevoorts were acknowledged patricians of the Dutch community in Albany, New York. Melville's grandfather, General Peter Gansevoort, died before Herman was born, but the legend of his heroism at the battle of Fort Stanwix in the Revolution formed an important ground of family pride, and it is not surprising that his grandson's second child should have been given the name Stanwix in his honor. The Melvill side of the house – the 'e' was added in Herman's time – receded into the mists of Scottish antiquity at least as far as Flodden Field, and had earned respect on American soil through the Revolutionary exploits of Herman's paternal grandfather, Major Thomas Melvill. Collector of customs in the port of Boston until removed from office in the Jackson administration (1829), the old veteran in his outmoded colonial dress was a living link between the infancy of the nation and the grandson who would end his own career as a customs inspector in an era of considerably diminished political prestige. Of the Gansevoort glory few memorials remain, apart from a street name in Manhattan and a statue in the public square of Rome, New York; but Major Melvill's memory is kept green by the fact of his participation in the immortal Boston Tea Party, which effectively launched the struggle for independence, and by the quaint picture of him in his ancient cocked hat and knee breeches which is forever preserved in Oliver Wendell Holmes's poem, 'The Last Leaf.'

Both Allan and Maria Gansevoort Melvill, Herman's parents, felt a pride of place never entirely justified by their own fortunes. Allan's losses and eventual failure as an importer and manufacturer may have hastened his death from somewhat ill-defined causes when Herman was only twelve years old. His widow had reason to be grateful for what affluence remained to the Gansevoorts to be drawn on in the bleak and uncertain years that followed. Herman, their second son and third of seven children, received among the influences of childhood a rooted anxiety about money, along with a solemn ethical conviction of its importance. Like his father, he was to support his family in genteel but precarious style and to be depressed at frequent intervals by the unrelenting pressures of need. As a child, however, he was shielded from the effects of lurking insecurity by a succession of household removals to excellent addresses in lower Manhattan and by the standard middle-class advantages of Irish servants and good schools.

In retrospect, none of Melville's childhood influences could have had more far-reaching effect than his earliest surroundings. The house in which he was born on August 1, 1819, stood within a block of Battery Park at the tip of Manhattan Island, on one side, and on the other the wharves and shipping offices of the South Street waterfront. Melville's first horizon was the Atlantic Ocean with a foreground of masts and rigging, cargo and sailors. No subsequent ambition, indeed nothing but desperation, was to drive him to sea; but when his collapsing fortunes carried him there, it would at least be to a world with which he had the earliest possible acquaintance. Meanwhile, pending that unforeseen development, he passed through a few lack-lustre years of conventional schooling, always in the shadow of his older and more aggressive brother, Gansevoort; helped, as much as a young boy in minor clerk-ships could, to relieve the distress of an impoverished and widowed mother; visited his Uncle Thomas, and briefly taught school, in Pittsfield, Massachusetts, where he would later spend his most crucial years; and dabbled in literature by joining a debating society in Albany and later publishing two volatile essays under the title 'Fragments from a Writing Desk,' in the local newspaper of Lansingburgh, New York, where the family had retreated to nurse its chronic insolvency.

In the spring of 1839 Melville faced the approach of his twentieth birthday with no resources and no prospects. Another teaching position could not be hoped for until the following autumn, and in the inter-vening months there appeared no alternative to idleness but to follow the example of several of his cousins who had met similar emergencies by shipping before the mast on merchantmen or whalers. In hard times such as those following the financial panic of 1837 the merchant marine was one segment of the economy with a seemingly bottomless capacity to absorb cheap transient labor. With the help of Gansevoort, then in New York to study law, Melville found a berth on the crew of the *St Law-rence*, a packet on the Liverpool run, and entered on the first phase of his true education. Although in later years he would credit a whaling ship with teaching him all he knew, his treatment of this exploratory ex-perience in *Redburn: His First Voyage* suggests that his four months on the *St Lawrence* constituted a more elementary but still invaluable schooling in the life that was to take shape in his novels.

The first mark of an exceptional nature in Melville was a reflective and imaginative response to experience that at best sustained and at worst stultified the mass of men who went to sea with no more than ordinary sensibilities. Although the gestation of that response required a decade of sailing and writing, the initial lessons were such as could only have been pondered in a self-contained floating world to which for the first time he found himself fully and independently committed. At sea he learned the necessity and satisfaction of hard manual labor, the arbitrary and intractable distribution of authority, the value of human sympathy, the squalor of forecastle and steerage, and the countervailing exhilaration of the maintop in fair weather and foul. Ashore, an equally instructive six weeks in the Liverpool docks and slums during the era of the Chartist agitations taught him dimensions of degradation and wretchedness unimagined by the penniless but genteel son of a less deteriorated society. To the shocking privations and inequities forced upon the young traveler's attention at every turn is owing some impetus to the social conscience which informed every book he was to write with a passionate, sometimes embittered empathy for the poor and the powerless. At the same time that he faced appalling realities on land and sea which could only reinforce the gloomy convictions of his inherited Calvinism, he breathed a liberating air at the masthead that opened his mind to transcendental prospects for the human spirit. If the sailor lives in more stringent confinement than the landsman, he also enjoys a wider horizon. The catalyst of latent energies, for Melville as for R. H. Dana, Jr, whose initiation preceded his by five years, was a certain 'witchery in the sea.' 'I have known a young man,' Dana wrote in *Two Years Before the Mast*, 'with such a passion for the sea, that the very creaking of a block stirred up his imagination so that he could hardly keep his feet on dry ground.'

Melville never described his own feeling for the sea in such romantic terms, but it is a fact that he did not keep his feet on dry ground very long. A dull winter as a schoolmaster, for which he earned no more than subsistence, was followed by a fruitless trip to Illinois, where his Uncle Thomas, now removed from Pittsfield, proved of no more assistance to him than his relations in the east. By autumn 1840 he was back in New York, full of interesting memories of the Erie Canal, the western plains, and the Mississippi River, on which he could draw for books then unimagined, but utterly destitute and faced with a final crisis of independence. He could follow the example of his brother Gansevoort and his closest friend, Eli Fly, and sink into an anonymous clerkship in a law office, or he could select what was for him as it would be for Ishmael in *Moby-Dick*, a more congenial 'substitute for pistol and ball,' and return to the sea. The first option remained a horror to him, its nightmare quality still unrelieved when he wrote 'Bartleby' twelve years later; the second was commended not only by his own experience but by Dana's classic tale of the landsman before the mast, just published and immediately devoured by the idle and searching Melville. In this way the most important decision of his life was made, and on January 3, 1841, he sailed out of Fairhaven, Massachusetts, in the new three-masted whaler *Acushnet* on a voyage from which he would not return for nearly four years.

Melville's odyssey to the South Pacific and back was a rich vein of exotic adventure which he eventually mined for five novels, a set of prose sketches, and a number of poems. Scholars have debated the degree to which these writings represent a direct transcription of events. Probably it is more productive to look for the ways in which the events excited his imagination to weave memories and ideas into the web of fiction under the pervasive influence of the intensive reading into which he dived after his return. It is in the broadest sense that one must read Melville's personal comment in the words of Ishmael in *Moby-Dick*: 'A whaling ship was my Yale College and my Harvard.' In conscious contrast to a Harvard-bred writer like Dana, such a remark might point with mild asperity to a felt deficiency in formal education. But in a positive light it reflects a more essential immersion in the raw facts and latent metaphors of ships, seas, islands, whales, and men.

The *Acushnet*'s maiden voyage took her over the accustomed sea route along the coast of South America to Cape Horn, and by that usually terrific passage into the Pacific Ocean where the best whaling grounds were to be found. By autumn she was cruising the waters about the Galapagos Islands, a cluster of volcanic cinders populated by sea fowl and tortoises, where a few years earlier Charles Darwin had pondered a book very different from the one Herman Melville was to produce on the subject. Six months after leaving those blasted shores the *Acushnet* again sighted land in the Marquesas, 3,000 miles to the west. The vision of those green gardens in the sea after a year and a half of bleak interment in the 'tyrannic ship' moved Melville, as it had countless other sailors of spirit, to lust for land as passionately as he had once lusted for wind and waves. On July 9 he and a friend called Toby disappeared into the jungle of Nukuheva and abruptly exchanged the rigors of the forecastle for the lurking terror of cannibalism among the little-known natives of the Typee valley. Within a few weeks, uneasy but intact, they made their separate escapes, and Melville found himself a refugee in a ship even more deplorable than the one he had deserted. At Tahiti a kind of

23

holiday mutiny set him free once more to roam the islands, this time in the company of a scapegrace, self-accredited ship's doctor, whose sardonic wit and casual erudition stirred the young sailor's imagination like a message from another world.

Two months later a third whaler, the *Charles and Henry* out of Nantucket, carried Melville among its transient recruits to Hawaii – then known as the Sandwich Islands – where he worked ashore through the summer of 1843 before signing on the navy frigate *United States* for the long voyage home. The fourteen months of that voyage, which he would compress in *White-Jacket* to three, taught Melville finally that methodical inhumanity and an iron stratification of power and privilege were not merely aberrations of the free enterprise system, suffered to fester beneath the decks of whaling ships, but were rather formal characteristics of the lawful structure of society. To the natural hardships of whaling Melville had responded with the stoical good humor of the pioneer; the self-justifying brutality of naval discipline roused him to indignation. Yet even in a floating principality as unjustly governed as the *United States* he found in the person of a petty officer a humane ideal that had been altogether lacking among the 'blubber boilers,' and a vital aspect of that ideal was an enlightened loyalty to a system gravely disfigured but not totally disqualified by oppression. It was Melville's crew chief, John Chase, who supplied his otherwise dispiriting education with this model of civilization. Dashing, articulate, magnanimous, Chase was an embodiment of the legendary 'handsome sailor' whom all about him love and admire. Nearly half a century after the *United States* dropped anchor in Boston Harbor Melville would dedicate the last of his writings, *Billy Budd*, to 'Jack Chase, Englishman, Wherever that great heart may now be/Here on Earth or harbored in Paradise.'

In all his travels Melville kept no journal, though he was to do so on two later and less eventful voyages after he had turned author and come to know the value of such records. What he carried ashore from his youthful wanderyears was a fertile but inchoate mass of impressions, usually in need of refreshment and enlargement by research when he set about converting them into books, but at once a matchless source of exotic conversation which enabled him, like Othello, to shine with tales of

> The Anthropophagi and men whose heads
> Do grow beneath their shoulders.

In fact, his audience included a Desdemona of sorts in the person of

24

Elizabeth Shaw, daughter of Lemuel Shaw, Chief Justice of the Supreme Court of Massachusetts and long-time friend of the Melville family. Although Melville did not marry Elizabeth Shaw until the summer of 1847, he benefited at once from her father's influential encouragement, and repaid the debt in the dedication of his first book, *Typee* – 'gratefully' in one version, 'affectionately' in another – to the Judge. Another valuable encourager to a literary career was Herman's brother Gansevoort, who in his absence had so progressed in law and politics as to be awarded the post of secretary of the United States legation in London, where he was conveniently situated to find an English publisher for Herman's first book. Gansevoort was dead of a sudden illness before the sequel to *Typee* was ready for press, but not before he had succeeded in bringing his brother's work to the attention of America's premier author, Washington Irving, and in selling *Typee* to Wiley and Putnam in New York as well as to John Murray in London.

The success of *Typee* was instantaneous and spectacular. Even the controversies generated by the indignation of missionary societies, and by the skepticism of readers suspended between fact and fiction, contributed to the notoriety of the romance and its unknown author. The fortuitous reappearance of 'Toby' in time to vouch for the veracity of his old shipmate's yarn of life among the cannibals provided substance for an expanded edition of *Typee* and heightened interest in the book-length sequel which appeared the following spring. With *Omoo*, another spirited and scandalous account of South Sea adventure, Melville consolidated a reputation never to be augmented, and never really to be corrected to accord with the profound changes he struggled to bring about in the character of his subsequent writings. One inevitable and fruitful result of sudden acclaim was the opening of doors in the literary establishment: he found himself being lionized by men like the Duyckinck brothers of the influential *Literary World*, to which he was soon contributing reviews and the one great critical essay of his career; and Cornelius Mathews, whose *Punch*-like humor magazine *Yankee Doodle* carried a series of ephemeral political lampoons by Melville. To these acquaintances, never perhaps quite ripened into friends, Melville owed his conversion from an amateur to a professional author and his introduction to other men of letters, most notably, in 1850, Nathaniel Hawthorne.

He also owed to these companions the stimulation of ideas and the access to books for which the years at sea had starved his mind. From old books which, as White-Jacket says, he had been able to 'pick up by chance here and there' in ship's libraries, he now plunged voraciously into major authors like Rabelais and Burton, Coleridge and Shakespeare. 'Melville reads old books,' Evert Duyckinck wrote to his brother George. 'He has borrowed Sir Thomas Browne of me and says finely of the speculations of the *Religio Medici* that Browne is a kind of "crack'd Archangel." Was ever anything of this sort said before by a sailor?' Unlike his first light tales of adventure, Melville's third romance was the sort of work Dr Johnson had in mind when he remarked that 'a man will turn over half a library to make one book.' It is obvious to every reader of *Mardi* that its author had devoured more books than he had digested; a work of fiction could hardly be more erudite or less assimilated. But the intellectual expansion and ferment of *Mardi*'s overflowing chapters signaled the new earnestness with which Melville had come to regard his art by 1848. It was to this period of his life and this process that he later referred in describing to Hawthorne how he had belatedly 'unfolded within [himself].'

The Melville of *Mardi* was unfolding, but also deeply divided as a consequence. The norm from which his third book had abruptly departed in mid-course was the effortless, almost reflexive yarn-spinning of a man who was, in Dana's words, 'incomparable in dramatic story-telling.' That nature had already made full disclosure of Melville's talents seemed plain to everyone who knew him. Nathaniel Parker Willis, a critic of some account, made an example of him in defining what he termed 'conversational literature':

> Herman Melville, with his cigar and his Spanish eyes, *talks* Typee and Omoo, just as you find the flow of his delightful mind on paper. Those who have only read his books know the man – those who have only seen the man have a fair idea of his books.

But Melville had not only 'sailed through oceans,' he had 'swam through libraries,' too, as he was to boast in *Moby-Dick*, and mere story-telling would never again be able to satisfy his ambition. To keep money flowing into the pocket of an author with a wife, a new baby, and a failed book, he impatiently dashed off two more easy retrospective narratives in rapid succession: *Redburn*, dealing with his earliest voyage to Liverpool, and *White-Jacket*, based on his final voyage in a man-of-war. Both were well received and paid him respectable returns, but their very success seemed an affront to his higher aims, and he treated them like step-children: 'beggarly,' 'trash,' 'jobs turned out for "lucre"' – as a wood-sawyer saws wood.' When he sailed to England and the Continent in the autumn of 1849, partly to find a publisher for *White-Jacket*, partly to find simple refreshment for his depleted resources, he took stock with wry ambivalence of the progress he had made in the world since his first inauspicious visit to British soil a decade earlier: *'then* a sailor, *now* . . . author of ''Peedee,'' ''Hullabaloo,'' and ''Pog-Dog.''' His masterpiece, *Moby-Dick*, had not yet been conceived, and he could only suppose, as he wrote to Duyckinck, that his next work was 'predestinated': 'I shall write such things as the Great Publisher of Mankind ordained ages before he published ''The World''.'

To R. H. Dana, Jr, now famous for his *Two Years Before the Mast*, it was clear that the ordained book remaining to be extracted from his friend's nautical adventures was the story of whaling itself, and by spring of 1850 Melville reported to him that just such a book was 'half way in the work'. To his English publisher Bentley, Melville described the work in progress simply as 'a romance of adventure founded upon certain wild legends in the Southern Sperm Whale Fisheries,' but to Dana he confided that it was turning into 'a strange sort of book.'

> Blubber is blubber, you know; tho' you may get oil out of it, the poetry runs as hard as sap from a frozen maple tree; – & to cook the thing up, one must needs throw in a little fancy, which from the nature of the thing, must be ungainly as the gambols of the whales themselves.

Before the book was ready for publication a year later Melville's whale would be 'cooked in hell-fire' as a result of a determination that grew upon him to put into it everything he knew. What converted a mere dissatisfaction with easy success into a consuming ambition to produce a masterpiece was his nearly simultaneous encounter, in the summer of 1850, with Hawthorne's *Mosses from an Old Manse* and with Nathaniel Hawthorne himself, at that precise juncture a close neighbor to Melville's new home in Pittsfield, Massachusetts.

Melville's response to the art of Hawthorne, recorded in a two-part pseudonymous essay in Duyckinck's *Literary World*, is an episode of professional discovery which invites comparison with Keats's reading of Chapman's Homer. Apart from a few scattered and unexceptional book reviews, 'Hawthorne and His Mosses' was Melville's only excursion into criticism, but it is a statement of landmark significance in the development not only of Melville's personal talents but of American letters at large. Reading it a century and a quarter after the moment of creative white heat in which it was composed, one readily sifts out and

27

dismisses its ephemeral elements, like the absurdly overstated literary nationalism which blossomed briefly in Melville's mind pending his inevitable recoil from chauvinism. What remains is a stirring intellectual drama unfolding through rising stages of conviction and commitment to a memorable climax of personal insight and historical prophecy.

In true romantic style Melville praises Hawthorne for the qualities of his heart, his 'humor and love,' and, as a concomitant of those spiritual riches, his 'great, deep intellect, which drops down into the universe like a plummet.' What the artist finds there at the bottom of things is no sentimental enlightenment but the kind of truth which is a 'blackness, ten times black'. The secret of such genius, at once the source and appeal of its 'power of blackness,' is 'that Calvinistic sense of Innate Depravity and Original Sin, from whose visitations, in some shape or other, no deeply thinking mind is always and wholly free.' It is not his immersion in Puritan history that calls up this rare power in Hawthorne, but his resemblance to Shakespeare, whose 'short, quick probings at the very axis of reality' make him master of 'the Great Art of Telling the Truth.' In his insistence that genius must have 'plenty of sea-room to tell the truth in,' Melville may have been thinking more of himself than of his ostensible subject, but his ultimate conclusion is that all genius is joined together by 'one shock of recognition.'

If Melville had met Hawthorne before he began to write his essay, he had only just done so. Nevertheless, he concluded his encomium with an attribution of influence as accurate as it was extravagant. 'Already,' he wrote, 'I feel that this Hawthorne has dropped germinous seeds into my soul. He expands and deepens down, the more I contemplate him. . . .' Not surprisingly, his response to Hawthorne the man was an outpouring of spontaneous affection unmatched even among Melville's normally genial relationships. The stimulation of the man and the art together formed an incalculable part of the cumulative creative excitement resulting, in the autumn of 1851, in the work published in England as *The Whale*, in the United States as *Moby-Dick*. It was dedicated to Nathaniel Hawthorne, 'in token,' Melville wrote, 'of my admiration for his genius.'

The euphoria attending such an effort was real, but so was the exhaustion. When the critical reception and the desperately needed sales of *Moby-Dick* failed to match the warmth of Hawthorne's personal appreciation, Melville was plunged into a despair exacerbated to bitterness by emotional fatigue and chronic eyestrain. *Pierre*, the novel that emerged from these conditions the following year, may have started life as the 'rural bowl of milk' he had promised Sophia Hawthorne, but it ended in being a travesty on the popular forms it imitated and a savage reprisal against the insensitivity of the very public on which its acceptance depended. Predictably, his New York publisher sold fewer than 300 copies in the first six months; and the entire printing went up in flames, along with the remainder of Melville's other books, in the Harper's fire of December, 1853. Hawthorne, whose college classmate Franklin Pierce had in that year risen to the White House, tried to help his new friend to some available consulate, but his influence was sufficient only to secure his own appointment to a consulship in Liverpool. Melville's liabilities now included three children, mounting debts, and a dwindling reputation. In these straits he turned to the popular magazines for ready income and began to write short stories.

In the next three years he produced fifteen sketches and stories for the monthly magazines published by Putnam's and Harper's. Although the short story was not his forte, several of the most substantial specimens, including 'Bartleby the Scrivener' and 'Benito Cereno,' have attained the status of classics. Two longer works – *Israel Potter*, based on the autobiography of an obscure Revolutionary War veteran, and 'The Encantadas,' a series of sketches incorporating recollections of the Galapagos Islands – appeared in serial form. At least one short story, 'I and My Chimney,' is demonstrably autobiographical and affords a glimpse, through a thin veil of fiction, of a middle-aged family man, ailing but unshaken, humorous and clear-sighted still, but so deeply oppressed by adversity as to move his troubled wife to send for their friend and neighbor Dr Oliver Wendell Holmes to stop in and examine his mental and physical health. During this period, as his best work lay ignored or fell, misunderstood, into early neglect, Melville's imagination ruefully wove tale after tale of frustrated hopes and blighted happiness. In 1856, as if to demonstrate that the melancholy of his themes was not a failure of nerve, he wrote *The Confidence-Man*, a taut and caustic novel which at once profoundly probed the spiritual malaise of mid-nineteenth-century America and brilliantly extended the range of Melville's art. But upon its appearance the following spring it would prove more baffling to its few readers than *Mardi* or *Moby-Dick*, and would be generally received as proof of its author's final lapse into eccentricity or down-right madness. It ends with the cryptic promise that 'something further may follow of this masquerade,' but it was to be the last work of fiction Melville would publish in his lifetime.

In October, at the urging of his family, he sailed once more for Europe, and this time the Middle East as well. In Liverpool, paying a final visit to Hawthorne at the outset of his wanderings, he took long walks by the sea with the one man to whom he had fully opened his mind, and moved the sensitive Hawthorne to record a penetrating memorial in his *English Notebooks*:

> Melville, as he always does, began to reason of Providence and futurity, and of everything that lies beyond human ken, and informed me that he had 'pretty much made up his mind to be annihilated;' but still he does not seem to rest in that anticipation; and, I think, will never rest until he gets hold of a definite belief. It is strange how he persists – and has persisted ever since I knew him, and probably long before – in wandering to and fro over these deserts, as dismal and monotonous as the sand hills amid which we were sitting. He can neither believe, nor be comfortable in his unbelief; and he is too honest and courageous not to try to do one or the other. If he were a religious man, he could be one of the most truly religious and reverential; he has a very high and noble nature, and better worth immortality than most of us.

The voyage was intended to rest Melville and restore his spirits; but the residual impression of his travels, perhaps partly a reflection of the mood he carried with him, was one of squalor and sterility. His notes are fragmentary and pessimistic, abounding in wasteland images. The stones of Judea haunted his imagination, and the teeming streets of ancient cities made him feel 'utterly used up . . . as if broken on the wheel.' Still, his pervasive despondency hardly inhibited the formation of images and ideas out of the sights of Egypt and Palestine, Greece and Rome. When he returned to New York in May, 1857, he brought with him the mental and emotional stock from which, in years to follow, he would draw thousands of lines of verse to fill the void left by the drying up of the springs of fiction.

Why the springs of fiction ran dry and why Melville's unexhausted creativity re-emerged in the form of lyric and narrative poetry are separate but related questions. The sources of his stories had been, really, not so much springs as pools, fed by the stirring experiences of his youth but largely unrenewed by subsequent events and only meagerly augmented by the cabin travel of his mature years. What remained when adventures ran out was the undercurrent of ideas and feelings that had always been vigorously present to enlarge his stories beyond their merely narrative bounds. In Melville there was always a poet waiting for encouragement. Once he had made up his mind to be 'annihilated' as a professional author, he felt free for the first time in his life to write as he pleased, unconcerned about public response and the income dependent on it. Shortly after his return from Europe he did make an abortive effort to publish a collection of verse, but nothing is known of it beyond a whimsical remark to his younger brother that he had sold his 'doggerel' to a trunkmaker for linings at ten cents a pound. While his latent poetic energies awaited the call of moving events to come, he occupied himself with lecture tours, speaking to whoever would pay to hear on Roman statuary, or the South Seas, or just travel in general. Then, in 1860, even that meager remuneration trickled to a halt. He took a sea voyage to the west coast with his brother Thomas, then captain of a clipper ship. He tried again, and failed again, to obtain a diplomatic post. The Civil War erupted; and Melville's faltering life seemed to pause, with the life of the nation, to be resumed in some deeply altered way when the demons were exorcised and the divisions closed, if not healed.

It was the war, finally, that moved Melville to practice the art to which he had committed himself in spirit. Battles and events of the national crisis that had stirred him took various experimental shapes of verse. And shaping them all into a unity of sorts was a belated master-plan to create a history of the war in verse, not answerable to journal standards of reportage, but woven into a loose chronology of the heart's participation in the tragic drama of conflict. True to his old habits of composition, he researched about a third of the seventy poems comprising *Battle-Pieces* in public sources such as *The Rebellion Record*, but many of the poems came out of his own deeply felt reactions to events of the war. The literary product can only be described as mixed. It may even be fair to conclude, with one merciless contemporary reviewer, that 'Nature did not make him a poet.' Certainly, few readers were willing to give money for what no critic could unreservedly praise. Happily, in the autumn of 1866, almost simultaneously with the publication of *Battle-Pieces*, Melville's long search for steady employment was rewarded by an appointment as inspector of customs in the Port of New York.

Perhaps 'reward' is a strong term for such modest employment, especially for a descendant of the Gansevoorts, inspecting cargo on the docks at the bottom of Gansevoort Street at four dollars a day. In happier days he had described one such 'friendless' fellow in *Redburn* as 'a man of fine feelings, altogether above his situation; a most inglorious one, indeed; worse than driving geese to water' (ch. 29). But Melville was not the first nor the last author to take refuge in that particular undemanding haven of support. His superior officer was Richard Henry Stoddard, a young poet who was to become one of the nation's leading men of letters; and Stoddard in turn owed his position to the influence of Hawthorne, who had occupied such positions in both Boston and Salem. Melville left no record of the nineteen years he spent as Inspector No. 75 on the New York waterfront, but both Hawthorne, in the famous 'Custom House' sketch with which he prefaced *The Scarlet Letter*, and Stoddard in his published memoirs, drew telling pictures of a deadening atmosphere of bureaucratic routine, intellectual stultification, and customary corruption. Surrounded by what Stoddard called 'incapable fogies' in an 'asylum for non-entities,' Melville performed his mechanical duties with a scrupulous rectitude that stood above the petty traffic in shippers' bribes, and by a sort of schizophrenic divorcement of energies went home each day to read Emerson or Arnold or Balzac and to spin out, Penelope-like, the long poem he would bring to fruition in 1876, or the dream books that would never be anything more than scribbled fragments of verse and prose. As he withdrew more and more from the world in which younger men like Stoddard were steadily rising, his interests became increasingly retrospective and far removed from a scene of life in which he had grown all but invisible to others and quite dead to ambition.

The harvest of twenty years' reflection on the stones of Judea was the stony poem *Clarel*, subtitled 'A Poem and Pilgrimage in the Holy Land.' It is his longest book, in his most uncompromising form, and altogether careless of its demands on the reader. He had no hopes, almost no concern for its success. He published it out of a deep necessity of his nature, by means of funds donated by Uncle Peter Gansevoort as the last of his many benefactions to the Melville family. How painfully private the composition of *Clarel* had been for Melville may be gauged by the ferocity with which he guarded and pursued his labors, even in the seclusion of his home, where the work in progress came to be for Elizabeth a 'dreadful incubus . . . [that] has undermined all our happiness.' 'Pray,' she wrote to her stepmother, 'do not mention to *anyone* that he is writing poetry – you know how such things spread and he would be very angry if he knew I had spoken of it.' After *Clarel* was published Melville never spoke of it himself, except to refer to it once as a 'what not . . . eminently adapted for unpopularity.' A two-sentence prefatory note, surely one of the briefest on record, announces laconically, 'I here dismiss the book – content beforehand with whatever future awaits it.'

In what remained of his lifetime no future at all awaited *Clarel* or any of the other writings it was left him to produce. To all the world, apart from his family and a few correspondents, chiefly English, who had with difficulty sought him out, the author of *Typee* was dead, his fame forgotten or associated with a lost antebellum generation. To a New York newspaper, reminded of his continued existence in 1886, he 'exemplifie[d] the transiency of literary reputation.' His very life seemed slipping away. By 1886, lately retired from his custom house post in failing health, he could count his blood losses: his mother, his brothers, two sisters, and both of his sons – one by suicide. Yet for the artist two volumes of poems lay ahead, and the drafting of a novel which would lie undiscovered in manuscript for more than three decades, but which when brought to light would rival *Moby-Dick* in the favor of unborn generations. The two slender volumes of verse appeared in private printings of twenty-five copies each: *John Marr and Other Sailors* in 1888, and *Timoleon* in the year of Melville's death. His finest lyrics are among the sixty-seven short poems in these collections. Of the making of *Billy Budd* no record remains apart from the fragmentary and partly illegible manuscript itself. It is a valedictory work of remarkable, seemingly undiminished vigor, drawing a tale of adventure out of the tragic events of a naval mutiny of 1842 in which Melville's cousin Guert Gansevoort had been a principal figure, and at the same time drawing a profound moral drama out of such inner resources as had always responded to *The Pilgrim's Progress* and *Paradise Lost*. His final effort thus focussed the leading influences of Melville's life and set the seal of greatness on a long and unsteady career.

Death came in September, 1891, a month after his seventy-second birthday. He was buried in an obscurity virtually undisturbed until a new century, with its own disasters and disillusionments, had seasoned the American consciousness to a maturity better able to understand his piercing vision of God and man than his own had been.

3

Travel Romance: *Typee* and *Omoo*

When Melville reconstituted his boyhood in *Redburn*, one of the earliest impressions he recalled was the excitement he felt when his aunt pointed out to him in church one Sunday the author of a book he had read about travel in Arabia. He thought he had never seen such interesting eyes in a man. He dreamed about them, grown steadily larger, and about the marvels they had witnessed. He 'fell into long reveries about distant voyages and travels, and thought how fine it would be, to be able to talk about remote and barbarous countries; with what reverence and wonder people would regard me, if I had just returned from the coast of Africa or New Zealand.' The tone is calculated to convey the naïveté of a child, but Melville knew he was addressing a nation of travelers who carried that child around inside of them clamoring for exotic scenes and books that could transport them to vicarious Arabias. No American writer could have known it better. For three years he had been living proof that an unknown sailor can instantly turn into a famous author if he has been to the South Seas and knows how to write about it.

With a sure gesture the opening pages of *Typee* lure the reader from his daily tedium into a summer world of adventure and irresponsibility.

> The Marquesas! What strange visions of outlandish things does the very name spirit up! Naked houris – cannibal banquets – groves of coconut – coral reefs – tattooed chiefs – and bamboo temples; sunny valleys planted with breadfruit trees – carved canoes dancing on the flashing blue waters – savage woodlands guarded by horrible idols – *heathenish rites and human sacrifices.*

The darker possibilities of the daydream are played on initially for whatever they can contribute to the appeal of suspense, but through most of *Typee* and all of its sequel, *Omoo*, the prevailing appeal is to a different kind of suspense – something more like the 'suspension of dis-

34

belief for the moment' which Coleridge said constitutes 'poetic faith.' Certainly the ability to charm a reader into acceptance of a totally fresh sphere of sensation is a more basic and enduring quality of Melville's first two books than the mechanical stimulus of temporary mystification. Consequently, the most notorious feature of these South Sea idylls, the melodramatic fear of being eaten, in the light of the author's evident survival must always be an attraction secondary to the gentler allurements of fantasy. The true atmosphere of Melville's Polynesia was one of 'hushed repose, which [he] almost feared to break lest, like the enchanted gardens in the fairy tale, a single syllable might dissolve the spell' (*Typee*, ch. 7).

If an appeal of this sort seems too delicate for the reminiscences of a sailor or for the expectations of the reader who lends his attention to such a narrator, it is worth considering that few concerns of civilized life can have more universal poignancy than the fragility and evanescence of pleasurable experience. The escape of an ordinary young man from the gray realities that oppress his days to the momentary respite of a perfumed and painted paradise is by nature a metaphor for the most common dream of humanity. It is less pointed an image than the spectacle of Hawthorne's Clifford Pyncheon blowing bubbles from the window of the ancestral mansion in which he is entombed in *The House of the Seven Gables*; but it has the advantage of being an easy vehicle for a whole volume – in this case, two volumes – of absorbing narrative.

Melville can never have had more congenial material to work with. Having lived an episode that remains for most people unimagined, he had only to recall and flesh out, with minimal assistance from the writings of previous travelers, the happiest adventures of his seafaring years. They lay fresh and blooming on the surface of a memory into which he would later be forced to dive for the richer substance of *Moby-Dick*. Moreover, they had the advantage of ample rehearsal for the telling, of having been repeatedly 'spun as a yarn,' as he remarks in the prefaces to both books. Nowhere in Melville's writings does he appear so simply the born story-teller as in these first books, where his art shows its most unmeditated spontaneity. Common sense led him to tell his essentially true stories in the first person, which would always be his most effective method, regardless of the degree of his actual identification with the narrator. And he had the good judgment, as he pointed out again in both prefaces, to avoid the 'pretensions to philosophical research' which was then characteristic of serious 'writers of travels among barbarous communities.' He did insist on an 'anxious desire to speak the unvarnished truth,' but every reader has rejoiced in his irresistible penchant for color and drama and humor in enlivening all the history and anthropology which he borrowed to embroider his story. Like the Mark Twain of *Huckleberry Finn*, 'some things he stretched, but mainly he told the truth.'

The stretching and embroidering cost him some initial difficulty with those publishers and critics who were confused or timid about such an indefinite mixture of fact and fancy, though to a later age, schooled to see in that very mixture the genius of *Moby-Dick*, the controversy that helped to give *Typee* its *succès de scandale* appears overblown and mildly ridiculous. John Murray, Melville's English publisher, refused to risk so racy a title as 'Typee' in his travel series, although he had included among his offerings Irving's more fanciful *Bracebridge Hall*. Instead, he brought it out under the ponderously prosaic title, *Narrative of a Four Months' Residence Among the Natives of a Valley of the Marquesas Islands; or, A Peep at Polynesian Life*. Melville's American publisher, more amenable to his wishes, agreed to call it *Typee: A Peep at Polynesian Life During a Four Months' Residence in a Valley of the Marquesas*. It is true that the first publisher to whom the manuscript was submitted in New York declined it on the ground that 'it was impossible that it could be true and therefore was without real value'; however, the issue in the United States was less the question of veracity than the dubious morality of the author's life among the 'savages' and his shocking disregard of the sensibilities of the American Christian missions. Hawthorne, reviewing *Typee* for the *Literary World*, referred discreetly and with becoming ambivalence to its 'freedom of view,' but narrower and more humorless minds found harder terms for the author's sexual candor and unaffected contempt for the follies perpetrated in 'Eden' by the religious agents of a more corrupted society.

Later in his life the corrosive repetition of such irrelevancies caused Melville to harden his resistance to demeaning compromises with his artistic intentions. At the outset he was too happy with his new-found success to stand on ceremonious principles, and he acquiesced in the production of a revised American edition which he himself consented to expurgate. For this reason all modern editions are based on the English version, with Melville's title restored, as it was by Murray himself in all subsequent printings. As for the problem of veracity, that was providentially solved by the partner of Melville's escapade, Richard Tobias Greene – the 'Toby' of the narrative – who learned of the controversy back home in Buffalo, New York, and came forward to attest the essential accuracy of his old shipmate's 'yarn.' Armed with Toby's testimonial and supplementary information about his part in the escape from Typee, Melville was able not only to muffle his critics but to write a formal 'Sequel' to his tale as an added attraction to subsequent editions.

The sequel most readers have more urgently desired, the true story of the fabulous Fayaway, was never so much as hinted by Melville in after years, and remains, despite all research, rumors, and conjectures, precisely the romantic mystery it ought to be. That lissome figure in the canoe, silhouetted against the native dress spread out for sail, has expressed the erotic fancy of generations of readers in conventional middle-class homes. Until well into the twentieth century it was Fayaway, not tragic heroes such as Captain Ahab or Captain Vere, who was Melville's most famous creation. At the heart of the unknown valley, after the pains and terrors of initiation, lay ease and plenty – and the nut-brown maiden. From the beginning, the soberest reader, when not inhibited by a need to defend morality or resist delight, succumbed to this elemental lure. 'Enviable Herman!' wrote an English reviewer, 'A happier dog it is impossible to imagine than Herman in the Typee valley.' The Longfellow family, not given to exotic indulgences, read *Typee* aloud and were so captivated by the life it described 'as to inspire a fancy for trying it.' Prominent New York attorney George Templeton Strong, normally a champion of realism against 'the cheap substitute . . . we call romance,' nevertheless confessed to his diary in 1849 an inclination to 'emigrate to Typee' and 'live on bread fruit and bananas.' With or without Fayaway, the Polynesian world Melville pictured was the last outpost of natural man in a state of ecological grace, where a farmer could be defined as one who 'owned several groves of the breadfruit and palm and never hindered their growing.'

At bottom, however, it is virtue and not ease that defined the primitive ideal for Melville. The controlling vision of society in the South Sea romances is Rousseau's. The overpowering first impression of the still interior of Nukuheva is that it has been 'untenanted since the morning of the creation.' The narrator, taking up his residence there, sheds his sailor name and is reborn as 'Tommo.' In this latter-day Eden it is innocence that forms the native character beneath the sloth that defaces it or renders it comical. The hidden thread that binds *Typee* and *Omoo* to later and less lighthearted books is the running contrast they draw between the representatives of Western civilization and 'the poor tattooed savage.' The evidences of English, French, and American influence which Melville observed in the Pacific in the 1840s were

37

chiefly military and ecclesiastical, and he makes little distinction between the physical and spiritual forms of imperialism that had alike, in his view, degraded the childlike islanders and brought into ironic question the very concept of civilization.

In passage after passage, excised or modified in the revised American edition of *Typee*, Melville reverted with the utmost earnestness to the theme that would agitate his mind to the last page of *Billy Budd*, where a man of simple-hearted virtue is suspended from a yardarm by the inexorable machinery of civilized morality.

> How often is the term 'savages' incorrectly applied! None really deserving of it were ever yet discovered by voyagers or by traders. They have discovered heathens and barbarians, whom by horrible cruelties they have exasperated into savages. . . . In a primitive state of society, the enjoyments of life, though few and simple, are spread over a great extent, and are unalloyed; but Civilization, for every advantage she imparts, holds a hundred evils in reserve. . . . I am inclined to think that so far as the relative wickedness of the parties is concerned, four or five Marquesan Islanders sent to the United States as missionaries might be quite as useful as an equal number of Americans dispatched to the islands in a similar capacity. . . . Civilization does not engross all the virtues of humanity: she has not even her full share of them. They flourish in greater abundance and attain greater strength among many barbarous people. . . . I will frankly declare, that after passing a few weeks in this valley of the Marquesas, I formed a higher estimate of human nature than I had ever before entertained. But alas! since then I have been one of the crew of a man-of-war, and the pent-up wickedness of five hundred men has nearly overturned all my previous theories. (chs 4, 17, 27)

In 1850 Melville went on to describe that microcosm of evil in *White-Jacket; or, the World in a Man-of-War*. In 1854, pondering an historic sea battle of the Revolutionary War in *Israel Potter*, he posed the rhetorical question, 'What separates the enlightened man from the savage? Is civilization a thing distinct, or is it an advanced stage of barbarism?' Seventeen years after his induction into the primitive community of the Typees the public lectures he delivered on the subject still bitterly contrasted their 'kindly and hospitable' nature to that of their would-be civilizers, 'the most barbarous, treacherous, irreligious, and devilish creatures on the earth.' In the light of this pervasive theme even Melville's earliest and sunniest romances have clear affinity with the somber works to follow as well as with the satirical writings of more caustic critics of society like Swift and Mark Twain. On its positive side the affinity is dramatized in the friendship of Tommo and Kory-Kory, which flourishes despite the tattooing that stands between them as the symbolic barrier of their cultures. A deeper brotherhood between the American Ishmael and a similarly decorated islander, Queequeg, is one of the leading strands of Melville's most mature romance, *Moby-Dick.*

The most essential difference between *Typee* and the otherwise continuous narrative of *Omoo* is that the Tahiti of *Omoo* is a fallen paradise, already corrupted by its infusion of European culture. To the wandering sailor Tahiti is a pleasure garden but no Eden. He himself is no Adam fulfilling a role, however honorary, in a community of innocents, but literally an 'omoo' or 'taboo kannaker' – a rover, without home, without status – an outcast of the islands. The dream-girl, Fayaway, undefiled in a state of nature, is transmuted to a succession of sophisticated flirts like Ideea, who proclaims 'by unmistakable gestures' that she is

A sad good Christian at the heart –
A very heathen in the carnal part. (ch. 46)

The white man typically assimilated into this society is not restored to integrity, but caught in a downward spiral of retrogression in which he adopts the facial tattooing of the natives and must live out his life with a bright blue shark, a mark 'far worse than Cain's,' emblazoned on his forehead (ch. 7). The renegade college professor Melville later described in his South Sea lectures, who lolled under the palm trees in a breech cloth with three native wives, was, to judge by Dana's account in *Two Years Before the Mast*, typical of 'half of the Americans and English who are adrift along the coasts of the Pacific and its islands.' It is a picture of what Melville's companion in the *Omoo* adventure, 'Doctor Long Ghost,' had become and of what Herman Melville, alias 'Omoo,' barely escaped becoming.

Even in the telling of the story the slide is apparent. Notwithstanding occasional detachable excursions into social criticism, there is a pervasive air of insouciance about the episodic yarning of *Omoo* that sets it apart from the more purposive and structured story-building of *Typee*. The narrator of both tales is a holiday figure, impelled by curiosity, but his earlier phase is directed and sustained by an interest unmistakably moral. The vagabond of *Omoo*, who casts his lot with mutineers in Papeetee harbor in order to be sociable and escape boredom, is different from the explorer who had sought something in himself along with the secrets of Nukuheva's primeval valley. There is exploration in *Omoo* as well as *Typee*, but it is a form of play indulged in idleness, a spectacular exercise in killing time. The unknowns encountered in *Typee* are desperate frontiers, full of risk and commitment. Its adventures generate questions. How will he cope with the mountain jungles to find haven in one of the valleys beyond? Will the valley he chooses be inhabited by friendly or hostile tribes? Are these people really cannibals, and if so can they ever really be trusted or admired? Will survival entail initiation by tattoo? Once in, how will he ever get out? *Typee* can hardly be credited with an invented form, but it has the advantage of all the formal interest that a novel derives from a plot. *Omoo* draws the reader along its loose thread of narrative by the power of charm alone.

The issue which *Omoo* contrives to evade is the central question of *Typee*: the validity of the idle life. Tommo among the beautiful, changeless aborigines is at once attracted and repelled by an existence without aim or effort. By the midpoint of this sojourn he has succumbed to the 'tranquilizing influences' of lush scenery, food, rest, and Fayaway: 'I forgot all my troubles, and buried for the time every feeling of sorrow' (ch. 14). *For the time.* In *Omoo* time seems suspended, and event follows event by almost casual displacement. But in *Typee* the suspension of time is a Damoclean sword.

> I gave myself up to the passing hour, and if ever disagreeable
> thoughts arose in my mind, I drove them away. When I looked
> around the verdant recess in which I was buried, and gazed up to
> the summits of the lofty eminence that hemmed me in, I was well
> disposed to think that I was in the 'Happy Valley,' and that beyond
> those heights there was nought but a world of care and anxiety. (ch.17)

The situation of Tommo, defined by Melville's allusion to the 'Happy Valley,' is precisely that of the Prince in Johnson's *Rasselas*, whose every want is satisfied and who is all too soon moved to discontent by discovering 'The Wants of Him That Wants Nothing.' In his reference to having 'buried' his sorrows and to being in consequence 'buried' himself in his 'verdant recess,' Tommo is expressing his latent dissatisfaction with the carefree life long before he encounters grisly hints of violence beneath its halcyon surface. Like Odysseus locked in the static embrace of the goddess Calypso, the lover of Fayaway savors his transient pleasures in suspended animation, and begins to long for the normal imperfections of home. 'With the Marquesans,' he observes, 'life is little else than an often interrupted and luxurious nap. . . . The history of a day is the history of a life' (ch. 20).

The three greatest natural retreats in the literature of the United States – Thoreau's sojourn at Walden Pond, Hawthorne's residence at Brook Farm, and Melville's visit to Polynesia – all took place at about the same time, in the same exploratory frame of mind, and were concluded for roughly comparable reasons: because they all thought they had, in Thoreau's words, 'several more lives to live.' When Hawthorne converted his experimental utopia to fiction, he too called it a Happy Valley: 'Blithedale.' His narrator, like Melville's – but unlike Thoreau, who wrote explicitly in his own person – had disappointments to account for and suffered a certain spiritual trauma in attempting to reconcile hope and fruition. He dramatized the dislocations of his spokesman, Miles Coverdale, by means of sicknesses of body or mind; and it is possible that Melville endowed his Tommo with a mysterious leg wound for a similar purpose. It is equally possible that the wound had been real enough on the leg of Herman Melville. In either event it is certain that the wound festers as Tommo stands apart from the community that holds him captive, enjoys a radical remission as he relaxes into contented identification with his captors, then reappears in all its virulence with the return of his longing for home and his determination to escape from his oppressive paradise.

A nostalgic poem which Melville published about his Polynesian interlude some forty years afterward adopted a conventional romantic title, 'The Enviable Isles,' but gave it an ironic application. The world it pictures recalls to mind that of the Lotos-eaters of Homer and Tennyson: the islands, though reached with difficulty, are immune to storms and wrapped in dreams – the 'trance of God,' which lulls alike 'all sorrow and all glee.' Living in this narcotic atmosphere, the inhabitants become

> . . . unconscious slumberers mere,
> While billows endless round the beaches die.

The Tahiti of *Omoo* offers even more evidence than Nukuheva of the natives' 'aimless, nerveless mode of spending life' (ch. 49); but when the narrator arrives at the last chapter of his adventure he is seized by no resolution, he has merely grown 'weary somewhat' of his current surroundings and, 'like all sailors ashore, . . . at last pined for the billows.' The result of such casual motivation is a narrative nearly devoid of the sort of tension which grips the reader in a cycle of escape to

41

captivity to escape, and which clearly tells in *Typee*'s favor as a work of art. On the other hand, while the effect of plot inherent in the material of the earlier story was an undeniable stroke of good fortune, it would surely be extravagant to credit Melville in his maiden effort with the conscious evocation of the myth of man's search for innocence. What he wrote of his method in the preface to *Omoo* rings true for both books: 'In a familiar way, he has merely described what he has seen.' In a world that has no more than it needs of good books, it is sufficient praise that he did that well. At their best his descriptions, however fortuitous, have the power to distill memorable images from inert anthropological phenomena; as when Tommo happens upon a royal burial ground where the effigy of a dead chieftain sits in a canoe, 'leaning forward and inclining his head, as if eager to hurry on his voyage.'

> Glaring at him forever, and face to face, was a polished human
> skull, which crowned the prow of the canoe. The spectral
> figurehead, reversed in its position, glancing backwards, seemed to
> mock the impatient attitude of the warrior. (ch. 24)

There, lacking a few years of practice and a compelling theme, speaks the author of *Moby-Dick*.

Taking *Typee* and *Omoo* for what they are, there is nothing to be gained by arguing a precocious profundity for them. Their claim to fame is precisely the summer ease that made their ambitious author soon impatient of a public character cramped to their limited measure. 'What reputation Herman Melville has is horrible,' he wrote to Hawthorne in 1851. 'Think of it! To go down to posterity . . . as a man who lived among the cannibals!' Still worse, he saw himself prospectively relegated to the minor status of a children's author: ' "Typee" will be given to them, perhaps, with their gingerbread.' Posterity has decided that he did not write for children. But in his first two books he did create a kind of children's world for adults to pine at, where a fortunate few had 'breathed primeval balm' in days before the discovery of the South Pacific by the tourist trade. Another of his nostalgic poems of 1888, seemingly addressed to his old companion Toby ('To Ned'), recalls that half-imagined 'paradise' of 'Pantheistic ports' –

> Marquesas and glenned isles that be
> Authentic Edens in a Pagan sea.

That simple myth survived in his memory without bitterness or irony, and his South Sea romances capture it for generations to whom it remains only as a gaudy dream in a Gauguin painting.

4

Philosophical Allegory: *Mardi* and *The Confidence-Man*

If in later years Melville himself tended to mythologize the experiences of his youth, early readers of *Typee* and *Omoo* could hardly be blamed for suspecting the author of selling them fantasy for fact. His immediate reaction to such a reception, however, was one of exasperation, aggravated by the impulse toward genuine fiction which was making ever more insistent demands on his imagination. The sense of irony mounted in his mind as he set to work on a sequel to *Omoo* in the summer of 1847. He longed, as he wrote to his English publisher John Murray the following spring, 'to plume [his] pinions for a flight, & felt irked and cramped, & fettered by plodding along with dull common places . . .'

> The truth is, Sir, that the reiterated imputation of being a romancer in disguise has at last pricked me into a resolution to show those who may take any interest in the matter, that a *real* romance of mine is no Typee or Omoo, & is made of different stuff altogether.

The new book, he had explained to Murray in January, 'clothes the whole subject in new attractions & combines in one cluster all that is romantic, whimsical & poetic in Polynusia [sic].' A year later, still negotiating with the reluctant Murray, Melville signaled the depth of his break with the past by instructing the publisher to omit mention of *Typee* and *Omoo* on the title page: 'I wish to separate *Mardi* as much as possible from those books.' Murray underscored the separation by declining to publish any more of Melville's work, and *Mardi* appeared, finally, in March of 1849, under the imprint of Richard Bentley, who saw enough advantage in Melville's reputation to justify his asking price of 200 guineas.

It was the publication of *Mardi* that inaugurated the career of Herman

43

Melville as a writer of fiction. For the rest of his life he would be impatient of every circumstance that forced him to retreat from the frontier of romance where he felt the greatest stimulations and rewards as an artist, sublimely irrespective of financial risks and the vicissitudes of public approval. The adventurous territory to which he was irresistibly drawn was a world of fantasy conceived in the service of ideas – what he himself christened, toward the end of *Mardi* (ch. 169), 'the world of mind.' Henceforth, Melville's writing would characteristically reflect an experimental amalgamation of fact and fancy, but two books stand out from all the rest by virtue of their extraordinarily bold departure from the balanced norms of dramatic narration. These exceptional excursions into the visionary realm of philosophical allegory were *Mardi* and *The Confidence-Man*.

In many ways these are radically dissimilar books, being separated not only by unlike settings, characters, and incidents, but also by every quality of tone and style that divides 'early' from 'late' Melville. Yet because they uniquely represent his efforts to construct a fable which should be utterly independent of the 'real' world, it is useful to examine them together, both for the common light that may be shed on their methods and themes and for the still greater illumination of the contrasts thus invited.

I

Mardi, to a more evident extent than any other of Melville's tales, was allowed to write itself. He had to find out what he could do, and this book was the workshop and the laboratory. Matthiessen called it a 'source book for plenitude,' a phrase which points at once to a fault inevitably involved in the very virtue it proclaims: *Mardi* is an unweeded garden; everything went into it but nothing came out. A concomitant fault (if fault it is) may as well be faced in the same preparatory glance: *Mardi* wanders, does not follow a self-consistent plan, is not by any standard a 'well-made' novel. Whether *The Confidence-Man* shares these traits, especially the latter, is a hotly debated question which may be addressed in time. What happened to *Mardi* along the way is not in doubt, because Melville himself paused to inspect his erratic course when it was nearly run and to reflect with exceptional candor on what he found. In the most widely quoted passage of the book he confessed to having 'chartless voyaged. . . . And though essaying but a sportive sail, I was driven from my course, by a blast resistless; and ill-provided, young, and bowed to the brunt of things before my prime, still fly before the gale' (ch. 169).

It is true that Melville announced in a little preface his intention to write romance, but the rules of romance, for writers who practiced that genre conventionally, were if anything more restrictive than the expectations loosely attaching to the sort of travel narratives Melville had so far published. Melville flouted those rules, not because he was ignorant or careless of them, but because he was tempted to try all the variations in one book: nautical romance, chivalric romance, oriental romance, philosophical romance, satirical romance. If he neglected any one set criterion, it was the requirement to imitate nature – to preserve the veneer of actuality which contemporary criticism labeled *vraisemblance*. That sweet deception of standard fiction, calculated to make everything seem 'real' to literal minds, was not likely to operate very compellingly on Melville's ambitious and unruly imagination. When the time came to move into fantasy in pursuit of his theme, he would invent a new geography and new races of men, physical and metaphysical, without compunction.

At the outset, however, *Mardi* is romantic only in the sense that the events recounted, though plausible enough to a point, did not actually take place. Curiously, even the early episodes aboard the whale-ship *Arcturion*, laid nominally in mid-Pacific, take place in a 'world of mind,' since they are the products, not of Melville's activity, but of his inactivity as a sailor. The animal monotony that had appalled him in Polynesia here oppresses him amid the extended calms and repetitive crossings of the Equator in slow search of whales. At sea, as in the islands, the days were 'endless and uneventful as cycles in space.' From this new mental and physical vacuum Melville staged another flight toward engagement – an engagement, as in the valley of Typee, all the more vital for embracing an unknown fate. The first and perhaps the last thing that can be said of the narrator of *Mardi* is that he is physically and intellectually fearless. The metamorphosis comprising his story is measured by the transformation of the first of those kinds of courage, as he faces the perils of an 'endless sea' at the end of chapter 12, to the second kind, as an 'endless sea' of a more ominous sort looms before him at the conclusion of the final chapter.

However complete in its break with historical fact, *Mardi* through its first thirty-nine chapters, or one-fifth of its length, develops a maritime adventure as wild and yet as credible as anything in English and American fiction. This portion of the book consists in turn of two equal segments. The first recounts the narrator's (nameless in this phase) adventures at sea in an open boat with his 'Viking' comrade, the phlegmatic and all-but-speechless Jarl. The second segment focusses on the events following the discovery and boarding of the drifting brigantine *Parki*. The *Parki* block (chs 19–39) represents a solid advance in the general artistic progress of the story, partly as a result of the sheer unity achieved by introduction of an episode substantial enough to offer consequences, partly by virtue of adding to a perilously attenuated cast of characters the fine comic inventions of Samoa and his domineering wife Annatoo.

Neither gain, as it happens, was exploited beyond the interval needed to introduce the narrator into the Mardian archipelago; in the end, the entire *Parki* block can be excised without loss of continuity and leave scarcely a seam showing. Like so many good things in *Mardi*, this interpolated skirmish in the war of the sexes carries its own justification as a set-piece. The reader of *Typee* or *Omoo* cannot be surprised to find in *Mardi* the prevailing manner of the sailor-author, which is yarn-spinning. Time and again, the teller must emerge from some by-channel of his tale to remark, as he does even in the midst of the *Parki* story: 'But all this is an episode, made up of digressions. Time to tack ship and return' (ch. 28). This characteristic discontinuity was a source at once of strength and weakness in Melville's art. It is nowhere more evident than in the two books under consideration, and in both he defended his practice in terms which every reader must weigh for himself when all the evidence is in.

A similar practice and a famous defense are among the hallmarks of *Moby-Dick* as well, and without prejudging their success there we may note in passing how effective a rehearsal *Mardi* provided for the richly digressive manner of Melville's masterpiece. In the first third of the book, before the principal 'Odyssey' portion is begun, no less than half a dozen chapters interrupt the flow of the narrative with extended essays on phenomena of the sea. Whether they 'belong' in the narrative is an open question for critics; that they are almost without exception both informative and entertaining is a matter of general agreement. A case in point is chapter 13, 'Of the Chondropterygii, and Other Uncouth Hordes Infesting the South Seas.' Here is a catalog of sharks as accurately observed and amusingly described as the whales in the greater work to come. Embodied in its style are already characteristic tricks of typing wild creatures in human terms, of elaborating the language of description by learned allusion and mock-rhetorical turn of phrase, of embellishing digression with digression as implications multiply and divide in the author's imagination. Just as the *Parki* episode is a tale-within-a-tale, so the paragraph on shark-hating in chapter 13 is an essay-within-an-essay. And themes as well as techniques unfold in such examples: ironic comments like, 'He who hates is a fool. . . . As well hate a seraph as a shark,' look forward to major developments in *Moby-Dick*'s sermon to the sharks and in *The Confidence-Man*'s brilliant chapter on Indian-hating.

With the sinking of the *Parki* in chapter 37 Melville left behind all safe havens and familiar decks and ventured, somewhat clumsily, into the uncharted waters of Mardi, his 'world of mind'. His minimum working needs were a motivating mission, a suitable plot mechanism, an appropriate cast of characters, and a setting in which the whole exotic contrivance could operate. It is customary for scholars to attribute the principal inspiration in solving these problems to Rabelais, whom Melville read as he worked on *Mardi*, and whose narrative method and style of writing are readily traceable in the finished product. It ought to be recognized, however, that a strong native and contemporary tradition also stood ready at Melville's hand, by which nautical adventure could be converted to various imaginary uses ranging from the frank fantasy of Poe's *Narrative of Arthur Gordon Pym* (1838) to the more subtle moral apologue of Cooper's *The Sea Lions* (1848; reviewed by Melville in 1849). According to Thomas Philbrick, a leading student of this tradition,

> No American writer of Cooper's day could have [been unaware] of the existence of a literary convention which fixed the South Pole as the destination of the allegorical voyage. The journey to a remote region where man can come in contact with a reality more meaningful, more nearly absolute, than that of ordinary life is, of course, as old as literature itself; but influenced by Coleridge's *Ancient Mariner* and limited by the fact that the South Pole was one of the few remaining unknown areas of the earth, American writers of the first half of the nineteenth century came to regard Antarctica as the special province of symbolic fantasy.

For his own purposes Melville substituted an imaginary archipelago in Polynesia for the *terra incognita* of the South Pole; but an allegorical voyage, a symbolic fantasy, was precisely what he had in view when he introduced a fairy princess, a melodramatic murder, a mysterious abduction, and a mythical kingdom into what had begun as a circumstantial fiction of the palpable world.

To see him risking so many assumptions of credibility in a narrative so far built on storms, sharks, mutiny and shipwreck is to watch an author in the grip of an almost uncritical compulsion to etherealize his art. And yet the really momentous event in this strange metamorphosis is not simply a shift in the character of the material, which continues to mix the real and the imaginary as effective metaphor must always do, but a transfer of narrative consciousness from the author to a persona. The radical move to the fantasy world of Yillah and the abstract network of mental islands through which she must be pursued necessitated the liberation of the narrator from his earth-bound author, and in this crisis Taji, 'the gentleman from the sun,' was born. He is a poor enough character, as literary *alter egos* go, but he merits some acknowledgment as the forerunner of a great gallery of self-chronicling Melvillian heroes: Redburn, White-Jacket, Ishmael, and the nameless Dickensian employer of Bartleby.

With the advent of Taji, two brief and largely functional blocks of chapters serve, first, to introduce the dream-maiden Yillah and to set the necessary problem of her disappearance, then to shift the action to Mardi and provide the personages required in the subsequent travels. With chapter 65 the main, or 'Odyssey,' portion of the narrative begins, and the remaining two-thirds of the story is played out within a variable but essentially homogeneous pattern. This pattern consists of four major skeins which may be described in terms of distinct and recurring functions.

The primary skein is that which defines the *mission* and keeps it going. It is the search for the vanished Yillah that propels the narrative and gives it the loose unity of an odyssey. Conceived as a skein, the mission in turn comprises several strands. First, of course, is Taji's simple, positive longing to recover his lost love. But this direct motivation is complicated by one that is negative and another that is equivocal. The negative strand is the pursuit of Taji by the avenging sons of Aleema, the old priest whom the narrator murdered in the act of liberating the maiden from her sacred bondage. Like all acts of violence, this blow is heroic or criminal as it may be viewed, and the protagonist finds himself pursued by the furies of guilt no less than he is drawn by the dream of innocence. Between the forces that push and those that pull is one that threatens to deflect: the determination of the mysterious Queen Hautia to lure Taji to her sinister realm by repeated symbolic embassies to his canoe in the course of the voyage. The distractions of Hautia may be thought of as equivocal motivation to the mission because the context strongly suggests an ambivalence in Taji's own desires which is merely dramatized by the periodic reappearance of the flowery heralds of a dark temptation. Research has long since established detailed symbolic significances in the floral messages of Hautia; the general symbolic import of Hautia and her relentless pursuit of Taji is part of the broad interpretative challenge of the book.

The second skein, which quickly takes on primary value in the mind of every reader, consists of the series of *visits* which Taji and his companions pay to imaginary islands in the process of their search for Yillah. If one interprets 'Yillah' as some sort of golden ideal, then a loose articulation is discernible between the central thrust of the mission and the slow, eddying dalliances in a score of crazy kingdoms, most of which represent by nominal proclamation familiar aspects of human folly. If any one theme predominates in this moral kaleidoscope, it is the instability and capriciousness of governments; but underlying all runs the more basic theme of the vanity of human wishes. Typical of the most interesting of the visits are those to the island of Maramma (chs 105–17), which represents the organized church in society, and to the island of Pimminee (chs 127–31), where the clothes philosophy of Carlyle's *Sartor Resartus* is put to hilarious use in demonstrating what fools these mortals be. The guiding spirit of the voyage is transparently Rabelais, whose peripatetic adventures of Gargantua and Pantagruel are sometimes directly imitated. What originality the visits have emerges mainly in a block of chapters (145–68) in which Melville departed from his fanciful geography long enough to send his characters on a quick tour of the Western World, with a stop-over in Asia and Africa. Under the thinnest of disguises (Dominora for England, Vivenza for the United States, and so on) a number of current and standing follies of the real world are pilloried, often with memorable wit. Among other things, Melville is effectively hard on British imperialism and American slavery; however, the historical particularity of the targets sets its own limitation on the life of the satire.

Linking all these visits is the third skein of *Mardi*, consisting of what may be called *promenades*, borrowing a term from the similar structure of Moussorgsky's 'Pictures at an Exhibition.' Given their function, there are about as many of these inter-chapters as there are visits, each one serving essentially to get the central characters from one island to the next. However, as Moussorgsky varies the form of his 'Promenade' in moving his music from picture to picture, so Melville varies the activities in King Media's canoe according to the Baedeker and the mood of the travelers. These travelers constitute Melville's 'chorus,' to draw an obvious comparison with the method of Greek drama. They represent the spectrum of intellectual society: Media the politician, Mohi the historian, Yoomy the poet, and Babbalanja the philosopher. As responders and supporters to Taji the searcher, they play their predictable parts in the continuous polemic of the voyage, commenting on islands past or to come, and with increasing frequency and intensity agitating the kinds of philosophic questions that Melville's friends and associates noted in his own conversation. As a product of the romantic sensibility, *Mardi* nowhere differs more sharply from its classical models than in its shift of emphasis from the utopia or anti-utopia under consideration to the inner life of the truth-seeker himself. In an important sense, all of the occupants of the Mardian canoe are aspects of the author and speak his thoughts on occasion. Especially is this true of the philosopher Babbalanja, who like his creator resists all easy or partial answers to the problems of life, and who is at once tormented and inspired by the sort of demon Melville associated with his own creative forces.

At the center of Melville's deepest involvement with his own (as distinct from Taji's) quest, a fourth skein enters into the complex fabric of *Mardi*. This skein consists of chapters suspended from the narrative, completely undramatized, and inserted with varying degrees of irrelevance in the manner of a short essay or prose-poem. There are four such *interludes*: 75, 97, 119, and 169. The last of these has already been cited as the *cri de coeur* in which Melville acknowledges with mingled surprise, anguish, and defiance that his book has run away with him into waters of untold depth and risk. The other three, though ostensibly on different subjects ('Time and Temples,' 'Faith and Knowledge,' 'Dreams') share a rhapsodic expansion of time, space, and consciousness that seems less assimilated to merely rhetorical models like Browne, Burton, or even Whitman, than to a psychedelic immersion in experience. Whether these interludes are profound or only bombastic each reader must decide. Melville himself, in *Moby-Dick*, made game of writers of his own stripe 'that rise and swell with their subject' and grow 'faint with their outreaching comprehensiveness of sweep, as if to include the whole circle of the sciences, . . . with all the revolving panoramas of empire on earth, and through the whole universe, not excluding its suburbs' (ch. 104). On the other hand, Hawthorne, shortly after meeting Melville, ventured a more equable judgment in remarking to Duyckinck that he found *Mardi* 'a rich book, with depths here and there that compel a man to swim for his life.' But he added, 'It is so good that one scarcely pardons the writer for not having brooded long over it, so as to make it a great deal better' (*Log*, 391).

Paradoxically, *Mardi* is the flawed work it is precisely because Melville brooded so long over it. But the brooding was not devoted, as Hawthorne's would have been, to questions of order and control.

> He did not build himself in with plans; he wrote right on; and so doing, got deeper and deeper into himself; and like a resolute traveler, plunging through baffling woods, at last was rewarded for his toils.

This description, so curiously apposite to the author of *Mardi*, is actually his own description of the creative methods of an imaginary poet named Lombardo, whose poetic masterwork 'Koztanza' is discussed by Taji's companions in chapter 180. The formal weakness which Melville knew his critics would fault in *Mardi* he assigned in anticipation to this interior model: 'But . . . the Koztanza lacks cohesion; it is wild, unconnected, all episode.' And then he supplied his own answer: 'And so is Mardi itself; nothing but episodes. . . .' The last of the many islands visited is named 'Flozella-a-Nina, or The-last-Verse-of-the-Song.' The whole voyage was conceived, Melville wrote, 'as if Mardi were a poem, and every island a canto.'

II

It is this un-novelistic quality of *Mardi* that is after all most helpful to bear in mind in reading the book, and it is this same negative quality that *Mardi* shares, uniquely among Melville's prose works, with *The Confidence-Man*. But if *Mardi* is a poem at heart, *The Confidence-Man* is a ballet. Like *Mardi*, it demands that the reader divest himself of the expectation of a dramatically consistent narrative of objectively imitated personages. Unlike *Mardi*, however, its action consists of the ritual movement and counter-movement of a succession of symbolically related figures – in other words, as the subtitle announces, a 'masquerade.' The importance of this masked-ball character of *The Confidence-Man* can hardly be exaggerated. The life that it pictures, as the Confidence-Man himself describes it in chapter 24, is a 'picnic en costume.' The costume varies, but the humanity that it masks remains constant. The action of the characters remains constant also, in the sense that it is rhythmical, significantly repetitive, taking its meaning and form from a reciprocal and patterned motion.

In this fundamental respect *The Confidence-Man* is the exact converse of *Mardi*. The earlier book was constructed of a limited set of fixed and discrete characters engaged in a large, theoretically infinite, variety of acts; the later work took shape around a large, theoretically infinite, variety of masked figures engaged in a limited, essentially identical, set of acts. It is nevertheless appropriate to refer to both works as allegories, since they are equally intended to dramatize ideas which are in one way or another embodied transparently in the identities and activities of their characters. If the books convey radically different impressions, it is because *Mardi* is a *static allegory*, operating on fixed equivalents and norms, whereas *The Confidence-Man* is a *dynamic allegory*, generating its meaning out of the moral flux of role-playing characters.

What unifies and propels *The Confidence-Man* is not character, since we are not permitted to identify with any individual or become concerned with his fate; nor is it plot, since what action there is is discontinuous and episodic; but rather it is the theme or subject of the book itself in which the reader must find the center of interest if he is to find one at all. Theme, in this case, includes setting, which provides the key to the allegory: the action takes place on All-Fools' Day (April 1) aboard the river-boat *Fidèle* (i.e., the 'Faithful,' the vehicle of Trust). On this world-ship the passengers – all fools, evidently – exhibit their skill at making wrong judgments as to whether to trust or distrust each other in a series of equivocal confrontations. It is not entirely clear whether Melville is saying that everyone has bad judgment or that there are no right answers, but it is clear that for dramatic purposes he regards the moral life as a two-valued proposition: either we live by Christ's assumption of good in man or by Satan's assumption of evil.

Melville's theme stands out sharply in an oblique light. Many of the authors he read in his later years, and in whose books he left the trail of his pencil, confirmed or crossed his views and so give us a reflected glimpse into his mind. When he read in the arch-optimist Emerson, 'Trust men and they will be true to you,' he scribbled in the margin, 'God help the poor fellow who squares his life according to this.' But in the pessimistic Schopenhauer he marked without comment: 'When two or three are gathered together, the devil is among them.' In Balzac's *Père Goriot* he found, thirty years after, a demonstration as eloquent as his own that 'the world is an assembly of fools and knaves;' and the satanic morality of Balzac's villain, Vautrin, is a virtual paraphrase of the way of the world he himself had painted in the second chapter of *The Confidence-Man*:

1 Herman Melville, aged 42

Gansevoort — May 13. '69

Mr. E. Dexter:

Dear Sir — That mezzotint,
The Healing of the Blind, which I left at
your place — pray, be good enough to cause
the Lettering at bottom, when cut off, to be
glued upon the back of the frame. — I am
glad, by the way, that my chance opinion
of that picture receives the confirmation
of such a judge as yourself. — Let me
thank you for the little print after Murillo.

Respectfully Yours,
Herman Melville

2 Autograph letter, 1869

Paris, you see, is like a forest in the New World, where you have to deal with a score of varieties of savages – Illinois and Hurons, who live on the proceeds of their social hunting. You are a hunter of millions: you set your snares; you use lures and nets; there are many ways of hunting. Some hunt heiresses, others a legacy; some fish for souls, yet others sell their clients, bound hand and foot. Everyone who comes back from the chase with his game bag well filled meets with a warm welcome in good society.

Most arresting of all are these lines from Matthew Arnold's 'The Buried Life,' which Melville did not mark but which, when taken out of context, perfectly describe the title character of his book:

I knew they lived and moved
Trick'd in disguises, alien to the rest
Of men, and alien to themselves – and yet
The same heart beats in every breast!

The theme of *The Confidence-Man* had its immediate roots in the thinking reflected in Melville's own *Israel Potter*, completed only the year before. The practical ethics of Benjamin Franklin, as Melville draws him in that novel, perfectly illuminate both the ambiguity of successful social relations in a world of treachery and deceit, and the self-contradictions which tend to betray even the virtuous man into hypocrisy. 'You can't be too cautious,' the wise man counsels young Israel, 'but don't be too suspicious.' 'I hate a suspicious man, but I must say I like to see a cautious one,' says the Confidence-Man to one of his prospective victims. As agent of the 'Black Rapids Coal Company' this particular operator illustrates as well the wit with which Melville fleshed out his allegory by clothing the devil in familiar commercial guises. The streets, then as now, were full of such operators. Melville's genius lay, not in portraying them only, but in seeing in them a metaphoric potential for dramatizing the moral crisis of his time. In its broadest frame of reference Melville's satiric apologue pictures the breakdown of Jeffersonian America, with its assumption of identity between public and private morality, and the rise of the post-Jacksonian society in which the impersonality of social mass required the replacement of mutual confidence by external mechanisms of control.

The world of *The Confidence-Man* is an America seething with expansionist and perfectionist schemes, a country in which the most transcendental optimism about the latent powers of mind and spirit

53

harmonized with the crassest sense of manifest destiny in commercial and governmental policy. The national temper was enthusiastic rather than critical; the national humor expressed itself characteristically in the practical joke and 'loading the greenhorn.' Even philanthropy confused the genuine and the spurious, and the motives of robber barons who repaid the sweat of labor with crumbs of charity were studies in ambiguity for any mind sturdy enough to penetrate the clichés and rationalizations of conventional rhetoric. Melville's attack on this society is multi-faceted. It responded with exemplary wit to such evangelical projects of the middle decades as that of the American Tract Society, whose formula for saving the world was to publish religious enlightenment to 'the entire accessible population of the United States' by means of domestic missionaries, known as 'colporteurs,' and others who by 1856 numbered around the world an estimated ten thousand persons. In chapter 7 of *The Confidence-Man* one of Melville's most entertaining operators, proposing to 'quicken [missions] with the Wall Street spirit,' sets forth a plan for a 'World's Charity,' predicated on 'doing good to the world once for all and having done with it.' An inventor as well as a philanthropic entrepreneur, this ingenious fellow has also prepared for market a 'Protean easy-chair . . . so all over bejointed, behinged, and bepadded, . . . that in some one of its endlessly changeable accommodations . . . the body most racked, nay, I had almost added the most tormented conscience must, somehow and somewhere, find rest.' Melville could have been inspired to this ludicrous masterpiece by a product popularly advertised in mail order catalogs of the day as the 'Rip Van Winkle Reclining Rocking Chair' and represented over a hundred years later by mechanical lounge chairs still offering the sitter '101 angles for resting.' At its best, the satire of *The Confidence-Man* is both apt and enduring.

Melville made it so partly by sacrificing the normal individuality of his fictional characters in favor of generic masks ('the barber,' 'the herb doctor,' or sometimes 'Mr Truman,' 'Frank Goodman'); partly by sacrificing the normal plot structure of a story, in which 'something happens,' in favor of a stylized, choreographed pattern of interaction which can only cease (not conclude) with his famous closing sentence, 'Something further may follow of this masquerade.' Yet it is a mistake to suppose that *The Confidence-Man* is formless. It has a structure as clearly defined as that of *Mardi*. In the beginning, two chapters of *introduction* establish setting and theme by means of a tableau-like scene on a river-boat, in which a Christ-figure's promulgation of New Testament ethics ('Charity') contrasts with a barber's proclamation of the tradesman's ethic, 'No Trust.' Then follows a sequence of interlocking but episodic *encounters* dramatizing various betrayals of Faith, Hope, and Charity among the passengers. Interspersed among these are four interior *fables* recounted by various characters to illustrate a point, although one is claimed by its teller merely to have been told 'with the purpose of every story-teller – to amuse.' At least two of these, the story of Colonel Moredock, the Indian-hater (chs 25–8) and the story of China Aster (ch. 40), are substantial, well-told, and brilliantly assimilated to the theme. Finally, three *interludes* are interpolated, in the manner of those in *Mardi*, to expound certain views of the author in the midst of the tale; in this case, aspects of the art of fiction: consistency (ch. 14), realism (ch. 33), and originality (ch. 44).

To the student of Melville's art these essays are of exceptional interest, the more since he had in general so little to say about the theory of his craft in relation to his own practice of it. To call them 'essays' may conjure suggestions of Henry James, but a glance at them will call up Henry Fielding instead. A playful air invests them, and, as in the case of the famous inter-chapters in *Tom Jones*, their very titles are framed in whimsy. Melville's are, among the chapter titles of *The Confidence-Man*, uniquely circular in character, a common distinction which points strongly to the careful unity of their conception. As for the apparent casualness with which they are dropped into the story, it is salutary for the hasty critic to observe the timing and preparation of the last of the interludes, which is the penultimate chapter, and which begins by picking up the concluding phrase of the preceding chapter: 'Quite an original.' This phrase not only links the comments that follow to the immediate context, but echoes the description of the first passenger to board the *Fidèle* on the first page of the novel. In his indirect and ironic way Melville then posits the uniqueness and universality of his archetypal figure and defines his center of meaning in memorable terms:

> The original character . . . is like a revolving Drummond light,
> raying away from itself all around it – everything is lit up by it,
> everything starts up to it, . . . so that, in certain minds, there
> follows upon the adequate conception of such a character, an effect,
> in its way, akin to that which in Genesis attends upon the
> beginning of things.

For the writer whose ambitious program was to 'penetrate to the axis of reality,' *The Confidence-Man* is a remarkable achievement. To have produced not one but two distinctive novels of ideas is more remarkable still, despite the relative inferiority of the earlier and less mature work. *Mardi* is a tragedy about an essentially comical subject, the follies of the world, and as such it labors under the besetting fault of romantic art. But *The Confidence-Man* is a comedy about an essentially tragical subject, man's moral failure, and the result is stunningly astringent, as a similar formula was for the most corrosive of all our moralists, Jonathan Swift. In both books Melville revealed himself to be, in a quite unintended sense, 'a man who lived among the cannibals.' Had he been able to trust posterity's capacity to see him in that altered light, he would have had less reason to fear his destiny as an artist.

5

Novel of Character and Initiation: *Redburn* and *White-Jacket*

After the easy success of *Typee* and *Omoo*, Melville had taken enormous risks with *Mardi*, and the bewildered reception of the book together with its disappointing sale made him feel like a gambler who has lost his stake. He felt 'stabbed at,' he confessed to his friend Evert Duyckinck; he complained that 'a hollow purse makes the poet sink'; and when he sent Duyckinck a copy of the book in February, 1850, he begged 'refuge' for it as a thing that 'almost everywhere else has been driven forth . . . into shelterless exile.' With an almost reckless perversity he dashed off *Redburn* and *White-Jacket* in the spring and summer of 1849, protesting to his father-in-law that his hopes for them sprang from his 'pocket' and not from his 'heart,' and that it was his 'earnest desire to write those sort of books which are said to "fail".' 'Failure,' he wrote a year later in reviewing Hawthorne's *Mosses from an Old Manse*, 'is the true test of greatness.' In *Mardi* Melville's reach had exceeded his grasp, and the less exhilarating effort of producing afterwards books he already knew how to write moved him to express a contempt for them which has unfairly shadowed their reputation.

That *Redburn* and *White-Jacket* were despised by their author should tell us more of him than of the books. Trapped as in a vise between relentlessly growing financial demands and the popular taste which alone could yield him the support he required, Melville reacted as he had to, and resented the unoffending instruments of his success in doing so. In his biased assessment of the literary quality of these semi-autobiographical sea stories, he may have misconstrued the facility of his task, taking the smoothness of conjunction between his subject and his craft as a fatal sign of shoddiness or insubstantiality. He certainly chafed at finding himself at the crest of the historic wave that had swept him to instant popularity with *Typee*. But if he worried over what his books would be worth when people tired of reading young men's adventures before the mast, or over the more pressing question of what he might give them to read when he had run out of adventures, his concerns were only those of every author who has awakened to find himself famous and wonders whether the connection between today and tomorrow will be as unpredictable as the connection between yesterday and today. The whole perplexing situation would soon become the subject of a chapter (bk XVIII) in *Pierre*, where he would contemplate in bitterness of heart the paradox that the best productions of men of singular genius, 'those which become the foolish glory of the world, are not only very poor and inconsiderable to themselves, but often positively distasteful; they would rather not have the book in the room.'

The same chapter reflects the root of his insecurity: that the instant success of a young author is 'almost invariably' the fruit of 'some rich and peculiar experience in life' which may accredit him with an originality he cannot sustain. R. H. Dana, Jr, Melville's chief model in the writing of *Redburn* and *White-Jacket*, was the perfect illustration of this observation, although Melville could not have known it at the time. Born to every advantage and gifted with exceptional capacities, Dana nevertheless owes the greenness of his memory to his casual account of a voyage undertaken as a therapeutic corrective to a life of proper Bostonian nurture and prospects. Happily, Dana's career did not depend on his following one book with another, and *Two Years Before the Mast* performed a historic service for literature that would mark it as unique had he written a hundred. It turned the tide of public taste away from the cosmetic romanticism of piracy, imperial exploit, and supernatural melodrama, and made possible an ethical and democratic treatment of life at sea. By focussing on the character and daily experience of the common seaman, Dana effectively brought the sea story out of its exhausted forms of satire and sentiment into modern literature.

Cooper, too, one of Melville's early and continuing enthusiasms, knew the sea at first hand and argued that true originality in the artistic treatment of the subject lay in portraying its realities. His *Ned Myers*, subtitled 'A Life Before the Mast,' came out in 1843 in the wake of Dana's success. In this tale Cooper not only anticipated the picture of maritime hardship which was to form the ground of Melville's sea stories, but built his narrative on the reminiscences of an erstwhile shipmate who had emerged, Toby-like, years later to refresh old experiences. The adventures of Miles Wallingford in *Afloat and Ashore*, the following year, look forward in some respects to those of Redburn, Israel Potter, and even Billy Budd. The vein thus opened, in which the intrinsic glamor of the sea is offset by a countervailing realism, is in fact anti-romantic; and it was in that spirit, rather than the opportune exoticism of the South Sea romances, that Melville conceived his middle tales of initiation into the merchant and naval services.

In terms of artistry, little of what his predecessors and contemporaries did could have pointed the way either to Melville or his potential readers. Miles Wallingford no doubt displays more signs of development than the static adventurers of Cooper's earlier novels; but Redburn at the center of his more unified world dominates the drama of his story like Huckleberry Finn. No doubt, too, Cooper's last nautical novel, *The Sea Lions*, goes far toward replacing action with character as the focus of interest; but Melville took no note of that development when he reviewed the book for the *Literary World* during the period when he was at work on *Redburn* and *White-Jacket*, and neither book owes any identifiable element of its artistic advance to the example of Cooper. In a sense, the seeds of these tales were implicit in what Melville himself had already done, and the progress of his art can be traced in the titles he most judiciously devised. In *Typee* and *Omoo* he had focussed on his scene and the actions peculiar to it; in *Mardi* the stage of action, still ostensibly the heart of the novel, was converted into theme by allegorical abstraction; in *Redburn* and *White-Jacket* he moved to character as his center of interest by infusing the actualities of nautical life with a search for meaning that places the springs of narrative within the consciousness of his protagonist.

Not only did he place his sailor-narrator at the artistic center of both books, he did so in a way that reflects the continuous conception natural to stories undertaken in unintermitted succession and completed within half a year. Whether by accident or design, the episodes he selected for these books were respectively the first and last of Melville's maritime career, and he made of them, not surprisingly, the alpha and omega of his own maturation through the years at sea. Read in tandem, *Redburn*, subtitled 'His First Voyage,' and *White-Jacket*, subtitled 'The World in a Man-of-War,' take on a relationship not unlike that of Blake's *Songs of Innocence* and *Songs of Experience*. Though structurally complete, each in itself, the two novels form sequential chapters in an enveloping account of spiritual growth, at first from naïveté and untutored sentiment to the dawn of self-knowledge and the tragic sense, then from self-absorption through a baptism of fire to a larger comprehension and acceptance of the social world as it is. It is perhaps risky to encapsulate such a theme, but a fitting epigraph for these novels could be taken from

Shakespeare, whom Melville was devouring for the first time while writing them. In chapter 65 of *White-Jacket* he makes Jack Chase praise the opening scene of *The Tempest* for its seamanship; his own reading of that play, however, responded more forcibly to the closing scene, where in his copy he marked and annotated the familiar exchange between the sheltered Miranda and her worldly father:

Miranda: O! Wonder!
How many goodly creatures are there here!
How beauteous mankind is! O brave new world,
That has such people in it!
Prospero: 'Tis new to thee.

Pondering this melancholy rejoinder of experience to innocence, Melville wrote in the margin, 'Consider the character of the persons concerning whom Miranda says this – then Prospero's quiet words in comment – how terrible! In ''Timon'' itself there is nothing like it.'

The epigraph which he did use in *White-Jacket* (there is none in *Redburn*) reinforces the dramatic focus on the narrator's ability to cope, as a nearly unaided individual, with the problems of a perilous and demanding environment:

Conceive him now in a man-of-war; with his letters of mart, well armed, victualed, and appointed, and see how he acquits himself.
Fuller's *Good Sea-Captain*

As a description of the narrator, however, this epigraph is either ironical or inappropriate, since the whole point about Melville's forecastle heroes is that they lack even the minimal supports with which Fuller's worthy sea captain might have hoped to sustain his role. They have no letters of mart, no arms; and Melville is at pains to establish at once, by identical metaphoric means, that they approach the testing circumstances inadequately appointed for the task. Whether anonymous to the world – White-Jacket is never given a proper name – or christened in a mode grotesquely unsuited to his station (Wellingborough Redburn), Melville's sailor-hero in both books is named anew by his shipmates according to his attire, a jacket so unique, so implausibly irregular, as to mark its wearer as 'a sort of Ishmael in the ship.' The words are Redburn's, as he finds himself ridiculed for a greenhorn on all sides, his proud name reduced to 'Buttons' in honor of the most notable feature of his old shooting jacket. White-Jacket, although he does not refer to himself as an 'Ishmael,' shares Redburn's experience of personal isolation through the ordeal of identification with a shroud-like linen garment, at once socially conspicuous and physically unserviceable.

Both jackets are suggestive of vulnerability. 'Buttons' Redburn, coming aboard ship in a landsman's outfit, is too 'green' to live. Having no fixed estimate of human nature, he wavers in his attitude toward the sailors with whom he is thrown, oscillating between enthusiasm and revulsion like a puppy alternately petted and spurned:

> Finding the sailors all very pleasant and sociable, . . . I began to
> think that they were a good set of fellows after all, . . . and I
> thought I had misconstrued their true characters; for at the outset
> I had deemed them such a parcel of wicked-hearted rascals that it
> would be a severe affliction to associate with them. (ch. 9)

His view of ships is no more realistic, having been formed by a parlor model of his father's made entirely of glass, accurate in every detail, but of a transparent fragility that doomed it over the years to shattered rigging and a broken crew. As a child Redburn had tried to peer into its painted interior, but had contented himself in the end with dreams of pirate treasure freighting its darkened hold. The homeward-bound White-Jacket, some 700 pages and five imaginary years later, reflects a drastically altered perception of both men and ships. Although his experience has not dispelled the mystery of good and evil, it has given him a level eye to look into the darkness and has stripped away the illusions of a youthful optimism.

> A man-of-war is but this old-fashioned world of ours afloat, full of
> all manner of characters – full of strange contradictions; and
> though boasting some fine fellows here and there, yet, upon the
> whole, charged to the combings of her hatchways with the spirit of
> Belial and all unrighteousness. (ch. 91)

> Outwardly regarded, our craft is a lie; for all that is outwardly seen
> of it is the clean swept deck, and oft-painted planks comprised
> above the waterline; whereas, the vast mass of our fabric, with all
> its storerooms of secrets, forever slides along far under the surface.
> (The End)

I

The starting point for this metamorphosis is the character of the boy Redburn, christened in honor of his distinguished uncle (Wellingborough) as Melville's elder brother (Gansevoort) had been, and reared in affluent gentility. Though attracted to the sea in a romantic way, his motive for shipping before the mast is not adventure or even the need that afflicts the family after his father's death, but spiritual crisis. On the one hand, as he says, all his 'young mounting dreams of glory had left [him],' and on the other he felt 'as unambitious as a man of sixty.' Redburn's beginning is thus a vacuum of the heart, a sense of life as merely 'bleak' and 'bitter cold as December.' In almost identical terms Melville would launch *Moby-Dick*'s Ishmael, the greatest of his searchers for meaning, in a 'damp, drizzly November' of soul. Again like Ishmael, whose depression takes the form of an impulse to knock people's hats off in the street, Redburn expresses his discouragement and sense of injury by glaring in open hostility at strangers who eye his patches with disdain, and by presenting his rifle at them in what he himself recognizes as a 'demoniac' display of resentment. That it is a form of injury that impels Redburn to go to sea and predisposes his life to tragedy is implicit in the imagery of 'blight' in which he describes the atmosphere of his departure. It is an interesting question whether a too-close identification with the younger self he was portraying might have predisposed the author to a sense of artistic blight upon his book.

Happily, the melancholy that rules in Redburn's heart is not allowed to darken the account of his initiation into the sailor's life. If he enters his urban and nautical adventures a stranger and afraid, he nevertheless possesses the psychic resilience to recognize his alienation as that of the greenhorn rather than of the pariah. To be a New Boy in the New World was matter for comedy rather than tragedy. Learning one's way around the great ocean in a sailing ship, no less than moving a 'prairie schooner' across the plains and mountains of the West, entailed enormous risks and perhaps for that reason encouraged a characteristic conversion of terror to mirth in the mind of the pioneer. For whatever reason, nothing has traditionally excited the laughter of the American so much as the plight of the uninitiated. The most humorous pages in Melville, apart from *Omoo*, are the early chapters of *Redburn* in which the green hand acquires his rude and often unanticipated education into the ways of ships and men. Deceived in everything – the smiling ocean that quickly turns to storm and stress, the simple tasks that suddenly take on esoteric names and pose superhuman challenges, the officers who mask contempt and arbitrary authority beneath a bland façade of mock courtesy, the older sailors who magnify the distance between their aplomb and the neophyte's discomfiture – Redburn is made to report the pains of his own ignorance and enlightenment with a balance of sympathy and self-derision often suggestive of the tone of *Huckleberry Finn*. That both Melville and Mark Twain had the judgment to put these tales into the mouths of their emerging innocents is one of the first marks of their genius. It is the extent and manner of the emergence, as much as anything, that differentiates the novels they achieved.

Huck Finn's life, like Redburn's, was not all freedom and joy, either afloat or ashore. On his raft there were the chicaneries of the 'King' and the 'Duke' to contend with; on land there were the malice of 'Pap' and the dark forces of ignorance and prejudice. Yet nowhere does Twain place salvation beyond the reach of good will and ingenuity, and rarely, apart from the pervasive curse of slavery, does evil loom larger in his pages than a social charade. Redburn's introduction to human wicked-ness is as different from Huck's as the sea is from the river. What for the boy on the raft is a game of wits with ethical stakes is for the lad in the forecastle an immersion in a society of 'black-hearted' men who are not only to be feared but 'loathed, detested, and hated.'

Focal point of this milieu of malevolence is the character of Jackson, a hideous seaman of indeterminate age, with a Satanic force of character and an 'infernal' eye that, the narrator tells us, 'haunts me to this day.' There is no doubt that the principle of pure (i.e., motiveless) evil in human nature haunted his author and led him to recreate versions of Jackson in book after book. In all of his forms he is at once a man – 'a Cain ... branded ... with some inscrutable curse' – and a spirit avowedly owing its conception to Milton's Satan. Though he has no redeeming qualities, he is nevertheless artistically redeemed by Melville's tragic insight into the burden of damnation:

> But there seemed even more woe than wickedness about the man; and his wickedness seemed to spring from his woe; and for all his hideousness, there was that in his eye at times, that was ineffably pitiable and touching; and though there were moments when I almost hated this Jackson yet I have pitied no man as I have pitied him. (ch. 22)

It is as though the frail and dying Jackson, in the very concentration of his rancor, bore somehow the intolerable weight of all the world's malice.

For young Redburn, in his school of life, it is only a step from the personal corruption of one hopeless sailor to the mass corruption of civilized society. Accordingly, the next lesson in Redburn's education is man's inhumanity to man. For nearly a hundred pages, or the central third of the book, the boy is allowed to roam the docks and streets of Liverpool, digesting his nearly indigestible impressions of the squalor and vice that had appalled his creator a decade before. The plight of the sailor, the degradation of the urban poor, the filth and dilapidation of the city, above all the extinction of sympathy in the grubby commerce of the inhabitants – all contribute to the erosion of the young visitor's faith and optimism. He is sobered and saddened by these observations, and personally embittered to find that his sort are not welcome in the fashionable quarter of town; but he is struck to the soul by the discovery, in the infamous alley called Launcelott's-Hey, that women and children can starve to death in the midst of life and the world do its level best to ignore the fact. Redburn's mounting horror and unavailing efforts to obtain help for a dying family have the lineaments of nightmare; the scene is engraved on the memory and imposed like a shadow on the whole of life. 'What right,' Redburn asks himself, 'had anybody in the wide world to smile and be glad, when sights like this were to be seen? . . . What are our creeds, and how do we hope to be saved?' Such an experience is Benito Cereno's and Israel Potter's in later and darker stories of Melville's. Here, the effect is registered on the perceptions of a boy, and it confirms the 'blight' with which adult reflection had marked the outset of his voyage.

From here on, the theme of Redburn's voyage is not adventure but survival. It is marked by repeated images of failure and death, conveyed in a style so sharply changed from the playful, mock-adolescent tone of the earlier chapters as to cause some critics to question its consistency. In all likelihood, the theme of the book could not be communicated at all without a distinct maturation of view in the course of the story, matched by a corresponding maturation of language. Mark Twain's method of imitating a boy's unmediated perceptions is not a credible method for an older Wellingborough Redburn recalling his youth across a crucial gulf of time which it is precisely his object to illuminate.

The tragic realities of failure and death are brought into focus with great dramatic skill. Chapter 19 ('A Narrow Escape') foreshadows these themes in the midst of the innocence of the outward vyage. A glancing collision with a passing vessel in the dead of night releases a train of memory and imagination: first, a simile likening the fatal impact of sailing ships to the death-struggle of antlered elks; then the recollection of a certain proud ship forced back to port with a shattered side, and of a vigorous acquaintance similarly brought down by a paralyzing stroke; finally, a philosophic expansion of the existential plight of ships and men 'quenched out of sight' by an unforeseen and devastating encounter. At the moral keystone and turning point of the book the theme of failure receives full dramatic embodiment with the introduction of Harry Bolton, the gentle and hapless English boy in whom Redburn embraces his own finer qualities, recoils from his latent weaknesses, and suffers vicariously a fate that might, but for the grace of God, have been his. In Harry, a brilliant, sensitive, dashing youth who is born to wealth but cannot manage money, who longs for adventure but cannot work, who faces circumstance with courage but is literally crushed by his destiny, Redburn recognizes the tragic discrepancy between a lust for life and a talent for living.

Reinforcing and advancing this awareness is a succession of images of hell, isolated in narration but concerted in effect. Two of these resemble the device familiar enough in epic poems: the descent into Hades as a spiritual crisis in the life of the hero. During the central Liverpool episode Redburn accompanies his new friend Harry to a London gambling house to witness in virtuous passivity the damnation of his companion. Later, on the return voyage, the steerage of the *Highlander*, into which Melville imaginatively crammed hundreds of emigrants in place of the score or so who were in fact aboard, is painted as a pesthouse, a 'cess-pool,' in which dying men, women, and children are confined by storm under closed hatches and unspeakable privations. Two related images, one on the outward voyage, one on the homeward, elaborate the pattern. In chapter 22 the *Highlander* passes a drifting hulk in mid-ocean, a sinister threat to shipping and a grisly horror to all who observe the moldering corpses lashed to its rail. Although the full tragic potential of this incident could be tapped only long afterward in a poem called 'The Aeolian Harp,' nevertheless Melville emphasized its bleakest implications through Jackson's vitriolic denial of salvation for the dead sailors: 'Don't talk of heaven to me – it's a lie – I know it – and they are all fools that believe in it.' Even more dreadful is the experience in chapter 48 of the 'Living Corpse,' which bursts into flame in the darkened forecastle, a plain enough case of 'animal combustion,' but to the horrified Redburn an unforgettable 'premonition of the hell of the Calvinists.' In the end, a sadder and wiser Redburn ponders the fundamental validity of the Christian's hopes: 'We may have civilized bodies and yet barbarous souls,' he says at the end of chapter 58. 'We are blind to the real sights of this world; deaf to its voice; and dead to its death.'

Dominating Melville's 'little nursery tale,' as he mockingly described it to Dana (October 6, 1849), is its central symbol, placed precisely in its middle chapters. This is the 'prosy old guide-book' which young Redburn has brought with him from home in the eager expectation of finding his way in a strange land by the directions his father had followed as a commercial traveler thirty years before. The discovery that the old landmarks are gone or changed beyond recall is a blow to a faith that seems somehow more deeply rooted than simply a naïve assurance in maps. His leather-bound guidebook with its 'cocked-hat corners' and 'fine old family associations' is for the youth a part of his inherited wisdom, yet in its silence on the constructions of his own generation, as well as in its confident testimony to vanished antiquities, it makes the whole world appear 'a deceit – a gull – a sham – a hoax!' The guidebook of the father is one of Melville's most natural and resonant symbols. It exactly balances and focusses the progress of youthful illusion and dependence toward awareness and self-reliance, and it makes of *Redburn* a 'nursery tale' in a sense that the author, even in irony, could hardly have intended. If it shows any mark of artistic immaturity, it is only in an unwillingness, common enough in Melville's time, to trust the reader to understand intuitively that 'the thing that had guided the father could not guide the son.' Indeed, a full paragraph of explication expands the moral to embrace books in general and allows only the Bible as a pious exception to what Irving before him had called the 'mutability of literature.'

II

Young Redburn surveys the world of change and defeat into which he has been initiated with a modest self-congratulation: 'I . . . chance to survive.' But he adds that he has 'passed through far more perilous scenes than any narrated in this, My First Voyage.' These more perilous scenes are narrated in the next two books, both of which significantly end, not merely with the hero's survival, but with a memorable suggestion of death-and-rebirth that elevates endurance to renewal. This change is one of the advances marking the approach to Melville's masterpiece, and one of the reasons for the affection many readers have felt for *White-Jacket* second only to that greater work.

The change with which a reading of *White-Jacket* must begin, however, is the subtle alteration in the feature selected by Melville as a personal emblem of both Redburn and his older successor – the jacket introduced in the first sentence of both books. Whereas young Wellingborough's shooting-jacket is pressed upon him by a protective older brother and appears to serve its brief initiatory turn well enough despite its extraordinary buttons, the makeshift garment of White-Jacket is a thing, and an identity, of his own devising, pieced together from available though unsuitable materials to shield him as best it might from the rigors of the voyage. The drama of its owner's life aboard the *Neversink* derives from the dual effects of the jacket's permeability and singularity. The opening chapter points to the function of the jacket as a metaphor of the narrator's individuality and a unifying device in a narrative which constantly threatens to disintegrate into episodes: indispensable 'next to [his] skin,' the garment is 'white as a shroud,' and a 'shroud it afterward came very near proving. . . .'

But *White-Jacket* is much more than a novel of personal destiny. It is a tale that looks outward, to a markedly greater degree than *Redburn*, to the nature of the society which forms the milieu of that destiny. The names of the ships say something: *Highlander* is simply a plausible name for a ship; *Neversink* is an ironic commentary on the real name of Melville's ship, the *United States*. The subtitles even more clearly indicate the shift of emphasis: from 'His First Voyage' to 'The World in a Man-of-War.' Technically, this shift signals Melville's first explicit use of the narrative device that was to become the hallmark of his art: the ship-microcosm. Though explicit in only one other work, *The Confidence-Man*, the trick of dramatizing a moral universe in a floating capsule is implicit in most of Melville's best stories. To those who argue the superiority of an open system of symbolic allusion to the closed system of metaphoric representation, *Moby-Dick* is a greater work of art than *White-Jacket* for the reason, among others, that the imaginative meaning of its voyage is less rigidly enforced than that of *White-Jacket*. But the meaning which *White-Jacket* enforces is a statement about life of such elemental clarity and power that its purposes might very well be subverted by greater subtlety or indirection of method. For *White-Jacket* stands out between *Redburn* and *Moby-Dick* like a wood-cut between paintings. In bold relief it draws the lines which delineate the classes of men, which channel and direct their relationships and their separations, which diagram the forces of authority, and which strip to its fundamental choices the career of the individual in the midst of an established culture. Within this oaken framework a multitude of details fill in the spaces in the action with pictures of men and events, of jobs and conditions and rituals, amply justifying the claim that 'a man-of-war is a city afloat, with . . . guns instead of trees' (ch. 18).

Most striking and first established features of this miniature world are its social hierarchy and its power structure. *White-Jacket* illustrates that well-known truth about successful works of art, that compression and selectivity make possible the articulation of ideas too numerous and too complex for literal communication. Within the narrow and highly regimented confines of the *Neversink* the vertical structure of society is literally, pictorially vertical, the ruling faction holding sway on the uppermost deck and the bottom of the pecking order bodily occupying the lowest. The highest authority is distinguished by his total seclusion from 'the people,' who feel his presence almost exclusively through fear of his imminent displeasure. Rewards and punishments are grog and flogging, alternatives distinct enough on a gross sensory scale but about equally stultifying to the spirit. The rules of the community are subsumed under the Articles of War, which culminate with Calvinistic insistence upon the threat of death, and the very heavens enjoy their regulatory functions by dispensation of the captain. The church is represented and formally honored, but 'the people' cannot understand the sermons. Life on the *Neversink* is in short an anti-society in which the reader is forced to see behind the transmutations of metaphor the very world in which he lives, founded in custom and prejudice, and functioning for its own perpetuity when it is not engaged in the destruction of another.

Since it is a human institution, however bad, Melville populates it with characters who sometimes rise, for better or worse, above the anonymity of the ant-like crew. Here and there emerges a full-fledged man whose qualities of undistorted nature call to White-Jacket's affections like heroism. The poet Lemsford, whose verses are stored in one of the guns and ultimately 'published' by it, is admired for his undefeated creativity; Nord is loved for his tacit self-assurance and Williams for his unaffected sociality; old Ushant, defending his beard in the teeth of a shaving edict, seems a saint ready to martyr himself for personal dignity. Above all, Jack Chase, legendary captain of the main-top, sustains the narrator's faith in the essential indomitability of the human spirit. Jack is a prime example of a Jeffersonian or 'natural' aristocrat, whose leadership among men asserts itself by force of character rather than, like Captain Claret's, by virtue of office.

But in *White-Jacket*, as in *Paradise Lost*, the most interesting characters are the evil ones. Of this gallery three may stand representative. The least of these, dramatically considered, had to be invented near the end of the book to stand for the fallen man in this 'Floating Hell' who is not a conscious agent of degradation but merely the cheerful victim of it. Like George Orwell's anti-hero in *1984*, Melville's Landless has been cowed and beaten into a happy insensitivity and 'loves Big Brother.' As his name suggests, his human roots have withered and he drifts about the oceans in a state of living death, 'without shame, without a soul' (ch. 90). The only other character described as soulless is the exact converse of Landless, 'an organic and irreclaimable scoundrel' who uses the office of chief law-enforcement agent on the ship to deceive his superiors and defraud the populace. This 'Knave in Office' (ch. 44) is named Bland by way of expressing both the ambiguity of his character and the ambivalence of his creator. Far more than the morally incinerated Jackson in *Redburn*, the urbane swindler Bland looks backward to Milton's Belial (if not his Satan) and forward to the Confidence-Man, to the more fully developed master-at-arms of *Billy Budd*, and to an array of lesser figures through which Melville explored the world's ethical masquerade.

In the notable gallery of *White-Jacket*, which, like the painting of Medusa, almost sickened the artist himself (ch. 91), there is no portrait more memorable than that of Cadwallader Cuticle, MD, Surgeon of the Fleet. Filled with a pride of profession that focusses on anatomical mechanics to the total exclusion of human sensitivity, Surgeon Cuticle seems better adapted than any of the naval officers to dramatize Melville's fundamental theme of organized inhumanity. Accordingly, he is allotted a sequence of three chapters (61 to 63) in mid-volume in which to canvass an injury, display his learning to a fawning staff, and perform an unnecessary amputation which costs the life of his patient. The mock brilliance of Cuticle displays the genuine brilliance of the author, for the mounting indignation and horror generated by the entire episode is perfectly balanced by an astringent humor that cauterizes the account and makes Melville's operation successful in precise proportion to Cuticle's failure.

> 'Tomorrow, at ten, the limb will be upon the table, and I shall be happy to see you all upon the occasion. . . .'
> 'Please, sir,' said the steward, entering, 'the patient is dead.'
> 'The body also, gentlemen, at ten precisely. . . .'

Moreover, one searches in vain in Melville's fiction for a more stunning example of characterization than his introduction of the surgeon through a moving description of the cast head of a tragically deformed woman which Cuticle keeps in his stateroom and uses for a hat-rack. Following the chapters on the keeper of this trophy comes strategically a chapter on

69

'Man-of-War Trophies,' in which institutionalized murder by an armed civilization is exemplified in the proud display of the emblems of bloody victory by an anecdotal Indian chief named 'Red-Hot Coal.'

Amidst the seascape of carnage and malice abides the man of feeling in his unique and permeable jacket of white. Six times in the course of his story he stops to comment on its qualities and effects in marking him out as an individual still in, but not of, the world. Once, indeed (ch. 19), it causes a chain of circumstances nearly resulting in a fatal fall from a yardarm. At last it does precipitate the accident foreshadowed, which forms the substance of the climactic and most brilliantly realized chapter (92) of the book. In the absolute rightness of its description, in the psychological penetration of the narrator's approximation to death, in the inspired symbolism of his escape from the encumbering jacket by cutting it off, 'as if I were ripping open myself,' this altogether masterful episode of the plunge from the main-top is a match for anything Melville ever achieved, and as clear an indication as might be that he was ready to undertake his greatest artistic challenge.

If the somewhat over-allegorical vehicle of his naval tale leaves something to be accomplished by way of structural fulfilment, he nevertheless brought to conclusion by this means a coherent account of the education of an American ranging through two novels unsurpassed in their kind of literature. In so doing, he brought himself to the point where it was now possible to create an Ishmael and an Ahab and the sort of universe they must inhabit:

> In our own hearts, we mold the whole world's hereafters; and in our own hearts we fashion our own gods. Each mortal casts his vote for whom he will to rule the worlds; I have a voice that helps to shape eternity; and my volitions stir the orbits of the furthest suns. In two senses, we are precisely what we worship. Ourselves are Fate. (ch. 75)

6

Epic Romance: *Moby-Dick*

By 1850 Melville had written five books out of the maritime adventures of his formative years, but in none of them had he touched upon the central experience of whaling to which all his other adventures were incidental. He had worked down to the heart of what he knew, and now had to face the ultimate question of whether all that oil- and blubber-hunting were really as contemptible as merchant sailors traditionally held them to be, or whether in fact the materials out of which a number of successful journalistic accounts had already been made contained the potential for romance. Having pictured a world in an island, a world in a canoe, a world in a man-of-war, could he now invent a poetically convincing world in a greasy, evil-smelling vessel devoted to collecting animal fat for industrial uses? In this dilemma he had to weigh not only the example of the pedestrian whaling books at hand, but the swarming themes and images and verbal rhythms of Shakespeare, Milton, and the host of lesser classics who had stirred him to emulation in the years following his return from the sea. Most imperative of the forces at work on him in 1850 was his sudden catalytic friendship with Hawthorne, which in the midst of his searching had made clear to him what he must do and so carried him to what he called the 'inmost leaf' of his unfolding genius.

I

It is a curious fact of history that the only other work of American fiction which is regularly granted equal stature with *Moby-Dick* is *The Scarlet Letter*, with which it contrasts in every significant way except ethical value and artistic power. The principal difference is suggested by the character of their central symbols, the A and the whale – one sharply defined, the other enigmatic; and by their settings – a tight colonial village versus the open primeval sea. Although Melville studied Haw-

71

thorne's art and learned indispensable lessons from it about 'the great Art of Telling the Truth,' in point of craftsmanship he had more difficult problems to solve than Hawthorne had because of the greater size, complexity, and public unfamiliarity of his raw material, and because of the radical disparity between the physical and metaphysical aspects of his theme. Hawthorne could educate his readers in a prefatory essay ('The Custom House'), and he could manage his materials through the disciplined formality of a style both traditional and perfected. Melville had to create a fictional world in a sphere foreign to the average reader (though less so in his day than in ours), and he had to extend an already experimental narrative style to express the scope and unruliness of his subject.

All of these problems had to be solved in mutually compatible ways if *Moby-Dick* was to escape the fate of *Mardi*, in which the reader marvels at the variety of books intended but regrets to find none of them fully realized. Put another way, the very richness of meaning at which Melville now aimed was in itself an enemy to the credibility which he had to achieve and maintain in order to keep his reader engaged. At the conclusion of chapter 80 Melville applies to himself as author the basic law of human relations which he has expanded from whale-hunters to the nations of the world: 'And what are you, reader, but a Loose-Fish and a Fast-Fish, too?' The reader, if he has persevered to that page, is still and for the moment a 'Fast-Fish,' but the wise author never allows himself to forget the tenuous character of that conquest and the imminent catastrophe of a flagging attention. Melville saw his problem essentially as a balancing act: a reciprocal levitation of fact and ballasting of fancy. Speaking again directly to his readers in chapter 45, he wrote:

> So ignorant are most landsmen of some of the plainest and most palpable wonders of the world, that without some hints touching the plain facts, historical and otherwise, of the fishery, they might scout at Moby-Dick as a monstrous fable, or still worse and more detestable, a hideous and intolerable allegory.

The irony of his tone makes it plain that a 'monstrous fable' is precisely what he is about and that he regards an allegorical meaning as not only tolerable but indispensable to its value. Here, however, he is concerned, as he had learned to be in the books that preceded *Moby-Dick*, with credibility – 'the reasonableness of the whole story' – not so that it might pass for truth, as *Typee* and *Omoo* had been expected to do, but so that the most ineluctable conditions of art might be met.

No one has described Melville's problem better than E. M. Forster, who placed *Moby-Dick* highest among the works he discussed in *Aspects of the Novel* (1927). It required for him a special category of fiction which he called 'Prophecy' and to which he admitted, besides Melville, only Dostoevsky, D. H. Lawrence, and Emily Brontë. The theme of such fiction, he said, is the universe itself, and its medium is not so much narrative as song. But the inevitable question is, 'How will song combine with the furniture of common sense?' and the answer has to be that 'tables and chairs get broken, and the novel through which bardic influence has passed often has a wrecked air, like a drawing room after an earthquake.' The formal irregularities at which it is possible to cavil in *Moby-Dick* could have no finer apology. In the book there is no evidence that Melville himself felt one to be necessary – beyond, perhaps, the sort of defense Walt Whitman was to offer for the similar transgressions of *Leaves of Grass*: 'I am large, I contain multitudes.' The plea of Melville, as of Whitman, is to respond to magnitude:

> One often hears of writers that rise and swell with their subject, though it may seem but an ordinary one. How, then, with me, writing of this Leviathan? Unconsciously my chirography expands into placard capitals. Give me a condor's quill! Give me Vesuvius' crater for an inkstand! Friends, hold my arms! For in the mere act of penning my thoughts of this Leviathan, they weary me, and make me faint with their outstretching comprehensiveness of sweep, as if to include the whole circle of the sciences, and all the generations of whales, and men, and mastodons, past, present, and to come, with all the revolving panoramas of empire on earth, and throughout the whole universe, not excluding its suburbs. Such, and so magnifying, is the virtue of a large and liberal theme! We expand to its bulk. To produce a mighty book, you must choose a mighty theme. (ch. 104)

Clearly, no book so conceived is 'just a novel.' The first effect of such expansiveness is the transformation of scientific report and journalistic narrative into something broadly identifiable as romance, but transcending that in the direction of epic. Such a story is of course liberated from the novel's usual commitment to mundane probabilities; but its liberation, instead of being a warrant for fantasy, is a commitment to the more demanding ends of myth. The narrative that claims a broader justification than the portrayal of particular lives obligates itself to portray lives of infinite validity, in which whole races of men may recognize their character and condition. Since whaling was one of the two pre-eminent physical adventures of Melville's America (the other being the conquest of the West), a modicum of literary power might have sufficed to make *Moby-Dick* a 'great American novel.' But the range of Melville's thought was no more narrowly national than Milton's, and less national than Virgil's. His theme was as encompassing of humanity as Homer's or Shakespeare's, and the novel, as he molded it to the larger purposes of such writers, became assimilated to their forms: epic, comedy, and tragedy. If such an ambitious combination seems too hybrid to succeed as an instrument of art, its validity must at least be judged, as one would judge the performance of an organ or a flute, in the light of the score to be played.

II

The 'mighty theme' which Melville humorously measured by the bulk of his whale was in truth even larger than that. It goes back to the whale-hunt itself and to the impulse that drove the restless hunters to their interminable pursuit. Though there were mean people in that 'liberal' calling and Melville fairly portrayed them in their place, still the meaning of whaling was expressed through those characters in whose breadth of view the sea itself was the ultimate challenge to humanity. Most arresting of these figures is the one named Bulkington, who seems to have been created solely to steer the *Pequod* out of port as, on Christmas night, she 'blindly plunged like fate into the lone Atlantic.' The voyage that is a unique venture to the narrator, as it had been for the author, is for Bulkington only another round in a continuous and compulsive career of voyaging in which the seeking of deep water and the shunning of land expresses a need of the soul, its 'intrepid effort . . . to keep the open independence of her sea; while the wildest winds of heaven and earth conspire to cast her on the treacherous, slavish shore.' That 'Lee Shore' represented for Melville a perilous safety, a 'craven' flight from the 'highest truth,' which is always 'shoreless, indefinite as God.' Bulkington, the professional whaler, who knows no home and wants no rest, thus becomes a man committed to an ideal of activity – Melville calls it a 'mortally intolerable truth' – in the grip of which 'the land seemed scorching to his feet.' The theme that Bulkington personifies in his apparently rootless and goalless questing is precisely the theme that Emerson had recently expressed in 'The American Scholar' (1837): 'The one thing in the world, of value, is the active soul.'

The question of how 'transcendental' *Moby-Dick* is, of how much and in what ways it bears the mark of Emersonian thought, is problematical. There is a good deal of literature on the subject, a fair consensus of which is that Melville owed more to the methodology of transcendental symbolism in his style of writing than to the idealism of transcendental philosophy in his thought. Nevertheless, the kernel of Emersonian faith just quoted remained a sentiment, even a conviction, of permanent appeal to Melville. Years later, after *Moby-Dick* and the rest of his fiction had been written, he carried on a strenuous and often amusing mental debate in the margins of Emerson's books as he acquired and presumably re-read them. And as early as March 1849 he asserted to his friend Duyckinck both his resistance to transcendental idealism ('I do not oscillate in Emerson's rainbow') and his genuine admiration of Emerson's personal vitality ('I love all men who dive').

III

If *Moby-Dick* owes something of the openness of its spirit to Emerson – or rather to a romantic dynamism for which Emerson was simply the most eloquent spokesman – it owes its character as fiction to quite other impulses and models. Much has been made of *Moby-Dick* as a 'metaphysical' masterpiece; but when the scholars and the critics have departed from the literary scene, it is as a drama of human life that every great novel must make its way. Melville knew what he was about when he praised Shakespeare as the writer who better than anyone else has penetrated to the 'axis of reality.' Transcending all other examples discernible in the voices and movements of Melville's best book is the creator of Shylock and Antony, King Lear and Macbeth, Timon and Hamlet, not to mention a gallery of clowns. Defining a center among these figures, and no less dramatic, is the image of Milton's Satan, bidding implacable defiance to a force sublimely superior to all he can threaten. Although it is by no means the whole story, the titanic struggle of Captain Ahab to avenge himself on the great whale that had reaped his leg is the dramatic heart of *Moby-Dick*, without which it would lack the mythic familiarity that makes it one of the world's best-known stories.

In this central drama, Ahab fulfils the classic role of the tragic hero as precisely as if Aristotle, substituting the ocean and the deck for his accustomed stage, had dictated the terms. By virtue of absolute authority in both his office and his person, the captain is noble, a man of highest consequence. Moreover, he is, though austere, a good rather than an evil man. Ahab is 'godlike.' He even 'has his humanities,' evidenced by a wife, child, mate, and cabin boy whom he loves and who honor him. His essential virtue, however, is deeply flawed by an excessive pride ('I'd strike the sun if it insulted me'), which leads him to presume on powers he cannot hope to match, with the inevitable result that he is brought down by a sudden reversal of fortune in the shape of the great beast he had sworn his life to kill. It is a plot Sophocles might have been happy to take in hand. The character of Ahab himself Melville modeled with the aid of both Christian and pagan images, images which at once describe and foreshadow. Ahab 'looked like a man cut away from the stake' (ch. 28), and tormented himself like one who 'sleeps with clenched hands, and wakes with his own bloody nails in his palms' (ch. 44). His character and fate are simultaneously portrayed in the livid scar which Melville describes in the manner of an epic poem or of a lyric chorus in classical tragedy:

> It resembled that perpendicular seam sometimes made in the
> straight, lofty trunk of a great tree, when the upper lightning
> tearingly darts down it, and without wrenching a single twig, peals
> and grooves out the bark from top to bottom, ere running off into
> the soil, leaving the tree still greenly alive, but branded. (ch. 28)

This protagonist, marked for high endeavor and foredoomed in it, is appropriately introduced by the author, not as an individual at all, but as an unnamed representative of 'all men tragically great' (ch. 16): 'a man of greatly superior natural force,' who speaks 'a bold and nervous lofty language' – 'a mighty pageant creature, formed for noble tragedies.' And to insure Ahab's qualification for membership in this exalted company, Melville locates the root of his character, 'dramatically regarded,' in 'a half wilful overruling morbidness at the bottom of his nature.' The Greeks called it *hamartia*, the tragic flaw.

Ahab's actual appearance on stage is effectively delayed until chapter 28, one-fifth of the way through the novel, following much foreshadowing through the talk of ship's agents Peleg and Bildad and of the crazy sailor-prophet Elijah. When he finally presents himself on deck, the narrator reacts with 'foreboding shivers. . . . Reality outran apprehension.' Braced upon his whalebone leg, Ahab instantly dominates the ship, and at the same time, through the 'determinate, unsurrenderable wilfulness of his eye,' takes unrelenting command of the crew and of the events which will absorb them all. At that moment Melville's first fully drawn sea captain enters the ranks of literature's originals, 'with a crucifixion in his face; in all the nameless regal overbearing dignity of some mighty woe.'

The magnitude of Melville's ambition for Ahab was possibly of more professional concern to him than the magnitude of his ambition for Moby Dick. The white whale, as he points out in time, has the inalienable advantage of his size and power and the added force of his charismatic color; the captain, on the other hand, remains 'a poor old whale-hunter . . . in all his Nantucket grimness and shagginess,' and not 'Nicholas the Czar' (ch. 33). Melville's solution to this problem lay initially in the development of a complex analogy, beginning in chapter 26, significantly titled 'Knights and Squires.' The chapter is devoted to the character of Starbuck, the first mate, and is followed by another identically titled which completes the roster of the ship's hierarchy; but its more essential function is to establish rank as a historical metaphor in which the honorary precedence characteristic of the Old World prefigures, sometimes ironically, the 'kingly commons' of the New. In this explicitly Jacksonian society everyman is elevated by a 'democratic dignity,' divine in origin and potentially heroic, which can invest 'the meanest mariners' with 'high qualities' and 'tragic graces.' Melville's elevation of Ahab, therefore, occurs less by virtue of the autocratic prerogatives of his office than by the power of his vision and the force of his will. It is Ahab the man rather than the captain of the *Pequod* who presides so magisterially over 'The Cabin-Table' (ch. 34), who moves his second mate not only to accept a kick but to dream that he has been honored by it (chs 29, 31), and who sways his entire crew almost hypnotically to commit itself to his private vendetta with nature (ch. 36). The reluctant assent of the one man with understanding and capacity to challenge Ahab on ethical grounds seals the captain's mastery as effectively as if he were indeed Nicholas the Czar. 'My soul is more than matched,' Starbuck reflects; 'she's overmanned' (ch. 38).

Even more important to the conception of Ahab than the democratization of the tragic hero was the articulation of the peculiar hubris that was to bring him down. A simple hatred of the animal that had maimed him, a lust for revenge, however meanly sustained, could have provided motive enough to drive Ahab's story along to some sort of melodramatic conclusion; but it could only have destroyed or made impossible the sort of epic romance that Melville was determined to achieve, and did achieve. The issue is joined, in precisely these terms, in chapter 36, where Ahab reveals his object and is challenged by Starbuck for the 'blasphemy' of seeking 'vengeance on a dumb brute.' In the rebuttal which follows, Melville causes his protagonist to define the symbolic perception that transmutes instinctive violence to existential frustration. Ahab modestly calls his perception 'a little lower layer' of meaning, but it categorically divides tragedy from melodrama. For Ahab is a transcendentalist: to him the things of this world 'are but as pasteboard masks, . . . a wall, shoved near,' and the whale he hates seems 'an inscrutable malice' through which he must strike in order to make his human response to the inhuman milieu of man's life. Sophocles defined tragedy as the encounter of man with more-than-man, and Melville in the single stroke of making Ahab a symbolist established the superiority of Ahab's antagonist on grounds transcending the merely physical combat of a hunter and his prey.

But 'be the white whale agent, or be the white whale principal,' Ahab's wreaking of hate upon him does not become hubris until impulse has been stabilized to principle. In chapter 41 Melville gives it at least a psychological stability by describing it as 'monomania,' a term which characterizes its singularity and inflexibility. Given Ahab's penchant for symbolic thinking, this rigidity of perspective not only leads him to see in his adversary 'that intangible malignity which has been from the beginning,' but also betrays him into an inflated sense of obligation to vent in his own single person 'all the general rage and hate felt by his whole race from Adam down.' Finally, these fatal generalizations gain force in Ahab's conduct through intense concentration and repression. All his very considerable powers become focussed on the conquest of Moby Dick, and then redoubled by the self-imposed discipline of simulated normality. When finally unleashed, Ahab's will rushes toward its awesome object with irresistible power and overreaching confidence. The portrait of the tragic hero is complete when Ahab refuses to pray to the 'great gods . . . as schoolboys do to bullies, – Take some one of your own size; don't pommel me!' (ch. 37). And the course and structure of tragedy are set when Ahab, in the same breath, announces defiantly, 'The path to my fixed purpose is laid with iron rails, whereon my soul is grooved to run.'

IV

The rest of *Moby-Dick* might be easily described as the working-out of Ahab's predestined catastrophe. Had Melville been writing a play it would no doubt have taken that form. But *Moby-Dick* is a novel, a tale told by a character who identifies himself as an actor in the drama of the *Pequod*'s fate. Whenever that happens it means that the reader must watch another, though sometimes shadowy, figure in the midst of the action, and must moreover remember that the impressions he gains of that action, however vivid and seemingly unmediated, are in fact transmitted through the filtering perceptions of the narrator. From book to book, and from time to time in any given book, these perceptions may be partial or distorted, according to the sensitivity and motives of the narrator; indeed, the narrator may be regaling us with a long and compelling tale intended, like the Ancient Mariner's, solely to anatomize his own career and exorcise his own peculiar demons. Melville had had plenty of experience with the first-person narrator before *Moby-Dick*; in fact, he had written in no other style; but never before had his self-projecting story-teller relinquished the center of the stage to another personage, real or imagined, and retreated so modestly to the role of observer. The reason is that never before had Melville created a theme and a character sufficiently commanding to displace his *alter ego* in the fabled segments of his recollected life. Even here, it is not evident in the first twenty-five chapters that he had done so, because those chapters belong altogether to the teller of the tale, one of the most memorable of literary self-portraits.

'Call me Ishmael,' runs the opening sentence, and with that introduction is issued an irresistible invocation to the reader to participate in the remembered life of one who endured in the teeth of disaster. Instantly the author is displaced by an authentic voice of witness, whose account of the despairing mood that drove him from the land and the half-defined longings that drew him to the sea compel the suspension of disbelief which is the primary precondition of successful fiction. What Melville accomplished with the name 'Ishmael', as with 'Ahab' and a host of other names throughout his books, is what any writer seeks to add to the complex work of characterization through the convenient mechanism of allusion. In this case, by that one inspired stroke, Melville brought to life the prototype of the human character with whom he felt the strongest affinity and whom he had in fact portrayed in every one of the central figures of his previous books: the character here termed the 'Isolato' (ch. 27), the outsider, the individual impelled to search for his identity apart from the conventional relationships in which circumstance has cast him. He is, in a special sense, a 'private eye,' not the confidential investigator, but a center of sensibility uniquely personal at once to author and reader, a vantage point equivalent, in romance, to the mediating chorus of classical tragedy. Not only does he beckon the reader to constant identification with the dramatic center of the tale he tells ('Ahab's quenchless feud seemed mine' (ch. 41)), but more profoundly he offers a qualifying angle of vision which enables the reader to govern and savor the experience that consumes Ahab and his ship. As Ishmael confronts the memory he is about to recreate, he seems to put aside a curtain before a drama fully as involved with his own inner life as with the stirring events of the *Pequod*'s voyage:

> the great flood-gates of the wonder-world swung open, and in the wild conceits that swayed me to my purpose, two and two there floated into my inmost soul, endless processions of the whale, and, mid most of them all, one grand hooded phantom, like a snow hill in the air. (ch. 1)

The interior drama of Ishmael parallels and explicates the exterior drama of Ahab. Whether one predominates over the other in importance – whether *Moby-Dick* is 'Ishmael's story' or 'Ahab's story' – is a question of perception or interpretation. More valuable is the recognition that neither story is in the last analysis separable from or possible without the other. The artistic object Melville had in view was as far beyond the self-destruction of Ahab as renewal is beyond defeat. The real essence of *Moby-Dick* is not so much tragedy as the tragic sense of life, a growth which could only take place in the narrator, and only through the failure of the leader with whom his own fate is linked. The enveloping pattern of *Moby-Dick* is death-and-resurrection, starting with the spiritual sickness of Ishmael, who flees to whaling as a 'substitute for pistol and ball,' and ending with his salvation by means of the buoyant coffin of his companion Queequeg.

Between these symbolic poles of loss and regeneration the drama of Ishmael is played out more in ideas than in deeds. So much more vital are the thoughts than the acts of Ishmael that his dramatized presence is allowed to lapse – whether by design or neglect is a matter of critical opinion – during extended sequences of the narrative. That is, the reader hears his voice, as distinct from the author's, only intermittently after the *Pequod* sets sail on Christmas night. Until Queequeg orders his momentous coffin in chapter 110, Ishmael visibly reappears about every fourth chapter, on the average; and when Ahab's quest is rushing toward its catastrophe in the final twenty-five chapters, there is no overt sign of a narrator's presence at all. He is there when Melville needs him, but when the tide of narration moves through the consciousness of Ahab, or into privacies not accessible to Ishmael, it would have hampered Melville to restrict his story-telling to the mechanical rigidity of a limited point of view, and he relaxed his method at the risk of technical inconsistency. It is a fault, if a fault, which will trouble only those concerned with literary technology. Through twenty-five unbroken initial chapters Ishmael establishes a palpable presence at the epicenter of the novel's action, and it does not vanish through periods of suspension or tacit assumption thereafter. It is difficult to see how a fictional narrator could be used with greater economy or to stronger effect.

Since Ishmael's function is to provide, not motion, but point of view, it will be useful to survey the accomplishments of his presence in building *Moby-Dick*'s structure of meaning. He is, of course, everything to the story in the first twenty-five chapters, most essentially through his basic identity as an 'Ishmael,' but almost equally in his developing relationship with Queequeg. It is his friendship with the 'savage' harpooner that counteracts his Ishmaelism, teaches him to search for character apart from the tattoos and grotesque manners that appal his bourgeois Presbyterian sensibilities, and in the end provides the means of his salvation. Several of the occasional reappearances of Ishmael in the foreground of action serve expressly to deepen and reinforce the meaning of this relationship, among them the episodes of mat-making (ch. 47), the monkey-rope (ch. 72), and the squeezing of sperm (ch. 94). In addition, it is four other reappearances during the voyage that erect the philosophic scaffolding of the novel. In 'The Mast-Head' (ch. 35) Ishmael expresses the transcendentalism ('the problem of the universe revolving in me') induced by his 'thought-engendering altitude' as a look-out. This is a sailor notion entertained by Redburn and White-Jacket before him. In 'The Whiteness of the Whale' (ch. 42) he offers a vital counterpoise to Ahab's paranoid view of Moby Dick, enlarging on the natural implications of that 'mystical cosmetic . . . of light' that 'by its indefiniteness . . . shadows forth the heartless voids and immensities of the universe.' In 'The Hyena' (ch. 49), following the first wild chase after whale, he links the physical perils of the voyage with his naturalistic vision of cosmic impersonality and formulates a 'genial desperado philosophy' by which all risks and difficulties are reduced to manageability through the saving mechanism of humor. Finally, at 'The Try-Works' (ch. 96) an apocalyptic vision of darkness and inversion teaches Ishmael to accept the preponderant tragedy of life without succumbing to woe, as Ahab in his madness had done. As a consequence of these crucial and cumulative reflections, the reader is prepared, when 'the drama's done' (Epilogue), to have Ishmael conclude his tale in the words of Job's servant: 'And I only am escaped alone to tell thee.'

81

V

If Ishmael and Ahab share the center of Melville's stage, they by no means exclusively occupy it. Part of the pervasive character of epic and romance in *Moby-Dick* is supplied by the fullness of its social gamut, which Melville appropriately presents in a pair of chapters titled 'Knights and Squires' (chs 26, 27), and in certain later chapters, such as the cluster 38 to 40, which imitate the style and form of a stage play. The supporting characters introduced in these sections surround the two principals in concentric rings, starting with the mates, Starbuck, Stubb, and Flask; closely followed by the harpooners, Queequeg, Tashtego, and Daggoo; and rounded out by a large and various crew, certain members of which, such as the carpenter and the blacksmith, are characterized in considerable depth. This cast, together with the complexity of its activities, contributes to the exceptional range and density that mark *Moby-Dick*. When Ahab achieves his fateful mastery over the wills of his men (ch. 36), the event is registered in part by the mob acceptance of the crew; in part by the representative fealty of the harpooners as their weapons are consecrated 'in nomine diaboli'; and in part by the sharply differentiated interior responses of the mates, whose outward assent blends into the general consensus. Everywhere the three mates yield standing commentary on events from three critical points of view: that of the scrupulous man (Starbuck), that of the careless man (Stubb), and that of what Ahab terms the 'mechanical' man (Flask), who has no attitudes but performs his role in life because it is there. The diversity of views on the hunt which is the focus of the *Pequod*'s cruise is most brilliantly dramatized in chapter 99, 'The Doubloon,' where each participant interprets the announced prize for sighting the white whale in terms of his own private values and aspirations.

A number of characters less central to the action than the mates and harpooners have nevertheless significant parts to play. The little black boy named Pip and the shadowy Parsee named Fedallah seem dramatically extraneous, yet they define important aspects of Ahab's character and foreshadow his fate in uniquely effective ways. As a victim of the very heartlessness of the sea which Ahab is sworn to defy, mad Pip comments with unconscious irony on the desperate quest, and elicits from his equally mad captain, as no one else can, those occasional flashes of sympathy and remorse which remind us of Ahab's tragic 'humanities.' Fedallah and his ghostly Oriental crew represent perhaps Melville's closest approach to the brink of absurdity in *Moby-Dick*, but even outlandish creatures are somehow at home in epic and romance, and the Parsee through his very exoticism succeeds in making credible the pathological need of Ahab for secret support and the superstitious reassurances of occult prophecy.

Along with these two minor figures aboard the *Pequod* are a series of figures outside it which cast ingenious and almost indispensable light on the meaning of the voyage. These figures are not persons at all but ships encountered by the *Pequod* in a succession of mid-ocean meetings which enforce illuminating contrasts with the state or mission of Ahab's ship. From the *Albatross*, whose spectral crew cannot communicate with the eager *Pequod*; through the *Enderby*, whose captain has lost an arm to the white whale and has sensibly concluded to leave him alone; to the *Rachel*, who true to her biblical character is searching in vain for a lost boat; the nine 'gams' have a dramatic character of both individual and cumulative impact in the story.

Engaging all these characters in a fabric of common enterprise is the great voyage itself, the narrative spine of *Moby-Dick*. Just as Ahab brings a career of indiscriminate whale-hunting to bear finally, with all its accumulated experience, on the pursuit and destruction of one creature, so the account of that climactic pursuit circles casually among the anonymous whales and the myriad procedures by which they are captured and reduced to marketable forms, then gathers momentum as the knowledge grows, until the reader is swept – and is ready to be swept – into the vortex of 'The Chase' in the final three chapters.

VI

A common complaint among modern readers, even some who find the drama of *Moby-Dick* most compelling, is that they are not swept into that climax swiftly enough. In chapter after chapter, through the long eddying middle of the tale, forward motion gives way to an interval of static reflection quite beyond the occasional need of the narrator for a moment of soliloquy upon the meaning of the chase. What has to be understood is that *Moby-Dick* is the kind of narrative best described as a symbolic poem in prose. Simply stated, this means that not only its characters and events but also the very texture of its materials are fundamentally and continuously metaphoric. At every turn the reader impatient to follow the hunt does well to heed the example of Ahab – surely the most impatient of all to follow the hunt – and pause to ponder what he calls 'the little lower layer' containing the meanings which are

83

merely masked by the appearances of things. 'O Nature, and O soul of man!' he observes in one of his reflective moments, 'how far beyond all utterance are your linked analogies! not the smallest atom stirs or lives on matter, but has its cunning duplicate in mind' (ch. 70). As in similar soliloquies of Ishmael bearing on a philosophy of perception, the voice of the author is heard behind the dramatic façade, and the literary character of the novel gains significant internal definition. The method is immediately recognizable to anyone familiar with Emerson's views on the relationship between words and things; or with the artistic practice of Hawthorne, whose stories can hardly be said to exist apart from the correspondences that form a fabric of linkage between acts and meanings. Such fiction, like poetry, can never yield itself up completely to paraphrase, but can only return a greater or lesser fraction of the reader's willing investment of imagination.

At its simplest, the analogical technique is no more than overt metaphor, applied in isolation for the illumination of a particular point. When the New Bedford preacher Father Mapple describes a ship's lamp hanging steady in its gimbals while the vessel beneath it rocks and pitches (ch. 9), he intends only to illustrate the operation of Jonah's conscience amid the contortions of his mind and the deviations of his conduct. It is a brilliant image, but it casts light in one direction only and has no more duration than is occupied in the telling. However, when Ishmael in the preceding chapter describes the prow-like pulpit of the chapel and the rope-ladder by which the preacher ascends to it, he moves at once beyond the range of visual illustration and concludes that 'it must symbolize something unseen.' In the ladder he senses 'spiritual withdrawal,' and in the ship's-bow pulpit ('what could be more full of meaning?') a pictorial suggestion of the very theme of his story and of the relevance of the coming sermon to the spiritual adventure to follow: 'The world's a ship on its passage out, and not a voyage complete; and the pulpit is its prow.'

In the same way, the tools and procedures of whaling are kept in constant figurative suspension, catching facets of light as they are turned by the narrator, and illuminating at once the process at hand and the larger life of which it is Melville's design to make it a part. A case in point is the description of the mat-making of Ishmael and Queequeg (ch. 47), in which the image of 'the Loom of Time' not only points outward with great wit toward the abstract constituents of fate – 'chance, free will, and necessity' – but inward as well to the mood of the weavers, their interdependence as participants in the deepening drama, and the cosmic

3 James Hamilton, *Capture of the 'Serapis' by John Paul Jones*. 'In view of this battle, one may ask—What separates the enlightened man from the savage? Is civilization a thing distinct, or is it an advanced stage of barbarism?' (*Israel Potter*, ch. 19)

4 (a) Arrowhead and its piazza, *c.* 1860

4 (b) Fireplace with inscriptions, Arrowhead, *c.* 1870

motion of which such fragmentary acts never hint outside the life of art. In *Moby-Dick* one has a growing sense that nothing exists in isolation. The most recondite facts of an exotic and now bygone occupation crowd into one's consciousness with insistent immediacy: 'All men live enveloped in whale-lines' (ch. 60).

Most striking of all is Melville's handling of the whale itself. The fact that the whale is commonly regarded as Good (God) or Evil by readers who are looking for an easy allegorical key to the book suggests the effectiveness with which Melville loaded his central figure with poetic values. Magnitude and mystery – these are the values generally invoked, and everything is bent to invoke them. The spout of the whale, first introduced as a spectral lure in the distance (ch. 51), is more nearly described as a kind of metaphysical vapor hovering over the head of the great beast like a meditation and 'glorified by a rainbow.' In like manner, thinks Ishmael, 'through all the thick mists of the dim doubts in my mind, divine intuitions now and then shoot, enkindling my fog with a heavenly ray' (ch. 85). But Melville is equally at home with less promising parts of the whale's anatomy. The next chapter begins by acknowledging the graces 'other poets' have praised in nature, but announces that he, 'less celestial,' will 'celebrate a tail.' Magnitude and mystery are the essence of that celebration, as of every other, and all are brought together in a conclusion that reinforces, quite without strain, the supernatural implications of the subject:

> Dissect him how I may, then, I but go skin deep; I know him not, and never will. But if I know not even the tail of this whale, how understand his head? Much more, how comprehend his face, when face he has none? Thou shalt see my back parts, my tail, he seems to say, but my face shall not be seen. But I cannot completely make out his back parts; and hint what he will about his face, I say again he has no face.

As to whether such descriptions are to render a divine spirit or a demonic one, Melville thoughtfully placed his advice earlier in the same chapter: 'it is all in all what mood you are in.'

One of the chief effects of magnitude and mystery is likely to be difficulty, not so much in interpretation of parts, as in comprehension of the whole. Many readers are affected by *Moby-Dick* as Ishmael was affected by the 'boggy, soggy, squitchy' painting that puzzled and fascinated him in the Spouter Inn (ch. 3). And perhaps the reader's problem is to be solved as Ishmael solved his: by discovering the identity of 'that

85

one portentious something in the picture's midst . . . even the great leviathan himself.' Everything else in the picture, and everything else in the book, revolves around that center and takes meaning from it. The myriad details of history, of anatomy and technique, the lowerings and the gams, the mounting drives and tensions of the chase, the encompassing microcosm of the *Pequod*, Ishmael's overriding search for the meaning of his life – all take their place, like the 'endless processions of the whale' in Ishmael's earliest dreams of the voyage: 'and, midmost of them all, one grand hooded phantom, like a snow hill in the air' (ch. 1).

Melville talks often and at length about his 'mighty theme' in *Moby-Dick*, but only twice, in short, isolated sentences, does he allude to the structure of his book. Both statements occupy separate paragraphs at the beginnings of chapters and therefore achieve considerable emphasis, but only when they are brought together, and in reverse order, do they give us what little information we are likely to get about Melville's own conception of the form his masterpiece was taking under his shaping hand. Nothing could seem more casual, less calculated, than the irregular movement of the chapters – from process to anatomy to narrative to history and back to process again; yet in the midst of just such a seemingly random sequence Melville opens chapter 82 ('The Honor and Glory of Whaling') with this laconic and unelaborated paragraph: 'There are some enterprises in which a careful disorderliness is the true method.' Despite an air of humorous irresponsibility about this self-justifying paradox, a high romantic principle of art emerges when it is explicated by the opening paragraph of chapter 63, the only other overt statement that Melville saw fit to make on this fundamental aspect of his craft: 'Out of the trunk, the branches grow; out of them, the twigs. So, in productive subjects, grow the chapters.' It is an artist's definition – impressionistic, figurative, undemonstrable. But it has the virtue of describing an organic work of art in organic terms. To search for a more mechanical structure is to look for the very method that *Moby-Dick* transcends. Like the strands in Ishmael's 'Loom of Time,' everything Melville was came together here in a marvel of coalescence and brought his art to a culmination few writers in English have equaled.

7

Social Novel: *Pierre*

Moby-Dick, the masterpiece that had been 'cooked in hell fire,' was not destined, in its own time, to be a success; but it had cost Melville a supreme effort, and it was characteristic of him to take a perverse satisfaction in its failure, which seemed to him the best evidence of an author's having genuinely tried to surpass himself. 'There is no hope for us in these smooth, pleasing writers that know their powers,' he had written in 'Hawthorne and His Mosses,' in apparent reference to Washington Irving, an author serenely and infallibly in command of his craft. Now Melville was to attempt a novel on the very subject of literary achievement. Its hero was to be a writer who first fails in success and then succeeds in failure. The book would turn out, like the life it pictured, a tragedy.

The paradox of success in failure, as Melville dramatized it in *Pierre*, was not for him simply an idea to be dispassionately manipulated into marketable form. It was an ironic concept deeply rooted in the ambivalences of his own emotional life. Nothing could be more telling than the juxtaposition of sentiments in his letters to Hawthorne at this time, at once rejoicing that 'as long as we have anything more to do, we have done nothing,' and fearing that in his own development he has 'come to the inmost leaf of the bulb, and . . . shortly . . . must fall to the mould.' These letters leave no doubt either that he knew the magnitude of his achievement in *Moby-Dick* or that, for that very reason, he despaired of its public recognition. It is clear from them too that he was both financially dependent on popular success and profoundly repelled by the kind of success he seemed fated to achieve. The five books published prior to *Moby-Dick* had produced an annual income of about $1,600, while Hawthorne was to do as well from *The Scarlet Letter* alone, a work that sold in its first six months more than twice as many copies as did *Moby-Dick* in its first five years. To say that *Moby-Dick* was a failure is not to weigh the reviews but merely to consider that the 2,500 copies disposed of in that time accounted for no more than half the sales needed to return a profit on the book. To add to the problem, what success Melville had enjoyed had come from a body of experience which was now nearly exhausted and from which in any case he now felt a desperate need to dissociate himself. Mainly, this need was simply what Conrad's was to be more than half a century later: a longing to escape from the irksome identification with nautical subjects and to establish himself before the world as a writer of prose fiction distinct from the nine days' wonder of a metaphysical sailor.

In his choice of subject for the book to succeed *Moby-Dick*, then, Melville was impelled by a determination to establish a story on dry land and to construct it on a model more likely to woo readers than the cosmic allegories of *Mardi* and *Moby-Dick*. The realities of the contemporary market showed clearly enough what it had to be. Popular taste was shifting away from the romance of adventure toward the romance of society – from Scott, as it were, to Bulwer and Dickens. But the popular American novel of manners in the decade now remembered as 'the feminine fifties' had little of the fiber of those strong British models. Although best-selling fiction was turned out by both sexes, it was Hawthorne's 'mob of damn'd scribbling women' who set the tone in books like Fanny Fern's 1853 sensation, *Fern Leaves from Fanny's Portfolio*, which sold 70,000 copies. Presumably most of them were bought by women, too, since fiction then was widely regarded as a kind of domestic adjunct, along with (as one contemporary magazine put it) 'the flower garden, the drawing room, and the nursery.' How sore a trial such a milieu must have been to more masculine and philosophical talents may be surmised from the tart exasperation of Hawthorne and the unstable amalgam of emulation and contempt in Melville's description of *Redburn* as a 'nursery tale' and of *Pierre* as a 'rural bowl of milk.'

Melville as a popular novelist in the 1850s was a square peg in a round hole: he was a hopeless misfit, but the fault was only half his. Modern critics are accustomed to saying that the violence which figures so prominently in contemporary fiction is as 'American as apple pie.' In the same way the repellent features of *Pierre* can all be traced to some infectious source in the adolescent art of the American popular novel. From the turn of the century, formula imitations of Richardson and Sterne had told stories of improbable domestic anguish in pietistic sermons, interminable letters and wooden dialogue. The most arrant travesties of reality claimed to be 'founded in truth,' and melodramatic sensation

88

shared the page hypocritically with moralistic repudiations of 'mere fiction.' A veiled (and therefore morbid) erotic element was often supplied by suggestive relationships such as seduction and incest, ostensibly introduced as object lessons to the licentious. Even worse than hypocrisy, because more insidious, was the endemic escapism of the popular novel, which 'fed the national complacency,' as one historian has written, 'by shrouding the actualities of American life in the flattering mists of sentimental optimism.' This prevailing frame of mind has not even the excuse of idealism, since it was all too patently rooted in a materialistic rationale: the United States was not simply the best of all possible worlds, it was the richest, which was even better. Catherine Maria Sedgwick was typical of those widely read social novelists who regarded the principles of free enterprise and equal opportunity as accomplished facts of the national life which, taken together with the Puritan identification of labor and virtue, had somehow produced a country where 'nobody sinks into deep poverty, except by some vice, directly or indirectly.' That bland assumption appeared in a novel called *A Poor Rich Man and a Rich Poor Man* (1836, 1843), a title suggestive of the more sardonic paradoxes of *Pierre* and of a pair of sketches Melville published in 1854 entitled 'Poor Man's Pudding and Rich Man's Crumbs,' narrated by a poet named Blandmour.

Such were the pieties of popular fiction confronting the writer who had produced half a dozen books more or less in the salty vein of R. H. Dana, Jr, and who had defined literature as 'the great art of telling the truth.' Moreover, the audience to whose approval he aspired seemed attuned, not to his sailor language, nor to the sonorous archaisms of his favorite black letter authors, but to a euphemistic and circumlocutory style in which the place of natural vitality was largely supplied by a declamatory elevation applied to stock sentiments. Somewhere in the conception of *Pierre* Melville invented his subtitle, 'The Ambiguities,' and that ruling notion nowhere applies more forcibly than to his own attitude toward the task to which necessity now impelled him. A self-deception indistinguishable from sincerity cries out from the letter in which, in April 1852, he made a last unavailing assault upon the commercial skepticism of the English publisher who had grown weary of losing money on Melville novels. Whatever might have befallen those earlier works, 'here now we have a *new book*,' he wrote, 'possessing unquestionable novelty, as regards my former ones, treating of utterly new scenes and characters; – and, as I believe, very much more calculated for popularity than anything you have yet published of mine – being a regular romance, with a mysterious plot to it, & stirring passions at work, and withall, representing a new & elevated aspect of American life. . . .'

No reader of *Pierre* would recognize that somber and perplexing work in such a description, however honestly intended. To see *Pierre* for what it is it is necessary to inspect objectively its structure, its materials, and the principal strands of thought and technique that comprise its fabric.

I

Architecturally, no book of Melville's is simpler: the story is divided into two approximately equal parts, the first located in the country, the second in the city, and the two joined together by a crucial – indeed, symbolic – journey. The pattern may be looked at in a number of mutually supportive ways. Culturally, Pierre's career is a movement from pastoral simplicity to urban complexity. Spiritually, it is a translation, such as Blake's poems express, from innocence to experience. Psychologically, it is a darkening inward progression like that of Hamlet or Raskolnikov. Mythically, it is the Dantean cycle in reverse, from Paradise through Purgatory to Inferno.

These allusions to *Hamlet* and the *Inferno* are neither arbitrary nor fanciful. Book IX, which attempts to elucidate the disillusionment and rebellion of Pierre, dramatizes his insights and responses in terms of his chance readings in those favorite books; they are made explicit touchstones of his sensibility at the turning point of his life. In so far as *Pierre* is a highly 'literary' novel, it is a saving grace that its level of imitation and allusion is not wholly defined by the ephemeral product Melville evidently mimicked by way of disguise. Much of the best literature fed this book, as it had all his books since *Mardi*: Byron and Scott, Rousseau and Goethe, Carlyle and DeQuincey – to name only a few – and of Shakespeare, not only *Hamlet* but *Othello*, *Romeo and Juliet*, and *Timon* as well.

The substance of *Pierre*, however, like that of all its predecessors, was Herman Melville. If as a writer he had already fished in nearly all the waters of his youthful travels, still he had not yet (as he wrote of Pierre) 'dropped his angle into the well of his childhood, to find what fish might be there' (XXI.1). What he found there of himself is a Freudian exercise in psychic recovery which can only be hinted at in a later portion of this chapter. What he remembered and brought back in names and places, persons and events, is a matter of record, most of it detailed in Henry Murray's admirable introduction and notes to the Hendricks House

90

edition (1949). Here are his aristocratic heritage, the family estates, the early death (in delirium) of his father, his uncle's French wife (and son Pierre), the traumatic blight of a disappointed youth, the alienation from a mother clinging to the pride of house, the struggle for independence, the eyestrain, the growing sense of isolation. In 'Saddle Meadows' he recreated the Pittsfield farm, facing Mount Greylock (formerly Saddle Mountain) and the Holmes estate of Canoe Meadows. In the 'Memnon Stone' he revisited neighboring Balance Rock, and in the rugged terrain in which he envisioned the Titan Enceladus he described the foothills of Greylock, to which (or whom) he somewhat sardonically dedicated the book. In the city it is easy to recognize Melville's lower Manhattan, from the old church on Nassau Street to the Battery. And in the bitter experiences of his cheerless apartment one can trace the painful birth of *Mardi* and *Moby-Dick* (including the 'chirographical incoherencies of his manuscripts') and the deteriorating relations with friends and publishers. It is possible that even the experience of syncope so brilliantly portrayed in XXV.4 may have been drawn from the memory of his own physical and emotional exhaustion.

The novel that Melville wove on this loom of memory and passion may, like *Mardi*, be examined, if not fully understood, in terms of four major skeins which constitute the pattern of the story. The first of these, though last to appear, is easiest to isolate and useful in defining a context within which the more pervasive themes of the novel may be grasped. What may be called the *professional* skein is introduced abruptly in book XVII, entitled 'Young America in Literature.' This short chapter, prefacing the tragic account of Pierre's literary debacle, is one of two satirical chapters – the other (XXII.1) deals with popular philosophers – which are sharply at variance with the prevailingly somber tone of the novel. Bearing as it does on the occupation of both his hero and himself, and transparently reflecting his own experiences as a young author in the market place, this low-comic disparagement of the contemporary New York literary scene leaves little to imagine in tracing the progress of Melville's artistic growth and disillusionment since the euphoric days of *Typee* and *Omoo*. The 'Young America' movement, which had stirred him to chauvinistic excesses in the late 1840s, had degenerated in his mind to a commercial circus. Friends, publishers, critics, readers and audiences alike are now lampooned with a contempt that borders on the very vulgarity he deplores in them, and in the increasingly bitter chapter that follows he indicts them all as hopeless worshippers of mediocrity. Two clear signs point to the intensity of Melville's personal involvement

these castigations: one is the prevalence in these chapters of the 'I'
hich he elsewhere held in check in this third-person narration; the
other is the 'incipient Timonism' which he attributes to Pierre and
which so eloquently describes the very air of his attribution.

The second skein of *Pierre*, less personal but more basic to the
continuity of Melville's writing, is the *political* skein. Despite his disappointment in the politics of literature, nothing in his life ashore had
changed the human sympathy of his sailing days for the man before the
mast. From the first page of *Typee* to the last page of *Billy Budd* Melville
was consistent in rejecting the sentimentality and hypocrisy of those
whose sensitivity to 'the picturesque in the natural landscape' becomes
assimilated to an appreciation of 'the *povertiresque* in the social landscape' (XX.1). The democratic bias of Pierre is militant in such language, as in his denunciation of the biblical acceptance of the haves and
have-nots (XVIII.2), and in his treatment of underdog characters such as
Delly Ulver and Charlie Millthorpe. The political theme seems at first
incidental in the perspective of the novel's romantic absorption in
personal catastrophe; but even the central tragedy of Pierre, whatever its
precipitants in bad judgment and unstable emotions, is deeply rooted in a
tradition of social injustice and pride of place. In no way is *Pierre* a more
direct or significant extension of *Moby-Dick* than in being a tragedy of
human pretension, of the vanity of human wishes, of the fall of princes.
Ahab was a natural aristocrat in an autocracy, Pierre a hereditary aristocrat in a democracy; but the principle of the self-destructive will which
Melville imputes to Pierre is equally applicable to both: *Nemo contra
Deum nisi Deus ipse* (No one prevails against God but God himself) (I.4).

The fate of Pierre, however, is an ironical and ambiguous one. Instead
of resulting from a display of hereditary power, or an indulgence of privilege, or a withdrawal into the sanctuary of class, the fall of the Glen-
dinning scion is caused by the precisely equal and opposite impulses to
challenge the sanctions of history, to rectify the unexpiated sins of his
father, and to exercise his congenital heroism by assaulting the very
bastion from which it dominated his world. The early chapters of the
story are wholly devoted to describing the 'noble pedestal' from which
Fate will topple the unsuspecting hero and to forewarning the reader that
he will find this aristocratic youth 'a thorough-going Democrat in time;
perhaps a little too Radical altogether to your fancy' (I.4). In this respect,
Pierre is the very model of a modern college rebel – although his mother
thanks heaven that she 'sent him not to college' (I.6). Unhappily, for the
novel as well as for its hero, general disaster turns out to be the only fruit

of rebellion and reform. However righteous the motives of Pierre, his destiny as a tragic protagonist reflects the follies of his mind more forcibly than the validity of his aims. Whatever character Pierre might have gained in Saddle Meadows as a champion of the oppressed is soon eroded in the city by moral vanity and sexual hypocrisy. Thus a potential victim, who might have shown certain affinities with the long-suffering Clifford of Hawthorne's *House of the Seven Gables*, becomes a villain strikingly reminiscent of the egotistical Hollingsworth of *The Blithedale Romance*. One possible measure of the failure of *Pierre* is that an admirable theory of the new society enunciated in its opening pages, in which the ferment of democracy is seen as a natural cycle bringing Life out of Death, becomes submerged, if not subverted, in a narrative which demonstrates nothing of the sort.

This apparent deflection of purpose brings us to a third, or *psychological*, skein of the novel. The skeins so far examined involve objective concerns; but the deepest concerns of *Pierre* are subjective. What the book is really about is Melville's writing of it. As early as *Mardi* he had formulated a high-risk theory of serious composition:

He did not build himself in with plans; he wrote right on; and so doing, got deeper and deeper into himself; and like a resolute traveler, plunging through baffling woods, at last was rewarded for his toils. (ch, 180)

In writing the life of Pierre – which is to say his own life – he was therefore determined to 'follow the endless, winding way, – the flowing river in the cave of man; careless whither I be led, reckless where I land' (V.7).

The river and the cave form the dominant image cluster of this remarkable pre-Freudian experiment in fiction. Sometimes the cave becomes a well or vault, as in the 'infernal catacombs of thought' to which Pierre's 'foetal fancy' lures him (III. 2), or the endless 'spiral stair in a shaft' which must be descended to 'find out the heart of man' (XXI.2). Or the river may appear as an 'Indian trail from the open plain into the dark thickets' (IV.5). But mainly the process Melville conceived was literally enough a stream of consciousness, partly associational ('The thoughtful river still ran on in him, and now it floated still another thing to him' (VII.8), partly a manifestation of what a Jungian would call the 'collective unconscious': 'unending as the wonderful rivers, which once bathed the feet of the primeval generations, and still remain to flow fast by the graves of all succeeding men' (VII.8). Pierre is keenly aware of this submerged life in him and tormented by the secret of its meaning. His problem of problems is that he quarrels with the mystery of his own nature as Ahab did with that of the universe. Pierre too will 'strike through the mask' (a visored knight in his case), 'tear all veils,' 'see the hidden things,' and enact the repressions of his 'hidden life' (III.6).

Masks take a number of forms for Pierre. Facets of his character are personified by his mother, by Lucy, by Isabel, and by Glen Stanly, all of whom make some symbolic identification with him, or he with them, or both. With all, his relationships are blurred and anomalous: his mother he treats as a sister; his sister he disguises as his wife; his fiancée is admitted to his home as a cousin; his male cousin, to whom he had been passionately attached in adolescence, usurps his fortune and his place, and the eventual murder of Glen by Pierre seems, like the murder of Poe's William Wilson, a form of suicide. Most important of Pierre's psychic masks is his dead father, with whom he most profoundly identifies himself. But his father is three persons, all represented by portraits: one formal, cherished by his widow; one informal, cherished by his son, until found to have been painted under the influence of illicit love; one unidentified, and perceived by Pierre as his father, by Isabel as herself. The resemblance which Pierre discovers between Isabel and his favorite portrait precipitates his catastrophe by demonstrating her secret paternity and moves Pierre to the crucial symbolic act of burning his father's picture. The erotic implications of these acts and relationships – the Oedipal pattern of life at Saddle Meadows, the incestuous ménage at the 'Apostles' in New York, the Gordian knot of Pierre's attitude toward marriage – these are questions perhaps belonging among the 'ambiguities' of the novel, certainly reserved to more specialized studies than this.

What appears on the surface of the action is a pattern of compulsive aggression and perversity springing out of Pierre's progressive disillusionment and sense of inadequacy in the face of mounting challenges to his judgment and courage. This behavior pattern is what might be called the 'hyena syndrome,' after the mechanism of psychic relief discovered by Ishmael in chapter 49 of *Moby-Dick*: 'There are certain queer times and occasions' ('some time of extreme tribulation,' he later adds) 'when a man takes this whole universe for a vast practical joke.' Commenting on certain madcap antics of Pierre, pointedly reminiscent of Hamlet's, Melville writes: 'If fit opportunity offer in the hour of unusual affliction, minds of a certain temperament find a strange, hysterical relief, in a wild, perverse humorousness, the more alluring

94

from its entire unsuitableness to the occasion' (XI.4). Inevitably, in Pierre's Gothic world, comic relief deteriorates to hysteria, and in the end, scribbling his mad book in utter despair, 'For the pangs in his heart, he put down hoots on paper' (XXV.3).

Framing this degeneratively neurotic career is a pair of remarkable episodes, brilliantly realized both as psychology and as art. Both are retreats – into nature and into his private self – for insight and renewal; both dramatize with agonizing clarity the extremity of his mental stresses. In the first, Pierre reacts to the discovery of a sister and of his father's secret life by visiting a boyhood haunt to ponder the most fateful decision he will ever make. Standing beneath the impending brow of the great hanging boulder he has named the 'Memnon Stone,' he speaks a Byronic invocation to disaster in the face of his determination to obey his moral imperatives (VII.4–6). In the second episode, he responds to the imminence of that disaster by a sudden loss of consciousness during which he is seized by a vision of another scene from his childhood. Carried back in mind to the day he had watched some youthful hikers attempt to unearth a massive rock half-buried at the foot of the Mount of Titans (Mount Greylock), Pierre recalls the impression of the mutilated giant Enceladus struggling forever in vain to hurl his vast bulk against heaven, and in his dream the armless Titan assumes 'his own duplicate face and features' (XXV,4). These chapters alone might suffice to keep *Pierre* on readers' shelves despite its grievous faults.

Most poignant, if not most compelling as art, is Melville's apparent identification of the Enceladus figure with his own self-image as a writer. In recognizing the stream of consciousness – the river of thought – which had to be followed in order to tell his story as it ought to be told, he railed against the shallowness of well-made books and praised those that mirror the 'unravelable inscrutableness' of life and so end as 'mutilated stumps' (VII.8). This tragic imperfection, Melville saw, was the fate of the thought-diver. The tragedy of *Pierre*, as he wrote it, was that fate. 'For the more and the more that he wrote, and the deeper and the deeper that he dived, Pierre saw the everlasting elusiveness of Truth' (XXV.3). If *Pierre* has a central theme, it is this 'elusiveness of Truth.' Beneath the Gothic trappings of plot and character and the involutions of normal and abnormal behavior, *Pierre* is, like Melville's other major books, a novel of ideas, and the durable pattern of its meaning is found in its *philosophical* skein. This is the dimension of greatness in *Pierre*, for which readers continue to endure its faults and wrestle with its difficulties. What is Truth? What is Virtue? are the ultimate questions the

95

novel asks; and its hero, who sacrifices everything for an answer, characterizes himself with pitiless precision as 'the fool of Truth, the fool of Virtue' (XXVI.4).

To understand that phrase is to understand not only *Pierre* but to a considerable extent the course of Melville's thought through the philosophical fiction that preceded it. The long unhappy life of Herman Melville is the record of an unremitting and unresolved struggle to reconcile the absolute values of Truth and Virtue with the relative incapacity of mortal man to realize them. Moral perfection and imperfection stood before Melville's straining vision as twin realities forever resisting all rational efforts to focus them in a single image. The reason we read so many references in his novels and letters to the warfare of 'head' and 'heart' is that he intellectually accepted the distinction but emotionally resisted it – as do we all, to a less painful extent. It was his personal agony and his artistic destiny to portray the 'courageous wrecks' of all the Tajis and Ahabs and Pierres who stalked his imagination in pursuit of his self-destructive ideals, while the self-preserving Ishmael in him suffered the spectacle of their fates but survived to write of them again and again, to – quite literally – the last syllable of his recorded thought.

In *Pierre* the war of ideas, in so far as it is waged outside the mind of Pierre himself, is most readily observed in the characters of the Reverend Mr Falsgrave and the philosopher Plotinus Plinlimmon. In the predicament of the former, the reader is invited to contemplate the discomfiture of the church as an institution attempting to be at once social and divine: to administer human affairs in accordance with chartered doctrines of sin and penance and at the same time to minister to human needs for compassion and rehabilitation. This problem is neither new nor subtle, limited to an early and merely illustrative subplot of the novel. It is in the person of Plotinus Plinlimmon that *Pierre* reaches its most memorable achievement as a novel of ideas. Starting with his very name, Plinlimmon (a mountain in Wales) is redolent with hints of philosophical detachment. He is immeasurably more complex than Falsgrave, and the machinery of his dramatization is correspondingly more imposing. The meaning of Falsgrave is conveyed in one Hawthorne-like gesture when, at table, his 'surplice-like napkin' slips to reveal a pin 'representing the allegorical union of the serpent and dove' (V.4). The meaning of Plinlimmon is conveyed not only by qualities of his personality – one might almost say by their absence – but by his abode, his society, and above all his writings.

On the first two of these features Melville achieved the best and almost the only comedy in his somber tale. The 'Church of the Apostles,' loosely presided over by Plinlimmon, is a brilliant metaphor of the intellectual community of Melville's New York. It is an abandoned inner-city church, adrift in a sea of offices and warehouses, and a makeshift sanctuary for a motley aggregation of rootless professionals. On the ground floor, with 'full purses and empty heads,' are lawyers; in the upper floors (with predictably empty purses and full heads) are assorted artists and philosophers; and in the tower perches a lone musician practicing his flute where formerly the church bells pealed (XIX.1). The impecunious occupants of this shabby warren are disciples of the guru-like Plinlimmon, who surveys his domain with bland and noncommittal gaze as his followers govern their wretched lives by faddish regimens of 'flesh-brush' bathing and starvation diets (XXII.1). There were of course specific objects of satire in these chapters, but Melville's broad target was the eternal illusion of utopian schemes for the perfection of man and society.

The central document of this indictment is also the keystone of the novel, forming the arch between the world of Pierre's pastoral innocence and the world of his urban experience. It is a fragmentary pamphlet by Plotinus Plinlimmon entitled 'Chronometricals and Horologicals,' which Pierre discovers by chance in the coach conveying him and his little family of social refugees to what they hope will be a new life. There are three problems connected with this pamphlet: one problem is what it means, a second is whether Pierre understands what it means, and the third is whether Melville espouses that meaning – whatever it may be. The book provides no sure answer to any of these questions, though all have been unflaggingly agitated in the critical literature for decades. They constitute the fundamental ambiguities in a novel that builds on dubiety as most fiction builds on fact. That inconclusiveness was intentional on Melville's part is clear from the fact that he prefaced the essay with the comprehensive title (ostensibly for a series of lectures) of 'EI,' which is Greek for 'if,' and that he terminated it with a torn page at the words, 'Moreover: if—'. 'If' is indeed the spirit of Plinlimmonism, which might be characterized as moral pragmatism. Simple enough in its statement, the pamphlet makes the case that virtue is relative by figuring Truth in terms of Greenwich time, which has absolute validity only in Greenwich (heaven) while local (earthly) time varies with geography. It is an ingenious but slippery metaphor, at once confirming the authority of Christ the 'chronometer' and denying the wisdom of its adoption by 'horological' man. The catastrophic career of Pierre is, of course, a running illustration of this principle: the effort to live a life of undeviating Christian virtue leads undeviatingly to what Plinlimmon calls 'strange, *unique* follies and sins, unimagined before.'

But does Pierre come to recognize this temporal wisdom? Or does he die in proud possession of his inflexible ideal? And which of those inner dénouements is intended or favored by his creator? These are questions which continue to make *Pierre* a fascinating puzzle even for readers who find it an exasperating novel. Some of the exasperation, without doubt, comes from a common unwillingness to accept the implications of the author's proclaimed 'ambiguities,' which are by definition puzzles. Perhaps what Melville says in his own person of the Plinlimmon pamphlet may be applied to the book as a whole: that though 'such mere illustrations are almost universally taken for solutions . . . to me it seems more the excellently illustrated re-statement of a problem, than the solution of the problem itself' (XIV.2). Ultimately, the reader of Melville's problem fiction has ample sanction for mystification in the author's own confession about this book-within-a-book: 'I myself can derive no conclusion which permanently satisfies.'

II

After the meanings and mysteries of *Pierre* have been pondered, the question remains for each reader whether this book belongs among Melville's masterpieces or among what he called his 'botches.' A critical compromise is to call it a 'flawed masterpiece,' or – a term that Melville himself would have favored – a 'magnificent failure.' Among the important defects that must be acknowledged, the most obvious is a confusion of aims. Melville's naturally discursive instincts as an artist posed some formidable difficulties for him in his chosen medium of fiction. It was perhaps as much by luck as by management that all of his earlier books had in one way or another been capable of accommodating that discursiveness: the loosely woven travel romances, the episodic sailor tales, the allegorical journey, the encyclopedic epic of the sea. In *Pierre* he had committed himself to the traditional novel form and devised a unified plot that restricted his options. When, at the major junction of the story, he encountered the confining limits of a merely conventional choice of narrative methods (time sequence or inner logic), he characteristically denied the issue: 'I elect neither of these; I am careless of either; both are well enough in their way; I write precisely as I please' (XVII.1). It might have been in his mind all along to make his hero a writer, but he waited

98

until this point, more than halfway through the book, to announce the fact, and then he used the chapter, as Sterne might have done, for a highly personal satirical essay on contemporary literature.

The decision to convert his country gentleman to a struggling urban novelist not only creates an awkward discontinuity in the plot but sharply reduces the artistic distance between the author and the protagonist, with whom he now unreservedly identifies himself. In an earlier chapter Melville had pointedly warned that 'the thoughts we here indite as Pierre's are to be very carefully discriminated from those we indite concerning him' (IX.1). Later, as both he and Pierre wrote deeper into themselves, they converged, with inevitable loss of perspective and control. The follies portrayed in Pierre become in the telling the follies of his creator. The ambiguities of tone attributed to the writings of Pierre become in the telling the ambiguities of Melville's. It may have been Melville's intention that this should occur; and if so, it can be defended by the same logic that justifies chaotic art as a mirror of a chaotic world. . The fact remains that the uncertainties of *Pierre* have taken their toll in the judgment of its readers.

Two aspects of the book are not in doubt: the pessimism of its outlook and the unevenness of its style. During the writing of *Pierre* Melville was in no mood for affirmations. The all-important 'resurrection' of Ishmael at the tragic climax of *Moby-Dick* was emotionally inaccessible to the author of *Pierre*, and the resultant darkness of tone brings to mind the warning of Ishmael, mastering this very crisis of spirit before the try-works: 'Give not thyself up, then, to fire, lest it invert thee, deaden thee. . . . There is a wisdom that is woe; but there is a woe that is madness.' The opening paragraphs of book IX of *Pierre* are very nearly a paraphrase of this passage. Since Carlyle's *Sartor Resartus* was a pervasive influence in the writing of *Pierre*, one way of assessing the philosophic disaster at the bottom of Melville's book is to observe its implicit reversal of Carlyle's familiar formula for the education of the soul: after his Center of Indifference, Melville moved, not to an Everlasting Yea, but to an Everlasting Nay.

Finally, even to a casual reader, the most glaring blemish of *Pierre* is its rhapsodic – one is tempted to say mock-romantic – prose. Whether Melville was trying to imitate or parody the fatuities of popular novelists is still in dispute, another of the damaging uncertainties of *Pierre*. What salvages the writing, of course, is that it is only intermittently bad. Many passages, some whole chapters, rise to equal anything Melville wrote. The Enceladus episode, for instance, displays a quality of prose-poetry that could hardly have come from anyone but the author of *Moby-Dick*; and in one remarkable passage at the beginning of XXII.4 the almost surrealistic collapse of time in the consciousness of the desperately laboring Pierre is expressed in a language experiment worthy of a Joyce.

Melville was not always in control of his craft in *Pierre*, but he knew what he was about. He knew the risks he incurred with his readers, and he knew the costs he incurred to himself. With a clear eye he saw his hero face the truth that now faced him:

> that the wiser and profounder he should grow, the more and more he lessened the chances for bread; that could he now hurl his deep book out of the window, and fall on to some shallow nothing of a novel, composable in a month at the longest, then could he reasonably hope for both appreciation and cash. But the devouring profundities, now opened up in him, consume all his vigor; would he, he could not be entertainingly and profitably shallow in some pellucid and merry romance. (XXII.4)

8

Historical Romance:
Israel Potter and
Billy Budd

After the failure of *Pierre* had dispelled Melville's last illusion of becoming a popular novelist, he returned to the novel form – or what might be more loosely described as long prose fiction – three more times. The first of these efforts, only two years later, was undertaken as precisely the sort of 'shallow nothing . . . composable in a month' that he had derided as so inferior to the imaginary profundities of Pierre's novel. The second, written after another two-year lapse, was that strange allegorical romance *The Confidence-Man*, for which he evinced not the slightest expectation of success. The third was the little sea tale that ripened in his mind nearly half a century and lay still unfinished among his papers at his death. Utterly unlike in most respects, the first and last of these, which remain to be discussed, share a unique characteristic among Melville's novels which makes it useful to examine them together: both *Israel Potter* and *Billy Budd*, and only those two, are based on real events in the past and may in that sense properly be called historical romances.

The term is not intended as a procrustean bed in which these vastly dissimilar books are to be forced to lie in comparative proximity. The house of fiction, even of historical fiction, has many mansions. Both of the works in question are of that general type which employ the atmosphere and known personages or events of a past epoch as a vehicle for an imaginary tale, a tale which takes some of its credibility from the verisimilitude of recorded facts but which remains free to adapt those facts to the primary aesthetic purposes of the author. Although Melville used his chosen materials more freely and with less overt obligation in *Billy Budd* than in *Israel Potter*, both books owe their raw substance, if not their artistic form, to specific documented actualities outside the personal experience or invention of Herman Melville.

Otherwise, these productions stand poles apart on the shelf of

Melville's work: *Israel Potter* a serialized pot-boiler, of all Melville's novels the most purely commercial in intent; *Billy Budd* almost a private novel, unpublished by him, and unmotivated by any need to publish. Moreover, they have been oppositely received by critics and the reading public: *Israel Potter* fallen into the deepest neglect of all Melville's novels, ignored by scholars, and until recently unreprinted in popular form; *Billy Budd*, undiscovered until 1924, risen at once to the forefront of acclaim and popularity, endlessly re-edited and reprinted, studied in every classroom, staged, filmed, and enshrined with *Moby-Dick* as a sort of 'Lycidas' to Melville's 'Paradise Lost.' These very contrasts are instructive and may lead to a suspicion of exaggeration in both reputations. In point of fact, both are serious novels, highly readable, with strengths and weaknesses, and linked surprisingly by a common thematic concern, which might be characterized as Melville's theory of history. Historical circumstances are used in both cases to dramatize an anti-hero, a sympathetic character who is a victim rather than a manager of his destiny. Human history, for the Melville of the 1850s and after, appears to have been less and less a record of heroic deeds, more and more an account of what happens to us. The title characters of *Israel Potter* and *Billy Budd*, different in all other respects, define the significant center of their stories by virtue of being enlisted men in the military microcosms in which they play out their losing roles.

I

Melville's very different approach to the two stories is itself a matter of history. The story of Israel Potter attracted him originally as matter for a simple adventure yarn for which the chief events would not even cost him the effort of invention or research. Sometime prior to his departure for England in 1849 he had picked up somewhere for pennies the 'sleazy' little volume entitled *Life and Remarkable Adventures of Israel R. Potter (a Native of Cranston, Rhode-Island) Who Was a Soldier in the American Revolution*, published in Providence in 1824. He got around to using it in 1854 as a serial contribution to *Putnam's Monthly Magazine*, for which he had been writing short fiction for nearly a year. There is no reason to question his own statement of intention in a letter to the publisher accompanying the first installment of the manuscript: 'There will be very little reflective writing in it; nothing weighty. It is adventure.' That Potter's story had a personal appeal for him, apart from its commercial promise, is implicit in the bitter record of the little man

102

whose best efforts go unrewarded as he stumbles from misfortune to misfortune down the precipitous slopes of failure: 'One brief career of adventurous wanderings; and then forty torpid years of pauperism' (ch. 3). What emerged from this protagonist in the deep natural process of his creation was a character thoroughly typical of those conceived in the declining years of Melville's fame: an anti-pilgrim engaged in an anti-progress through a world both dark and bright, but predominantly and finally dark.

The structure of *Israel Potter*, often dismissed as 'episodic,' does suffer from that defect, but not demonstrably because of its serialization. The nine installments of the novel were all determined by page length rather than by any intrinsic considerations. Logically, the novel has six parts – four major and two minor – stitched together after the picaresque fashion by the peregrinations of the central character. Chapters 1 through 6 constitute what may be called the *refugee block* made almost exclusively of the materials provided by Old Soldier Potter, from his pastoral New England childhood, through the battle of Bunker Hill, to the hare-and-hounds experience of a prisoner of war on British soil. This initial section makes no secret of emphasizing incident at the expense of characterization, but brings them into some rough balance in Potter's encounter with George III in chapter 5. Chapters 7 through 11, comprising a *Paris block*, follow a sharply rising line of interest based chiefly on the prominence in the action of Benjamin Franklin and John Paul Jones, the two most fully realized historical figures in the book. This strongly sustained section is followed by a *Brentford interlude*, two chapters of Melville's raciest comedy, marked also by the inexorable progress of Israel's degradation as he drops to the status of a scarecrow in an English field.

Chapters 14 through 20 reintroduce John Paul Jones on the stage of action in a *Naval block* which he effectively dominates. Here Melville had free play among the recorded exploits of America's first authentic naval hero, culminating in the bloody moonlight conquest of the *Serapis* by the *Bon Homme Richard*. This stirring battle moved Melville to one of the most insistently recurrent questions of his career: 'What separates the enlightened man from the savage? Is civilization a thing distinct, or is it an advanced stage of barbarism?' (ch. 19). Perhaps the last chapter in this block, entitled 'The Shuttle,' deserves independent status as an interlude. Not only does it link two unrelated portions of the tale, but it achieves in itself a small masterpiece of farce which manages to comment in effortless counterpoint on the tragedy of dispossession which is the serious theme of the novel. Structurally, the two succeeding chapters are

103

dissociated from the plot and constitute an *Ethan Allen interlude*, dealing with the captivity of the hero of Fort Ticonderoga, and concluding a patriotic motif itself interwoven, in the manner of a 'shuttle,' with the darker threads of the old soldier's tale.

The concluding five chapters, seen collectively as a *waste land block*, are heavy with the imagery of despair and damnation. It is here that the continuity of *Israel Potter* with *Pierre* and *The Confidence-Man* becomes indisputably clear, despite Melville's conscious efforts to confine himself to a work of pure entertainment in which, as he had promised his American publisher, there would be nothing to 'shock the fastidious.' The account of Israel's near-slavery among the brickmakers offered irresistible opportunities for reflections on 'vanity and clay' in human existence, and for a metaphoric description of the kiln in which certain tiers of bricks are ruined by over-exposure to the fire, others by under-exposure, and some protected and brought to perfection between the two extremes. In addition to this little sociological parable, Melville saw in the analogy between social and architectural edifices a reflection on the slight historical value of the individual, which led him to observe that 'brick is no bad name for any son of Adam.'

The moving focus of this dehumanized conception is the black and blasted heart of London itself, swarming with faceless and hopeless multitudes and characterized by allusions to Erebus, Avernus, Phlegethon, and the Cities of the Plain. 'Not Marble, nor flesh, nor the sad spirit of man,' Melville concludes, with an ironic nod toward Shakespeare, 'may in the cindery City of Dis remain white.' Bound to a descending spiral of doom in this urban wilderness, Israel is spared a degradation merely obscene by a brilliant device of hallucination, reminiscent of Pierre's Enceladus vision, which superimposes on the old man's shattered perceptions the halcyon memory of feeding 'Old Huckleberry,' the favorite horse of his rural childhood. When Melville does bring his career full circle in the final chapter, it is in the manner of 'Rip Van Winkle,' with the poignancy of a twenty-year absence more than doubled through (as Melville's subtitle announces) 'His Fifty Years of Exile.'

Israel's less than triumphal return to his native land takes place on July 4, and in an overweight irony Melville has him nearly run down by an Independence Day parade in honor of the veterans of Bunker Hill. But irony was not Melville's sole motive for labeling the serial version of his novel 'A Fourth of July Story.' Whatever he may have believed about man's fate, he was still in 1854 a patriotic democrat and an unreconstructed optimist concerning the good seed of American national character. One of the leading themes of *Israel Potter* is St John de Crèvecoeur's old question, What is an American? Melville's answer is given in terms, not of the social pawn to whom for better or worse the center of his stage was given over, but of the three notable Revolutionary figures whose secondary roles have already been outlined.

One not inconsiderable achievement of Melville's 'negligible' novel is our best literary portrait of Benjamin Franklin – not to be compared, perhaps, to the great self-portrait of the *Autobiography*, but the best we have in fiction. Franklin is a difficult character to draw because he is at the same time simple and complex, an ambiguity reflected in the range of benchmark figures called into comparison in these chapters: Jacob, Hobbes, Plato, Machiavelli. The keynote is his ability to 'act any part' in the world. Implied are both adaptability and superficiality, achievement and fraud. 'Jack of all trades, master of each and mastered by none,' he is 'the type and genius of his land' – the quintessential American. While there is humor in this portrayal, there is no scorn. Melville's lone but signal reservation about Franklin is that he was 'everything but a poet.' The principal quality reflected in this assessment is a sublime confidence in assiduity, an emphasis increased by repeated citation of Poor Richard's maxim, 'God helps them that help themselves.' Melville's own radical divergence from this facile principle is implicit in the whole dismal career of Israel Potter, and it is on this ground that his picture of Franklin veers into satire. Benjamin Franklin was for Melville a remarkable anomaly: the philosopher *manqué*, 'household Plato,' world's champion purveyor of portable wisdom, prophet of a burgeoning American breed whose identity Melville could only dimly adumbrate in *The Confidence-Man*. 'Sly, sly, sly,' was Israel's word for him, and he reminded his creator, as had the Reverend Mr Falsgrave before him, of the combination of 'apostolic serpent and dove.'

The sophistication which is at once the strength and the weakness of Benjamin Franklin is notably lacking in Melville's second great American, John Paul Jones, whose character calls forth such terms as 'savage,' 'barbaric,' 'not altogether civilized.' He is an 'Indian chief in European clothes,' 'an untrammeled citizen and sailor of the universe.' If *Israel Potter* can boast one fully heroic figure, it is John Paul Jones, a man Melville might have liked to be. The relation of his brand of superiority to Franklin's is clear in the observation that he had a 'bit of the poet as well as the outlaw' in his nature. This dimension of Jones is displayed in his reckless aspiration, his very unpolitical discontent with the possible. Though he possesses some of the arrogance of Ahab, he also possesses humor, which reduces the arrogance to brashness; and his retreat in humility from the shadow of Ailsa Craig in chapter 15 demonstrates that he understands his place in nature. Hewing to the facts, in part as reported by Jones himself in his historic letter to Dr Franklin of October 3, 1779, Melville retells the rousing story of Jones's expeditions in both the *Ranger* and the *Bon Homme Richard*. In recasting this rich material, Melville had three objects in view. First, of course, he wished to advance his narrative, which involved assigning Israel a major but unhistorical role in events (he captures a sloop single-handed), in battles (he lights the fires at Whitehaven), and in the councils of the mighty (he suggests naming the flagship for Poor Richard). Second, Melville wished to take full advantage of the dramatic possibilities of the battle of Flamborough Head, and in fact succeeded in making of it an exemplum of organized brutality that gives his treatment more substance, and possibly more literary power, than Walt Whitman's exactly contemporary handling of the same material in the 'Song of Myself.' Finally and most importantly, he wished to extract from the personality of John Paul Jones another aspect of his composite American. What he found in him was 'a type, a parallel, and a prophecy. . . . Intrepid, unprincipled, reckless, predatory, with boundless ambition, civilized in externals but a savage at heart, America is, or may yet be, the Paul Jones of nations' (ch. 19).

The terms of his own formula might well have reminded Melville of that most spectacular of all Revolutionary 'savages,' Ethan Allen, who like Israel Potter had written his own account of captivity in England. For the sake of continuity Melville places Israel in the vicinity of Pendennis Castle at the time of Allen's arrival there, but he arranges no meeting and makes no use of Allen in the narrative other than to reinforce the theme, more and more feebly fed by Potter himself, of Americanism. The character Melville gave Allen was that of a 'Samson Among the Philistines,' a 'wild beast . . . unsubdued by the cage.' To an even greater extent than Jones he is 'frank, bluff, . . . convivial,' and he meets adversity with 'barbaric disdain' – exactly the 'wild, heroic sort of levity' originally exercised by Ishmael in his 'Hyena' moods and by Pierre as an alternative to spiritual capitulation. This sheer pagan vitality, always for Melville the best kind, is now finally identified as something fundamentally alien to the strains of his own people, the merchants and politicians of the Eastern establishment. Ethan Allen's spirit, notwithstanding his New England origins, was 'essentially Western; and herein is his peculiar Americanism; for the Western spirit is, or will yet be (for no other is, or can be), the true American one.'

The headlong frontier qualities of Ethan Allen and John Paul Jones seem equally removed from the pragmatism of Benjamin Franklin and the mere endurance of Israel Potter. Yet all are parts of Melville's composite American, having in common perhaps nothing more than their basic loyalty to the flag, the only subject on which Israel is allowed to be as articulate and intrepid as the rest. When all is said, Melville's three great Americans are known quantities and have their medals in hand. It is Israel who represents – more and more with passing time – that anonymous enigma, Everybody Else. It is difficult to be certain how purposefully Melville drew his picture of the old soldier as an anatomy of the common man. The raw material, or his manipulation of it, permitted no intimate domestic insights, no close emotional approaches to his rambling and uncommitted outcast, and as a result Israel never really rises above his initial role as an aimless victim of circumstance. Yet, as he follows his largely involuntary trajectory through misfortune to neglect, he seems to force his creator's confrontation with the plight of the unheroic hero:

> The gloomiest and truthfulest dramatist seldom chooses for his
> theme the calamities, however extraordinary, of inferior and
> private persons; least of all the pauper's; admonished by the fact,
> that to the craped palace of the king lying in state, thousands of
> starers shall throng; but few feel enticed to the shanty, where, like
> a peeled knuckle-bone, grins the unupholstered corpse of the
> beggar. (ch. 26)

At a later stage in history the Marxist angle of vision might have given some thematic thrust to the predicament of the proletarian hero victimized by society; but the revolutionary bias was far from Melville's mind, as he used his romance to praise American democracy and laid the woes of his Everyman at the door of what Mark Twain was to call 'the damned human race' rather than of any particular political or economic system. Granted that he regarded poverty as a 'weed which but grows on barren ground; enrich the soil, and it disappears' (ch. 23). Still, his wasteland, his 'City of Dis,' is a Sodom or Gomorrah whose essentially spiritual ills are not amenable to any doctrinaire programs of reform. Modern civilization, however it is organized, is full of Israel Potters. Their literary prevalence may be taken to suggest that traditional heroism is extinct, or perhaps that it was never more than a romantic myth. One of the interesting meanings of *Israel Potter* is its implicit equation of the ethical impotence of the common protagonist, the Man Without Qualities, and the functional impotence of the vestigial hero, the atavistic Ethan Allen or John Paul Jones, who rises briefly from the ruck of history to revivify an ancient ideal of human possibility, or accomplish some impossible dream of moral force, only to fall back through corruption or erosion of sustaining power. Between these poles of failure bustles the third element, the Benjamin Franklins, running the world as best they can by practical ingenuity.

It is of course important to note that Melville did not in fact make Benjamin Franklin the residual hero of his story. He contented himself with portraying a world in which men who act and men who are acted upon are equally liable to frustration and defeat. If a common theme were to be found to link *Israel Potter*, *The Confidence-Man* and *Billy Budd*, it would be this; and if it were to be expressed by a common subtitle, it would be: 'The Way Things Are.'

II

When we turn to *Billy Budd*, however, we are confronted by a novel which has been for many years a critical battleground. More than any other of Melville's books *Billy Budd* has excited readers to partisan dissension about its author's attitudes and intentions. To some extent the disagreement may arise out of uncertainties inherent in a work which the author was still revising at the time of his death; but more fundamentally it reflects the degree of Melville's success in creating a fictional situation that matters. The reason *Billy Budd* is debated is that it touches a nerve; it dramatizes, but does not resolve, a dilemma which Melville correctly perceived to lie at the very 'axis' (his good word) of human experience. *Billy Budd* is a problem novel – that is, a novel about a problem. The artistic difficulty the author encounters in such a novel may be not so much how to make the problem clear as how to prevent it from being so clear that it is simply transparent. Even more than in *Pierre*, and quite as much as in *The Confidence-Man*, Melville was dependent on the quality of ambiguity for the effectiveness of his story. If the reader or viewer of tragedy is not torn by vicarious agonies of decision in contemplating the available alternatives of conduct, he has missed the heart of the aesthetic experience. In this tragedy of justice at sea Melville invited his readers ('the snug card players in the cabin') to assume in imagination 'the responsibilities of the sleepless man on the bridge' (ch. 21). The interpretation of such a work is a function of moral participation. Commentary must be content to describe the text and elucidate the facts of composition.

The unique, and uniquely important, feature of *Billy Budd* among Melville's novels is that it has come to us in a posthumous manuscript and that it is the only one of which the manuscript has been preserved. What this means is that all the prior novels and stories have their existence in printed texts prepared and approved by the author, so that each work is final as it stands, but *only* final; that is, the record of how that final text evolved (particularly important in the case of *Moby-Dick*) is forever closed to us. *Billy Budd*, on the other hand, exists as a sheaf of hand-written sheets, scribbled, revised, corrected, shuffled and annotated by Mrs Melville, then stowed away in a trunk until resurrected by an enterprising scholar a generation after her death. The record such a text provides is exactly the reverse of the other: it preserves the process of the novel's growth but only hints at what its finished form might be. The information this particular manuscript contains has been wrested from it slowly and with the greatest difficulty on account of its perilous approach to illegibility.

Three major efforts have been made to decipher it: the original heavily flawed transcription by Raymond Weaver of Columbia University in 1924; the improved but still erroneous revision of F. B. Freeman of Harvard in 1948; and the corrected and currently authoritative edition of Harrison Hayford and Merton M. Sealts, Jr, published by the University of Chicago in 1962. The accuracy of whatever version one has in hand of this frequently reprinted work can be ascertained by three quick tests, using the most visible alterations of the latest editors: its title should be 'Billy Budd, Sailor (an inside narrative)'; the ship on which the action takes place should be HMS *Bellipotent*, rather than *Indomitable* as in earlier versions; and the story should begin at once with chapter 1, not with a short historical 'Preface,' as was previously thought. No single emendation, however, is of transforming importance, and it is better to read a faulty text than not to read *Billy Budd* at all. Helpful as many of the recent changes are, the major contribution of modern textual scholarship has been, not the correction of errors, but the establishment of a 'genetic' text – that is, a reliable picture, almost archeological in character, of the stages by which the conception of the novel grew. At least part of the answer to the persistent question of what Melville had in mind in writing *Billy Budd* could only come, and now happily can come, from watching him write it.

Almost as though he anticipated his ghostly audience in the next century, Melville carefully dated the process of composition: 'Friday Nov. 16, 1888./Began,' he wrote at the head of his first chapter, and beneath that, 'Revise – began/March 2d 1889.' Last of all, he wrote, 'End of Book/April 19, 1891,' though in fact he continued to work on the manuscript until his death on September 28. In the interval the complex little fable as we have it, concluding with the rude ballad 'Billy in the Darbies,' took shape, not toward that end, but precisely in reverse. The earliest sheets bearing the name of Billy Budd are those relating to the draft of that ballad, along with other 'old sailor' verses and paragraphs of Melville's last years. In that first incarnation Billy was an older seaman of lower station than Melville's symbolic foretopman, and the hanging celebrated in the ballad evidently followed a real enough conspiracy to mutiny: the line (11) ultimately generalized to 'all is up' began as 'the game is up.' Melville's original interest in the ballad, beyond the brief and cryptic verses he had turned in imitation of maritime folk art, was to make a story behind the story, to piece together a 'true' history of his hanged mutineer. What he had in view, apparently, was a kind of biography of his little ballad, its 'inside narrative,' and the first condition of such a dramatic reconstruction was the moral purification of his sailor.

A new phase of creation had clearly been entered when Billy took fresh shape as a spiritual innocent, more sinned against than sinning. As his moral profile clarified, a vacuum developed around the need for an evil principle in the story, and John Claggart, Master-at-arms, was born, at first in outline, then fuller and fuller in detail as Melville pursued the mystery of his malice and duplicity. The clearing of Billy's guilt as a mutineer, the placing of a false accusation in the mouth of Claggart, and the transformation of Billy's crime to murder are easy steps in the logic of the creative imagination. All that remains to the essential framework of the great parable in the making is the judge, the all-powerful authority to whose lot it falls to pronounce upon the moral character of the acts he has witnessed and upon the fate of the transgressor. Only at this stage, evidently, when the conception of the troubled captain had added a third dimension to his developing drama, did Melville begin to flesh out a historical scene, to paint the stage of time and place on which his tragic collision of moral forces could achieve human credibility. It is at this point, finally, that *Billy Budd* takes on its semi-polished character as historical romance, a tale of the Revolutionary summer of 1797.

In constructing this quasi-factual backdrop of events Melville strove for two kinds of credibility. In the most general sense he was concerned, as he had always been, that his story not be dismissed as a 'monstrous fable,' the fate he had feared for *Moby-Dick*, but that it be accepted as 'a narration essentially having less to do with fable than with fact' (ch. 28). What he meant by 'fact,' as he explains in the next sentence, was 'Truth uncompromisingly told' – a definition which, in broadening rather than narrowing the field of reference, left him as much freedom for romance as if he had chosen the term 'fable.' What he wished to avoid, he wrote in chapter 11, was mere plot juggling or manipulation of events for some preconceived outcome, such as contriving a prior relationship between hero and villain in order to rationalize the enmity that moves them toward catastrophe. What he sought was a romance compounded of the sort of 'mysteriousness' with which the very reality of life is charged: in this instance, a drama rooted not in mechanical causes but in the profound enigmas at the bottom of such natures as those of his three 'phenomenal' principals.

What history, or a show of history, gave him was not documented certainties of the past, but verisimilitude and motivation. For these purposes he did as much research as he had to and no more. His principal sources were William James's *Naval History of Great Britain* and Robert Southey's *Life of Nelson*, and most of what is specific and authoritative from those sources he worked into chapters 3 to 5. His first object was to establish an atmosphere in which the moral crisis of his story could grow. This atmosphere was admirably supplied by the tensions resulting from, on the one hand, the grave blow to British naval morale in the unprecedented mutinies of Spithead and the Nore in the spring of 1797, and on the other hand, Britain's crucial need of her sea power as a last line of defense against the rising power of France and Spain in the succeeding months and years, culminating in Trafalgar. He located his action on a 74-gun ship-of-the-line with the British fleet in the Mediterranean; he made use of contemporaneous evils such as impressment and the enlistment of criminals, as well as the disciplinary trauma of threatened mutiny; and he seized on the shortage of scouting frigates of which Nelson complained in that campaign to explain the detached service which was to force Captain Vere into the isolated role of judge and executioner. In addition to these solid historical aids, he used the character of Nelson himself as a touchstone of naval heroism, establishing as his primary virtue an impassioned sense of duty.

At some point in the developing conception of his plot, though not at first as was once generally believed, Melville recalled and adapted to his purposes another chapter of naval history, the notorious execution in

111

1842 of three suspected mutineers on the United States brig *Somers* by order of the captain, Alexander Slidell Mackenzie. The deeply moot question of the captain's authority and procedure was impressed on the American public at large by the fact that a young midshipman among the victims of Mackenzie's summary justice, though less virtuous than the legendary 'Handsome Sailor,' was the son of the Secretary of War; and it was impressed on Melville in particular by the fact that the first lieutenant, whose advice and consent was demanded by the captain, was Melville's cousin, Guert Gansevoort. The trial scene (ch. 21), at the conclusion of which Melville explicitly cites the *Somers* case as an analogue, is shot through with echoes of a story which he had known and pondered for nearly half a century. Even Billy's famous last words, 'God bless Captain Vere,' reflect those of one of the *Somers* men, who cried, 'God bless the flag.'

The place where Melville tampered with history, or simply worked from inadequate research, was in establishing the legal framework of his plot. In point of fact, neither Mackenzie's action nor Vere's, had Vere been a real captain of a British man-of-war in 1797, was required or even sanctioned by law. But such action was at least consistent with the spirit (if not the letter) of the Mutiny Act, and no doubt Melville would cheerfully have falsified his facts if necessary in order to provide the statutory rigors indispensable to the dramatic dilemma he wished to create. The difference between history and historical romance is that for the reader of the latter a 'fact' is whatever the author says it is. In the case of *Billy Budd* the facts had to be such, and so arrayed, as to constitute a moral vise constricting the heart and mind of Captain Vere between polar absolutes of sympathy and obligation. It is precisely Melville's genius as an artist that led him to select the facts that conduced to this illuminating crisis of soul and to alter those that did not or invent others to take their place.

In the last analysis, *Billy Budd* is a collage, made of many pieces of history, but also of many pieces of poetry, drama, and fiction, some of it his own. More than any other work of Melville this last brief novel is nostalgic, a kaleidoscopic play of memory over old loves and hates, yearnings and despairs. Most poignant is the dedication of his story to the 'Handsome Sailor' he had really known in the maintop of the *United States* in 1843 – Jack Chase, 'wherever that great heart may now be/Here on Earth or harbored in Paradise.' Much of the 'Man-of-War World' of *White-Jacket* necessarily came back to the forefront of his mind as his guileless peacemaker, Billy, was removed from the *Rights of*

Man to the *Bellipotent*, where his innocence and his stammer exposed him to abuse much as the white jacket had exposed his earlier counterpart. The Machiavellian master-at-arms came partly out of that memory, too, as the polished cynicism of the *Neversink*'s Bland coalesced with the vitriolic malice of *Redburn*'s Jackson to form the matrix of the satanic Claggart.

Least traceable of all the elements in *Billy Budd* is the complex and unprecedented character at the heart of it, Edward Fairfax ('Starry') Vere. The other two leading characters pose far simpler questions. About the sculptured figure of 'Baby' Budd there is the primal simplicity of myth: he is Hercules, Apollo, Isaac, Adam, Christ. He is not all of these at once, of course, but he is all in succession as Melville rotates him to the light of events and displays the essentially static facets of virtue. Claggart, though more problematical within, is of equally monolithic singularity in his social behavior. If he is a deeper character than Billy, it is because of the mysteries that hedge about a 'depravity according to nature.' The finest of tints color his psyche with suggestions ranging from homosexuality to the envy of Satan in the Garden. Still, his external posture is as diagrammatically simple as that of the innocent he accuses with studied lies in the cabin of the *Bellipotent*. But Vere, whose understanding must encompass them both, is a mystery inside and out. An impossible combination of soldier and philosopher, he is a puzzle to his associates, an enigma to generations of readers who have debated and will continue to debate his conduct, and fully understood only by that other 'phenomenal man' whom he condemns to death and by whom he is blessed in his moment of truth. Whether Vere is judged to be a martyr or a traitor to morality – and it does make a difference – he stands in all his excruciatingly human ambiguity as Melville's capstone achievement in fiction.

9

Short Stories and Sketches

Melville's short stories constitute a distinct phase in his career, as sharply grouped as if the fifteen separate pieces he published between 1853 and 1856 had been fifteen chapters in another novel. Even the nine installments of *Israel Potter* merged almost imperceptibly with the separate stories and sketches appearing during this period in *Putnam's* and *Harper's* monthly magazines. Except for the historical material of that novel and the recollected or researched material of 'The Encantadas' and 'Benito Cereno,' everything about these stories bespeaks the inwardness of Melville's thought following the publication and failure of *Pierre*. Financially and emotionally wounded, drained of the narrative substance that had flowed from his mind continuously for seven years, he turned to his own inner condition for the themes of the periodical contributions he had to sell in order to live – and in order to sustain himself as an artist. For this reason, the most revealing, if not always the most accomplished, of the stories are those which are overtly autobiographical.

I

Two tales, both written in 1856, signal their personal character, not merely by their first-person narration, which they share with all but two of the fifteen, but by their undisguised references to Arrowhead, the Pittsfield home where they were written. 'The Piazza' was created expressly as a preface to the collection of *Putnam's* stories which was brought out in 1856 under the title *The Piazza Tales*. Its purpose was to set the personal stage, to establish a point of view. The model of Hawthorne's prefatory sketch in *Mosses from an Old Manse* is visible enough in it, but with the difference that Melville's focus is on outlook rather than atmosphere or sense of place – functionally the difference

114

between a piazza and a manse. What he made of his title story was a parable of imagination embodying both his philosophy and his method as an artist. From his chosen vantage point the world is lighted by the play of sunshine and shadow upon a dark mountainside where, under certain conditions, he can detect 'one spot of radiance where all else was shade.' His aesthetic mission – he calls it his 'inland voyage to fairy-land' – consists in seeking that spot, only to find it occupied by the shabby cottage of a lonely girl who entertains fantasies of the shining house in the valley, which he recognizes as his own. Here is Melvillian irony in almost diagrammatic form, expressed in his characteristic dichotomy of bright and dark. As Melville uses those values, brightness is 'illusion . . . complete,' while at 'night, when the curtain falls, truth comes in with the darkness.'

Even more patently autobiographical than 'The Piazza' is 'I and My Chimney.' As the title indicates, the story is an elaborate metaphor equating the man of the house and the imposing architectural 'backbone' of his home. Paralleling the serio-comic battle between the narrator and his wife over the remodeling or dismantling of their great central chimney was the very real crisis at Arrowhead over Melville's back pains, which precipitated a physician's consultation ludicrously comparable to a master mason's visit in the tale to poke about the base of the chimney and prescribe its alteration. Elizabeth Melville's brief memoir of the historical episode attributes to it the loss of her husband's 'former vigor and strength,' but Melville's symbolic chimney and the tone of the debate over it suggests a crisis less physical than spiritual. 'The old smoker' who defends the integrity of his counterpart at the core of his house is transparently the indomitable author who had dedicated his last two novels respectively to Mount Greylock and the Bunker Hill Monument. Yet 'I and My Chimney' takes its literary character from humor, not bitterness. It is an entirely social sympathy that is aroused by the spectacle of a man whom love and friendship would like to make over – to rescue from himself – insisting with utter serenity on remaining his awkward and uncompromising self.

II

'The Piazza' is about point of view; 'I and My Chimney' is about identity. These highly personal themes combine to produce a series of tales at one remove from autobiography, all having to do with the delicate counterpoise of illusion and reality and with the inviolability of the defeated personality. All three of the tales in question, written within little more than a year, speak with eloquent insistence of Melville's obsessive concern after the failure of *Pierre*: how to be happy though unappreciated.

The first and least skillful of these is as bald as its title, 'The Happy Failure.' It is a mere skit played out, like amateur theatricals, among an impractical inventor, his grumbling but faithful black servant, and a narrator of convenience in the role of a nephew. Plot and dialogue are of childlike simplicity. The peculiarly Melvillian twist comes in the old man's response to the inevitable collapse of his ten-year project. Suddenly relieved of the long tension of striving, like one whose fever has broken, he cries, 'Praise be to God for the failure!' The recovery of good sense and the release from compulsion have brought peace, for which the loss of his dreams is not too great a price.

If 'The Happy Failure' has few claims as literature, the next attempt at the same theme, 'The Fiddler,' represents a considerable artistic advance. To begin with, the central figure of Hautboy, the child prodigy grown old in obscurity, has an aptness and credibility that draw the reader into more sympathetic identification with the author's attitude. The plot, though simple enough, is built on genuine suspense, the release of which drives home directly the theme of the story. Hautboy too is a 'happy failure,' but since his failure is public rather than private, his response to it is more subtle and complex than that of the foolish uncle who has only to face the natural consequence of his lack of genius. What Hautboy lacks is not genius but the recognition of it, and the deep, almost Pan-like happiness of his character has to arise from a simple pleasure in what he is, quite irrespective of the rewards that may or may not accrue to him. In this ruddy, twinkling old man the exhausted Melville reconstituted an invulnerable loser, serenely sufficient unto himself and equal to all events.

Nowhere in all his writing does Melville make it so clear as in this story that he is creating a model for himself. In the character of Helmstone, the narrator, he pictures a disappointed and embittered poet who inclines to think that only shallow people are happy, until he meets Hautboy, a forgotten but still radiant genius of the violin, and determines to abandon poetry for fiddle lessons. The point about Hautboy is that he is not a mere happy-go-lucky like Stubb in *Moby-Dick*, but a person of fully developed sensibilities whose deep content is rooted in a reality purged of vanity and illusion: 'He saw the world pretty much as it was, yet he did not theoretically espouse its bright side nor its dark side.

116

Rejecting all solutions, he but acknowledged facts.' Hautboy represents an existential ideal sharply distinguished from mere mediocrity, all too obviously dramatized in the character of Standard, who is happy because he has no reason to be otherwise. In the neglected genius Melville saw a 'tumbled temple of Fame' covered by 'the vine and the rose.'

The ruined temple, the vine and the rose are all recurrent motifs in Melville's later writings. The last, in fact, is the central feature of the third and best of these three related tales, 'Jimmy Rose.' This is the longest and most fully developed of them, the least perfunctory in the setting of scene and the elaboration of character. The figure of Jimmy Rose is a memory evoked, with superb artistic tact, by a faded and once magnificent wallpaper. The urban scene, already used to good effect in *Pierre* and 'Bartleby,' foreshadows the theme of affluence fallen to decay; and a narrowing, almost cinematic focus on a room with ruined rose-and-peacock walls revives the image of its former owner – 'poor Jimmy Rose.'

The recollected story-within-a-story employs basically the *Misanthropos* or Timon plot, but takes a sharp turn into capitulation and social adjustment in order to make Melville's very different point. All three of Melville's failed men undergo a radical change of heart to bring them to a happy ending, though in each case Melville evades the dramatizing of the change, as he was to veil the crucial accommodation of Billy Budd to his death and to his judge. The consistency of the evasion suggests a weakness of craft, or a certain trepidation in the face of a turning point deeply felt or wished for but dimly understood. In any case, we have the wealthy and open-handed Jimmy, stricken with loss of property and society and driven to bay among his paper roses and peacocks, yet miraculously converted during a quarter-century hiatus into a charming, threadbare free-loader who sustains a fiction of independence by the charity of his friends. He is not a wholly admirable character, as Hautboy is clearly intended to be, but his survival – with 'roses in his cheeks' – is a triumph as well as a tragedy.

He is a memory of things past but also, for Herman Melville in 1855, a projection of things to come. In the nostalgic refrain the author inserted at three intervals ('Ah, poor, poor Jimmy – God guard us all – poor Jimmy Rose!') is a plain implication that 'There but for the grace of God go I.' Although the skillful use of symbols, especially the eloquent wallpaper, effectively generalizes the story, still no one who has read *Moby-Dick* can fail to hear in the opening phrases of 'Jimmy Rose' the accents of the man who once called himself Ishmael: 'A time ago, no matter how long precisely, I, an old man . . .'

III

In most of the substantial stories of these years the narrator adopts the pose of an 'old man' or identifies with one. Nowhere is this singular feature, or the prevailing theme of failure, more evident than in Melville's first and most famous short story, 'Bartleby,' which opens with the deceptively straightforward pronouncement, 'I am a rather elderly man.' Whether that fact, and the proclamation of it, make of the narrator a Solomon or a dotard there will always be readers to debate. No other story of Melville's has proven so enigmatic, so tantalizing, as this. As a consequence, the interpretive literature on it exceeds that of any other short work of Melville's except 'Benito Cereno,' which rivals it in complexity and reputation.

One issue that plagues this tale, but not the later one, is the question of its autobiographical content. 'Benito Cereno' is based on a known historical document, part of which is overtly adapted to the text of the story; 'Bartleby' is of unknown origin and read by many critics as a parable of the author's inner life. Whether Melville portrayed his own frustration as an author in the defensive withdrawal of his strange and silent clerk is not susceptible of proof. Perhaps such conjectures only impede the process of imaginative enlargement which alone can open the appeal of a work of fiction to all its readers. What clues Melville gave to his intention, however applicable to his own situation, are the opposite of restrictive. He made his title character a 'scrivener,' which may be a writer, but which is also a type of the repetitive and uncreative worker in a commercial society – all of those masses of men who, as Thoreau said, 'lead lives of quiet desperation.' For this reason it has as cogently been argued that Melville was thinking of Thoreau as that he was thinking of himself.

There is no objective reason to suppose that he was thinking of anyone in particular, but only of a way of life that had repelled and appalled him since, in the winter of 1840–1, he had signed aboard a whaling ship and left his friend Fly to copy in a New York law office, 'where he has incessant writing from morning to evening.' He joked about the suicidal character of his own choice, but there was never any doubt that he found life and vista on the open sea, especially at the mast-head. In the blasted Galapagos it was the towering Rock Rodondo that enabled him to rise above the desolation of his subject; in the Middle East it was the minarets of Constantinople that dispelled the depression felt in the knotted byways of the city; and in the period of 'Bartleby' it was the outlook from the

118

Arrowhead piazza that contrasted so sharply with the lower Manhattan residences he resorted to from time to time and so poignantly recalled in the city scenes of *Pierre* and 'Jimmy Rose.' Nothing stands out so plainly in 'Bartleby' as its author's tendency to claustrophobia. In book after book Melville invited his readers to pity the man who is afraid of heights, but a wholly different order of artistic pressure is brought to bear on our sympathies in this story for the man who is mortally vulnerable to enclosure.

'Bartleby,' Melville announces in his subtitle, is 'A Story of Wall Street.' He means, of course, the financial district of New York where the narrator has his law offices and where the action takes place. He also makes clear in his imagery that he means a street of walls, a forest of buildings shouldering each other in the crowded spaces and making a mockery of windows. The inspiration of Melville's story is the vision of a society trapped in this jungle of brick and paper. The Wall Street clerk, forever copying legal documents in a somnambulistic haze of boredom, had been prefigured in 'that hopeless, sallow tribe' of Sub-Sub-Librarians to whom he had credited the 'extracts' on cetology which introduce *Moby-Dick*. It is precisely one of that mass of invisible men whom he chose to make visible in Bartleby.

The method by which Bartleby is made visible – he can hardly be said to be brought to life – is analogous to the principle of polarized light. The plane of expectation is rotated, the assumption which controls his behavior is reversed, and with one revolutionary gesture the pale and silent scrivener springs into sharp relief against the field of action. The plane of expectation is the commercial establishment itself; the basic assumption is its work ethic, its axiomatic doctrine of reciprocal productivity. When Bartleby utters the words, 'I would prefer not to,' he proclaims a posture of free will totally subversive to organized society. Without fire, sword, manifesto, or even a raised voice, this meek copyist, who simply draws a line for himself, stands like Childe Roland before the dark tower of our dehumanizing culture. Unfortunately, Bartleby's 'No' is something less than a battle cry or a plan of action, and the moment of his resistance is the extent of his victory. The system sweeps on and Bartleby is its first victim.

As the mute, defeated clerk lies curled in a foetal position before his final wall, it may be supposed that he is simply another of Melville's failed men, a rabbit whose response to the hounds is to freeze in his tracks. But the story is not wholly focussed on Bartleby. Like Ahab in *Moby-Dick*, he occupies the center of the stage but not the center of sensibility. That center is defined by the elderly attorney who tells the tale and who measures by his own frustration and enlightenment the meaning of Bartleby's bizarre denial of life. If the essence of Bartleby is the inversion of expectation, the essence of his employer is the affirmation of it, the embodiment of all the conventional assumptions society makes about the mechanics of its own survival. Here we stand, Melville's nameless old lawyer seems to say to us; what are we to make of the lone striker whose stepping aside shows us the treadmill we are on? Melville aids our perceptions, if not the narrator's, by providing foils, again in a manner reminiscent of *Moby-Dick*, to guide an assessment of the central character. Turkey and Nippers, the comical clerks who alternate function and dysfunction in the operation of the business, are almost allegorical half-men. Performing with normal efficiency, or a parody of normal efficiency, they hilariously caricature the compromises of the real world while Bartleby pursues the inexorable logic of his private truth. We recognize in Bartleby, even without the narrator's eyes, another face in Melville's gallery of absolutists, for whom he was shortly to discover the perfect image in the obstinate Galapagos tortoise. What the narrator does for us is to direct and control sympathy, to express both the resentment and the charity that struggle for ascendancy in the mind of the average reader, who performs his own leaden tasks even though he too, perhaps, 'prefers not to.'

Ambivalence lies at the heart of 'Bartleby.' It is not a story of good and evil, of hero and villain, but a parable of the human condition. It is to be understood, not in terms of who is right and who is wrong, and certainly not in terms of Herman Melville's putative quarrels with God, society, or the profession of letters; but in terms of the human anguish of an insoluble spiritual dilemma, suddenly dilated by art to a predicament that touches us all: 'Ah, Bartleby! ah, humanity!'

IV

Neither Bartleby nor his employer is a wholly sympathetic figure. Despite the normal inclination to side with one or the other in their irresolvable antagonism, in the end it is the antagonism itself that occupies the center of the tale, an ineluctable fact of economic civilization, driving the employee in a downward spiral of dependency as a consequence of his very effort to break free. Just beneath the fictional surface of 'Bartleby' lurks the resentment and incipient rebellion of an author writing himself blind for his friendly publishers in order to feed and clothe a family that kept augmenting itself with almost mechanical persistence. Always in debt, never liberated from the necessity of promoting an advance on the next book, Melville ground out his stories and left in their themes and characters the traces of his distress. Scattered among the tales of failure and the strange private victories wrung from discouragement is a revealing series of sketches about people in poverty and privation.

The earliest of these, published in *Harper's* in the winter of 1853 as 'Bartleby' was appearing in *Putnam's*, is easily the strangest of all Melville's excursions into short fiction. It bears the title 'Cock-a-doodle-doo!' and expands to considerable length an idea essentially no more complex than the irony of a poor man's possession of a magisterial rooster. The melancholy narrator, cheered by the triumphant crow of a distant cock, traces him to the hovel of a poor woodcutter, where he watches the entire family die of general inanition even as the cock continues to fire a false joy in them by the tumultuous optimism of his voice. Since the cock thereupon drops dead too, there cannot be much doubt of the true value of his inspiriting powers. A parody of the sort of transcendental exhilaration which was always irritating to Melville's moody sensibility, the cock 'Trumpet' is portrayed with almost hysterical exaggeration as a creature of sound and glory, signifying nothing. His owner, a noble pauper named Merrymusk, commands this clamorous delusion with the compulsive insistence of a drug addict. A more rounded presentation of the narrator and his problems is hardly sufficient to compel sympathy or belief, and the emotional force one feels in the tension of the writing remains undirected, inconclusive. Clearly heralded in the tone of the story is its author's abiding contempt for shallow optimism, yet the narrator emerges at last a convert to the cock's gospel of cheer, forever cured of his 'doleful dumps.' Whether confused, insincere, or doubly ironic, 'Cock-a-doodle-doo!' is an unconvincing story, hopelessly at odds with its own thesis. It is one of a number of writings which tell a good deal about the inner Melville but owe their survival as art entirely to the fame of their author.

The failure of 'Cock-a-doodle-doo!' is plainly a failure of craft, an inability to embody in the short story form a passionately felt sympathy with a human predicament he all too perilously shared. Whether he thought he could manage the allegorical machinery as Hawthorne might have done – whether Hawthorne himself could have brought it off – is useless to surmise. All we can know is that when he addressed himself to the same theme a year later he very nearly abandoned the effort to make fiction of it. What he produced instead was a pair of 'Pictures,' as he called them, in which he discovered a more congenial format in contrasting, but unconnected, dramatized essays. 'Picture First,' entitled 'Poor Man's Pudding,' places Melville's customary first-person narrator in the position of testing the reality behind his friend Blandmour's sentimental rationalizations of poverty, by which every form of privation, every meager substitute for comfort and well-being, is disguised as a blessing of nature, somehow superior to the effete luxuries of the wealthy. The reality of Poor Man's Pudding, of course, is a nauseous mess, and the stoicism with which Melville's paupers stomach it leads him to end the sketch with an editorial polemic on the condition of 'the native American poor.' Though physically identical the world over, that condition, as he sharply perceived, was the source of greater misery in a democracy than elsewhere because of the open contrast between the political, economic, and social ideals universally shared and the gross, irremediable inequities of actual circumstance. The benign evasions of the poet Blandmour, signaled perhaps too heavily by Melville's favorite trick of naming, provide just the right turn of irony to give dramatic force to the naked moral of the story: 'Of all the preposterous assumptions of humanity over humanity, nothing exceeds most of the criticisms made on the habits of the poor by the well-housed, well-warmed, and well fed.'

'Picture Second,' entitled 'Rich Man's Crumbs,' neatly if predictably creates a converse scene. Drawing on the aristocratic customs and assumptions of the old world, Melville recalls the London of his 1849 visit, turns back the calendar another thirty-five years, and portrays a Lord Mayor's Charity, which admitted the city's paupers to Guildhall the day following a royal banquet to scavenge among the leavings of the feast. The subject was distasteful to Melville, and he vented his distaste in descriptions as repellent as a nightmare. The inevitable irony which is the hallmark of his treatment is generated by an English guide who assesses the brutal 'charity' at face value and displays it with pride. Otherwise 'Picture Second' is less impressive than its counterpart; but taken as a co-ordinated set of variations on a theme, the pair of sketches constitutes a diptych with a cumulative effect perhaps greater than the simple sum of its parts.

Evidently Melville was intrigued by the possibilities of the diptych format, for he used it on two further occasions in dealing with the same general subject. The first of these was enlivened, but also doomed, by the idea that a pauper would find a warmer welcome in the gallery of a theater than in the pews of a fashionable metropolitan church. *Putnam's* editor reluctantly declined 'The Two Temples,' frankly fearing to offend his affluent church-going readers, and the story never got into print. But in a pair of sketches called 'The Paradise of Bachelors and the Tartarus of Maids,' which appeared in *Harper's* in 1855, he found another sort of contrast and produced a social commentary transcending the simple theme of poverty. The idea of setting off the ease of a bachelor dinner with a group of London barristers at the Temple against the hardship of a group of working girls in a New England paper mill has an obvious and perhaps primary economic focus. But it is the contrast of the sexes in their social roles that caught Melville's imagination and more deeply shaped these tales.

The first of the two sketches, though pleasant reading, is little more than a familiar essay in the manner of Dickens or Irving, given thematic direction by an emphasis on irresponsibility. It is not the wealth of his bachelor lawyers that Melville stresses, but their lack of family ties 'to give an anxious thought,' their utter removal from 'those two legends,' pain and trouble. The factory girls, on the other hand, know only pain and trouble, and something about the nature of their work suggests to the imagination that their burden is not so much their penury as – in contrast to those carefree males – their sex. The paper mill, as Melville describes it, is a perfect paradigm of the gestation process, from the 'albuminous' pulp through the 'abdominal' machinery to the inexorable emergence, precisely nine 'minutes' later, of moist sheets of 'blank fool-scap.' On the last point Melville could not forbear pointing to his latent metaphor by reminding the reader that he had borrowed John Locke's image of the *tabula rasa*, the blank state of the human mind at birth. In the main, he contented himself with erecting a scaffolding of puns around his literal narrative: Woedolor Mountain, Blood River, a guide named Cupid. Having discovered what he is about, the reader who returns to the opening pages of this sketch may see the extremity of the risks Melville took in playing this little game with his conventional magazine public. The imagery implicit in the topography of his scene – Black Notch, Devil's Dungeon, Mad Maid's Bellows-pipe, and the like – could have precipitated more editorial compunction than a few satirical thrusts at the prosperous parishioners of Manhattan's Grace Church. 'The Tartarus of Maids,' with or without its companion piece, is an amusing and pointed exercise in *double entendre*. How far the sexual parallels may be pressed is a question of interpretive discretion. The imagery of mechanism and frigidity pose interesting problems, though perhaps more biographical than literary.

V

The dramatization of Melville's inner life in these stories of the 1850s was accomplished largely with the use of odd scraps of memory and experience left in the wake of the sea novels which had drained him of so much of his primary material. Three times during this period, however, he returned to the sea for the substance of his writing, and it is a sufficient confirmation of his *forte* that two of these three maritime stories enjoy a reputation shared, among his shorter works, only by 'Bartleby.' The last of the three, a familiar essay entitled 'The 'Gees,' calls for little more than passing mention. It is a lighthearted piece of comic ethnology, reminiscent in both matter and manner of the Marquesan Melville of the 1840s, and for that very reason as interesting as a crocus in autumn. But it masks no depths and asks only to be read and enjoyed. The other two sea stories, while no less enjoyable, are major works of complex design and problematical meaning, requiring fuller attention.

There is some evidence that Melville planned at one time to publish 'The Encantadas, or Enchanted Isles' as a book; but when he got down to writing his recollections of the Galapagos archipelago, where the *Acushnet* had paused on its way into the Pacific in 1841, they took the form of ten interrelated sketches rather than a unified sequence of chapters. Or rather, since a certain kind of artistic unity is demonstrable in these sketches, what they lack should be described as narrative continuity: they do not constitute a 'story' in the conventional sense. What unites the segments, apart from their common subject, is an imaginative treatment signaled by the general title and the epigraphs of the successive sketches. Adopting the popular Spanish name for the islands instantly endows his descriptions and anecdotes, however miscellaneous, with an ironic theme; and prefacing each one with an apposite quotation from Spenser's *Faerie Queene* extends the idea of enchantment in the direction of moral allegory. These barren volcanic outcroppings in the southern sea are Melville's wasteland, his palpable hell on earth, as those other enchanted isles in Polynesia had been the heaven: 'In no world but a fallen one could such lands exist.'

In Melville's Dantean imagination they formed another of his microcosms, blasted by some nameless malignity and populated by the immemorial tortoises that dragged themselves with 'penal hopelessness' across the vitreous earth. These ancient and torpid creatures, 'solitary lords of Asphaltum,' are the resident spirits of the islands, putting him in mind at once of the souls of the damned and the mythic bearers of the universe. They form the first focus of attention, and in the second sketch give rise to two reflections of critical importance. For one thing, as the title announces, there are 'two sides to a tortoise,' the 'dark and melancholy' shell and the yellow breast-plate revealing a sunnier side beneath: 'The tortoise is both black and bright.' For Melville this dual aspect was a model of life, recalling the vision of Ishmael at the try-works, and implicit in all his images of the world since *Mardi*. Comic and tragic views are intermingled in 'The Encantadas,' and the one attitude that persists through the shifting moods of the sketches is that neither may be denied. Another characteristic of the tortoise, even more striking than his contrasting surfaces, is his 'strange infatuation of hopeless toil,' his inflexible commitment, whether through stupidity or resolution, to make his undeviating way against all obstacles, however immovable. The creator of Taji and Ahab, Pierre and Bartleby, was almost morbidly fascinated by what he called 'the crowning curse' of the Galapagos tortoise – his 'drudging impulse to straightforwardness in a belittered world.' And yet it is a mark of his deep ambivalence that he termed this stubborn quality 'heroic' even as he made fun of it.

As the tortoises provide a philosophic outlook, the Rock Rodondo supplies a physical, one might almost say a dramatic, one. In a series of three related sketches (Three through Five) Melville first pictures the strange, towering chimney of stone that dominates the approach to the islands, then enlarges upon the prospect of the archipelago from that vantage point, and finally recounts a historic episode connected with the rock and its 'enchantments' that sets in motion the chain of anecdotes to follow. It is a plan as purposeful as a plot and as compelling as a guided tour. In addition – and it is here that Melville set his special mark on 'The Encantadas' – the Rock Rodondo takes on a metaphoric quality that gives it a poetic as well as a geographical command of its surroundings. Like the 'Bell-Tower' of a great Italian cathedral, which was to form the subject of a later story, the Rock rises precipitately to yield a view as of 'the universe from Milton's celestial battlements.' With pointed irony, Melville calls it 'a Pisgah View from the Rock.' But the outlook remains somehow secondary to the arresting imagery of the structure itself; although it is a natural formation, it is as a tower, symmetrically erected and hierarchically populated, that it takes hold on the imagination. With his characteristic blend of humor and allegory Melville draws his Rock as a series of concentric layers or shelves, each a distinct class system ascending from 'Nature's failure' the penguin, to the pelican, the albatross, and so on through rising 'thrones, princedoms, and powers' of birds to one 'snow-white angelic thing' at the pinnacle of this created order. Around the base, beneath the water, mysterious creatures in shadowy grottoes mirror the teeming orders of life in the air above. The Rock Rodondo is another of Melville's microcosms.

The last five sketches erect on this general symbolic foundation a disproportionately fragile superstructure of episode and anecdote. Sketch Nine, which paints the Caliban of the islands, Hermit Oberlus, is an exceptionally vivid delineation of character; but only Sketch Eight, 'Norfolk Isle and the Chola Widow,' has the weight and power of Melville's best short stories. The character of Hunilla is charged with genuine pathos, and the tale of desertion, cruelty, and endurance that unfolds around her develops the haunting quality that was latent in another story about a widow which Melville had outlined to Hawthorne two years earlier, but which neither of them ever used. 'Norfolk Isle and the Chola Widow' contains some of Melville's best writing, and as august a critic as James Russell Lowell praised the moving artistry of this story's concluding sentence:

> The last seen of lone Hunilla she was passing into Payta town, riding upon a small gray ass; and before her on the ass's shoulders, she eyed the jointed workings of the beast's armorial cross.

From such a level the final sketch is, not surprisingly, anticlimactic. However, it is suitably focussed on the ruins and relics of the islands. It concludes with a 'doggerel epitaph,' half-serious, half-comic, and as final as the folk ballad that terminates *Billy Budd*:

> Oh, Brother Jack, as you pass by,
> As you are now, so once was I.
> Just so game, and just so gay,
> But now, alack, they've stopped my pay.
> No more I peep out of my blinkers,
> Here I be – tucked in with clinkers!

The total effect of 'The Encantadas,' notwithstanding its darkness of tone, is casual and anecdotal, rising as easily out of old memories as the travel romances with which Melville had begun his literary career. His only other important use of nautical material in these magazine stories is of a radically different character.

'Benito Cereno' is the longest and most ambitious of Melville's

126

shorter works. Although leisurely in pace by modern standards, it is more tightly controlled by the unity of its plot than any other of Melville's writings, simply by virtue of its being in effect his only mystery story. 'Benito Cereno' is a good deal more than a mystery story, but it starts with the appeal of a puzzle and makes its most immediate impact through the familiar mechanisms of deceptive appearances, misread cues, hinted horrors, rising tension, and a sharply turned moment of truth which hangs on the verge of error before falling into a clarifying dénouement. Apart from its lax economy, it is the one story of Melville's most likely to have won the approval of Edgar Allan Poe, had that master of effect survived to read it. That it should have so many strictly literary virtues is the more remarkable for its owing more of its substance than any other work of Melville, even *Israel Potter*, to a historical source. The tale of the slave mutiny aboard the *San Dominick* and of its discovery by the Yankee captain Amasa Delano in 1799 is a twice-told tale, having its origin in Delano's own *Narrative of Voyages and Travels in the Northern and Southern Hemispheres*, published in Boston in 1817. Melville's transformation of that factual account is one of his most impressive achievements.

Mardi, *Pierre*, even *Moby-Dick*, offer demonstration enough that Melville did not always plan well or know precisely where his imagination would take him; but the opening paragraphs of 'Benito Cereno' signal a mature artist in command of his material. Neither Poe nor Hawthorne, America's reigning experts in the short story form, could have painted a scene more potent in atmosphere than the 'gray' paragraph with which the action of this narrative begins, though perhaps both of them would have avoided the overt directive in Melville's concluding sentence: 'Shadows present, foreshadowing deeper shadows to come.' The next paragraph yields character and theme at a stroke. The 'undistrustful good nature' of Captain Delano is at once the key to his character, to the point of view of the narrative, and to the meaning of the story. Obviously, a certain kind of innocence, a certain constriction of vision, is a precondition of mystification: as Conan Doyle understood this classic pattern, Watson must retard and misdirect the reader's perceptions if Holmes is to have a clear field to shine. Melville's mystification, however, called for a constriction of *moral* vision, and it is that dimension of the resulting puzzle that elevates it to the seriousness of allegory. That which Captain Delano is unable to perceive in the strange scenes that unfold before him is the principle of 'malign evil in man' which alone can explain the events that perplex him. 'Benito Cereno' was written only a year before *The Confidence-Man*, and its plot perfectly prefigures the confrontation of trust and deception which was to form the matrix of that novel.

This theme, the contrapuntal interplay of innocence and corruption, is implicit in every misinterpreted act, every ironic gesture and word, every facet of the uneasy triangular relationship among the optimistic American, the morose and frightened Spaniard of the title, and the obsequious slave Babo. Veiled meaning hangs in the air of the story, like the shrouded figurehead which is both the climactic revelation of the plot and a metaphor, however unintentional, of the story's structure. Clues, at once physical and metaphysical, abound in the symbols found or invented to deepen the mystery and make it resonate. The ships are the *San Dominick*, bearing its decayed culture like a ruined castle afloat or 'a white-washed monastery after a thunder-storm,' and the *Bachelor's Delight*, neat, trim, and well-disciplined, like the young nation it represents. Everywhere the *San Dominick* bespeaks dissolution: in the deserted state-cabin with its sealed dead lights and rotting balconies; in the ancient stern-piece, carved to represent two masked figures in a tableau of mastery and subjugation; most tellingly in the grisly figure-head with the ironic motto, 'Follow your Leader.' Moreover, the decay such images project is the decay of a civilization; it is the House of Usher, subtly altered from a psychic myth to a political one. An especially brilliant scene in the cabin, in which Babo shaves his master, using the Spanish flag as an apron, emphasizes the point. On deck revolution simmers under Delano's unsuspecting nose as the blacks pick oakum or scour hatchets, and a white sailor tries desperately to communicate a hint through a useless and fantastic knot.

After the stunning climax of the story, as cinematic as anything in Melville, the pace and medium of narration shift with a suddenness that many readers have found disconcerting. His mystery exposed, Melville elected to fill in the antecedent action by recourse to a lengthy deposition which was a part of his source material. He made few changes, except for the excision of some irrelevancies, and obviously wished by such authenticity to – quite literally – document his story. Undeniably, the document is tedious and clogs an already overlong tale. On the other hand, its length is at least proportionate, and its inclusion is defensible as 'the key to fit into the lock of the complications which precede it.'

In any event, the mystery is unraveled by that means and the story brought to an aftermath or epilogue of considerable importance to Melville's themes. Chief of these, perhaps, is the inversion of good and

128

evil beneath the mask of appearances, a failure of perception that moves both captains to retrospective wonder. Next, by direct implication, is the failure of communication, the mutual isolation that divides men in a world where things are not as they seem. Finally, there is the irremediable trauma of evil, which haunts the Spaniard to an early grave but is incomprehensible to the resilient American:

'You are saved . . . what has cast such a shadow upon you?'
'The negro.'

It is an enigmatic response, which some readers may understand as little as Captain Delano. At the least, it is the remark of a weak man frightened to death by a clever and ruthless adversary who happens to have been black. At the most, which is likely to be a good deal too much, it is a glaring emblem of the black race, which converts the tale into a pre-war tract on slavery; or it is a secret symbol for Melville's hostile critics, about to drive him to retirement on his own 'Mount Agonia'; or any number of possible but tiresomely arbitrary interpretations. 'Benito Cereno' is not without faults and problems, but it is too good a story to be read on any but its own terms.

VI

Three more stories remain to be mentioned. All positively require the sort of allegorical reading which ought to be resisted or adopted with utmost caution in interpreting Melville's best tales. In addition to a strongly allegorical cast, all three share as well a subject matter linking the moral life with some aspect of science or technology. All suffer by comparison, not only with Melville's own best work, but with classically successful efforts in that kind by both Hawthorne and Poe.

Of 'The Lightning-Rod Man' perhaps the title contains its own sufficient elucidation. In a world beset by risks, physical and spiritual, the salesman of lightning-rods is a merchant of fear, counseling a virtually paralytic withdrawal from the dangerous business of living (shades of Bartleby) and peddling his fraudulent averter of apocalypse in the familiar manner of the Confidence-Man. The symbolism is intriguing, whether or not it extends to a commentary on Calvinism, as some have claimed; but for whatever reasons, it did not receive from Melville either the structural or stylistic attention necessary to fabricate a satisfying tale.

'The Bell-Tower' clearly received serious attention in the making; to how satisfying an effect each reader must decide. Its theme and materials are of engrossing value, inescapably reminiscent of several of Hawthorne's finest tales. To read 'The Bell-Tower' in the full perspective of Hawthorne's fiction is to catch continual echoes of 'Rappaccini's Daughter' from the Italian Renaissance setting; of 'The Artist of the Beautiful' or 'The Birthmark' from the labor and character of the artisan Bannadonna; or of 'Ethan Brand' from the crime and fate exemplified. The plot is the very stuff of allegory: a famous craftsman in his pride erects a uniquely lofty bell-tower; he places in it a great bell flawed in the casting by the blood of a workman he had struck down in anger; and he himself is struck down in turn by an automaton devised to ring the bell. The telling of the story partakes perhaps too much of the heaviness of the flawed bell, the iron giant, and the fallen tower; but even without the finer touch of Hawthorne 'The Bell-Tower' justifies the weight of its ideas and the penetration of its symbolism.

Melville's last published short story, 'The Apple-Tree Table,' is less solemn and portentous than 'The Bell-Tower' and partly for that reason easier of movement and more credible as fiction. Its plot, borrowed from a folk tale which Thoreau had also used in the conclusion of *Walden*, is a ready-made parable of resurrection and spiritual renewal overlaid with a thin veneer of scientific hocus-pocus concerning the emergence of long-dormant insects from old wood. It is the comic potentialities of this material that Melville chose to develop, capitalizing on the distance between simple entomology on the one hand and the superstitious implications of spirit-rapping and the 'providences' of Cotton Mather's *Magnalia Christi Americana* on the other. Melville wisely allowed this story to take shape as domestic farce, a sort of companion piece to 'I and My Chimney,' which was written just two months earlier. Its humor is genuine but dated, as the literary playfulness of bygone generations tends to be, and the story closes Melville's brief career as a short-story writer on a pleasant but suitably modest note.

The unalterable fact is that Melville was by nature a discursive writer. He lacked the inclination of Poe and Hawthorne toward the spare discipline of short forms. There is much evidence in Melville's stories that they were composed in admiration, possibly in imitation, of Hawthorne's. But despite some clear and memorable successes, the short story remains as secondary to Melville's peculiar genius as the long romance is to Hawthorne's.

10

Poetry

The last of Melville's literary ventures, and the latest to be recognized and evaluated in our own time, is his poetry. To an even greater extent than his prose writing, Melville's poetry is uneven in quality, the best of it fairly assured of a place of honor in the national literature, the worst of it recalling to mind his own wry observation in *Mardi* that 'Genius is full of trash.' The primary fact to bear in mind in reading Melville's poetry is that it represents in the strict sense an amateur enterprise. Melville may have written occasional poems from an early age; indeed, the evidence of an unpublished poem called 'Immolated' suggests the existence at one time of many 'children' of a 'happier prime' which were later consigned to the fires of disappointment or self-criticism; but no poems saw the light of publication until Melville had abandoned professional authorship and ceased to regard the constraints of popular taste and the literary marketplace. In order to understand the poems, then, it is useful to look for the spiritual imperatives and aesthetic conceptions that guided Melville into poetic expression in general and through the exacting composition of four very different volumes of verse.

I

The essential motive to poetry, its 'inspiration' in an almost literal sense, Melville explained in terms of the familiar image of a whole generation of romantic poets: the wind-harp. He made the analogy quite explicitly in prose in the preface to his first volume of poems, *Battle-Pieces and Aspects of the War* (1866):

> Yielding instinctively . . . to feelings not inspired from any one source exclusively, . . . I seem, in most of these verses, to have but placed a harp in a window, and noted the contrasted airs which wayward winds have played upon the strings.

Later, perhaps as much as twenty years later, he reverted to this master image in a poem of great depth and complexity entitled 'The Aeolian Harp,' which he included in *John Marr and Other Sailors* (1888). The poem is revealing both of the persistence of the idea and of Melville's characteristic poetic process.

'The Aeolian Harp' begins and ends with the wind in the strings, making a poignant music that first reminds the poet of a tragic scene at sea, then expresses the human meaning of the scene in 'Thoughts that tongue can tell no word of.' Between these lyric and thematic poles the descriptive center of the poem paints in longer stanzas the picture of a drifting hulk, 'deadlier than the sunken reef,' lifeless itself and a constant threat of destruction to all who cross its random, unmarked course. That this image literally haunted Melville's imagination is not in doubt, since he first incorporated it into chapters 19 and 22 of *Redburn*, drawing either on an actual experience common enough in the days of wooden ships, or on his reading of a similar episode in the opening essay of Washington Irving's *Sketch Book*, or both. A purely emotional logic links the sound of the wind-harp with the tragedy at sea. But in Melville's hands the linkage itself lends an additional dimension of meaning to the poem: the mental recall responding to the sound becomes a 'hint' of the nature of 'the Real.' The true horror of the 'craft that never shows a light' is that it runs 'pilotless on pathless way,' invulnerable itself and 'fatal only to the *other*!' The wreck thus expands through metaphoric extension to an emblem of blind chance; not of hostile intent, but of what Ahab called the 'inscrutable malice' of circumstance. What began as a romantic lyric ends as an existential tragedy, without losing any of its initial character. The last line echoes, consciously or unconsciously, Wordsworth's 'Thoughts that do often lie too deep for words.'

The language and structure of verse were not, perhaps, among Melville's native gifts, but poems like 'The Aeolian Harp,' not to mention the symbolic cast of his prose, demonstrate that he had a fine sense of the relationship between the real and the ideal which underlies all imaginative art. Long before he turned to poetry as an expression of that relationship he defined it with perfect accuracy in *Moby-Dick*: 'fact and fancy, half-way meeting, interpenetrate, and form one seamless whole' (ch. 114). The entire history of modern poetry, from Coleridge on, is a gloss on that deceptively simple principle. In sharp contradistinction to the vast majority of nineteenth-century poets, who were content to let fact and fancy merely coexist illustratively or ornamentally in their verses, Melville aligned himself as if by instinct with the poets of the future for whom meaning was to be the product of a fusion rather than a juxtaposition of elements. It was this sense of the true difficulty of poetry, fully as much as the weight of his tragic themes, that made the writing of poems during the last quarter century of his life, not the pastime of a retired author, but the climactic struggle of a powerful mind to mold words and ideas into new organic shapes.

This implication of profound exertion, physical and spiritual, is Melville's own, and suggests how much of the poet's labor lay ahead of him after the wandering winds of inspiration had stirred his latent creative energies. The poem Melville wrote on this subject has justly achieved a fame unmatched by any of his other writings in verse.

> 'Art'
> In placid hours well-pleased we dream
> Of many a brave unbodied scheme.
> But form to lend, pulsed life create,
> What unlike things must meet and mate:
> A flame to melt – a wind to freeze;
> Sad patience – joyous energies;
> Humility – yet pride and scorn;
> Instinct and study; love and hate;
> Audacity – reverence. These must mate,
> And fuse with Jacob's mystic heart,
> To wrestle with the angel – Art.

Poetry was not only an intellectual effort for Melville but a dramatic and religious one as well. The controlling images came together again in the description of Nathan in *Clarel*, a poem both dramatic and religious, and concerned not at all with the problems of art:

> Alone, and at Doubt's freezing pole,
> He wrestled with the pristine forms
> Like the first man. (I.xxvii. 194–6)

The word 'form,' which these lines share together with the imagery of struggle, has significant prominence in still another small poem of Melville's, which is expressly about the subject of art.

> 'Greek Architecture'
> Not magnitude, not lavishness,
> But Form – the Site;
> Not innovating wilfulness,
> But reverence for the Archetype.

In these lines the emphasis is on craft rather than the spiritual struggle of the artist, and the imagination of the reader is invited to attend more to the model than to the creative sensibility that contemplates it. Moreover, the very qualities that distinguish Melville's fiction, its size and exuberance and experimental boldness – all qualities traditionally associated with his romanticism – seem here to be repudiated, or placed in subjection to a strictly classical decorum. No doubt both impulses were present in him and were held, along with other 'unlike things,' in that creative tension which is the subject of 'Art.'

II

Like other romantic poets, Melville looked in his heart when he wrote, and he wrote about what he found there. However, the subject that inaugurated his career as a poet was the most objective phenomenon to which he ever addressed himself: the Civil War. His approach to this subject could not have been even as personal as his approach to the sea had been, since he was never in uniform and never in battle. His nearest participation in the conflict, apart from a brief visit to the front in 1864, was through reading *The Rebellion Record*, a running archive which left its journalistic track in many of his topics and lines. Though he may have composed isolated poems about the war in its earlier years, the conception that unites *Battle-Pieces* is a late-blooming intention to produce a kind of verse-history of the national tragedy. More deeply, *Battle-Pieces* is unified by a theme, an insistent point of view, that makes the term 'tragedy' in that context considerably more than a synonym for 'disaster.' He saw the Civil War as a monstrous and deeply shared fraternal sin, altering forever the character of the nation, and requiring an expiation as universal as the guilt. He expressed this view directly in the prose 'Supplement' to the book, which, for readers now much removed in time and place from the smoldering immediacy of the subject, may well be read as a foreword rather than as an afterword to the poems.

Despite its brevity and modesty, the 'Supplement' breathes a statesmanship not unlike that of Lincoln's second inaugural address, and like that address it takes for its theme reconciliation and the application of Christian principles (i.e., forgiveness and the Golden Rule) to national policy. It stresses shared guilt and shared responsibility, both for disasters past and for redemptions to come. Above all, it displays an understanding of historical meaning that has its roots in the perspectives of art as well as in the intensities of personal feeling: it assumes that the common catastrophe 'ought to disarm all animosity,' and concludes with a prayer that the 'tragedy of our time' may instruct the nation 'through terror and pity.' With a God's-eye impartiality, Melville at once denounced slavery as 'an atheistical iniquity' and pled for a generosity toward the erstwhile oppressors of the blacks that alone could forestall, 'among other of the last evils, exterminating hatred of race toward race.' Although his writings contain no single work devoted to the subject of race, Negroes and other ethnic minorities occupy places of prominence and dignity in Melville's books. In *Battle-Pieces* only one short poem, 'Formerly a Slave,' represents Melville's sympathy for blacks, whom 'now too late deliverance dawns upon,' and his measured optimism for redress 'far down the depth of thousand years.' Most characteristically, beneath his utterances on this and all subjects of anguished division, is a sense of what he called in the 'Supplement' a 'sacred uncertainty' in human society. In the embattled causes of his time Melville was never a 'blind adherent' because it was his settled conviction that 'to treat of human actions is to deal wholly with second causes.' With or without reference to the prose 'Supplement,' it is impossible to read *Battle-Pieces* without feeling the magnanimity of the author's mind. Although many of the poems are partisan enough in their point of view – Melville made no secret of his detestation of both slavery and secession – nevertheless the passion that animates the poems is one of principle and of sympathy, often of tragic impersonality, never one of hatred or recrimination.

Both the technical range and the thematic unity of *Battle-Pieces* can be seen by looking at the first and last poems, as Melville arranged them. What one notices first is chronology, the elementary dramatic continuity in starting with a premonitory piece entitled 'The Portent' and ending with an elegiac 'Meditation.' 'The Portent' stands as vestibule to Melville's moving museum of war. Its two seven-line stanzas present a single stark image, the hanged body of fanatical abolitionist John Brown casting a gently swaying shadow across the land. A cap veils the face, with its prophetic anguish, but beneath it flows the famous beard, 'the meteor of the war.' The verse has an incantatory formality, in its strict balance and in its ritual repetition of the name 'Shenandoah.' And spotted through the lines, like whispered asides or antiphonal comments, are parenthetical phrases, in two parallel instances pointing to the sacred identity of the hanged man, and in a third citing the ambiguous 'law' by which men placed that body at the end of a rope and nature set it in its slow pendulum motion. It is a poem remarkable for the economy and force of its brooding evocation; it opens the implied drama of *Battle-Pieces* with both cinematic clarity of scene and symbolic embodiment of theme. By contrast, 'A Meditation' is more discursive, with longer lines and a slow march of stanzas, empty of all tension except the bitterness of recollection, and almost devoid of memorable expression. What gives the poem its weight is its emphasis on the mutuality of fratricide, the even-handedness of human loss and culpability. Much of it, taken in isolation, is conventional enough ('But shall the North sin worse, and stand the Pharisee?'); and yet the ending is an image fully as indelible as the swinging corpse of John Brown: a picture literally and precisely drawn and left to speak its volumes in the heart.

> When Vicksburg fell, and the moody files marched out,
> Silent the victors stood, scorning to raise a shout.

The second poem in *Battle-Pieces*, like the first, is short – again, two seven-line stanzas – and strongly compressed. Entitled 'Misgivings,' it is the first of several poems employing the imagery of storm. In the middle of the first stanza, like a stroke of lightning, a single image ('And the spire falls crashing in the town') establishes a metaphor of war striking down the citadel of faith in the midst of a terrified society; and the poem culminates in three startling lines, first picturing the devastation of the tempest, then linking it to an ominous sequence of cause and effect, and finally arresting the whole process of historical necessity in twin images as bold and elliptical as Donne's:

> With shouts the torrents down the gorges go,
> And storms are formed behind the storms we feel:
> The hemlock shakes in the rafter, the oak in the driving keel.

It is worth noting that, as 'The Portent' moves in short, equal, pendulous lines appropriate to their grim burden, so in 'Misgivings' the lines which move toward expanding violence grow in each stanza from four stresses to five and finally, almost painfully, to six. What is some-times merely roughness in Melville's verses seems calculated irregularity in the carefully balanced hammer-blow line that concludes the first stanza of this poem:

> The tempest bursting from the waste of Time
> On the world's fairest hope linked with man's foulest crime.

Another short poem employing storm imagery is ' "The Coming

136

Storm'',' one of the most unusual and significant pieces in the collection. In reading this poem it is important to read a period at the end of the third line of the second stanza rather than at the end of the fourth, as some editions have it, and to understand the background cryptically indicated in the subtitle. The title itself is printed in quotation marks because it is the title of a painting which attracted Melville in the National Academy of Design exhibition in New York in the spring of 1865. This painting by Sanford Gifford is of particular interest for having been the property of Edwin Booth, Shakespearean actor and brother of John Wilkes Booth, who had just shot and killed President Lincoln. In that context it is immediately clear that Melville's subject is tragedy. Edwin Booth's heart, the heart of anyone who has plumbed the depths of Shakespearean tragedy, is mirrored in Gifford's darkling scene, at once placid and ominous. Prescience is part of wisdom in Melville's demanding philosophy – 'Such hearts can antedate' – and the wise man is a Man of Sorrows because he 'knows' what must happen. The vision of the try-works (*Moby-Dick*, ch. 96) is here, and the 'power of blackness' he had long ago imputed to Shakespeare and Hawthorne. Although it is not immediately apparent, '"The Coming Storm"' is Melville's elegy for Lincoln, less direct but more poetically compelling than 'The Martyr,' written just before with overt reference to the assassination. The two poems are related somewhat in the fashion of Whitman's familiar Lincoln elegies, the one conventional in technique almost to the point of self-parody (Melville's 'The Martyr' might have been written by Kipling), the other brooding, oblique, symbolic. The logic of '"The Coming Storm"' is inexorable but it is also emotional and associational, having nothing but grammar in common with the statements of prose. Like 'The Aeolian Harp,' it is an evocation, which is to say that its author, for all his faults, was indeed a poet.

At bottom, the tragic sense is an ironic sense, and it was the ironies of war that most deeply moved the poet in Melville. The gulf between innocence and experience that had fired his dramatic imagination in so many novels and short stories created even more poignant tensions in his mind as he contemplated the flux of young idealism and partisan hopes against the grim background of monolithic forces and the surge of historical 'Necessity' that 'heaps Time's strand with wrecks.' This characteristic thought and image appear in 'The Conflict of Convictions,' but the mood is pervasive in all the poems about war. This one achieves an effect of dialog or of echo by means of stanzaic statement and counter-statement, returning again and again to the center-line of divine impartiality. Like Emerson's 'Hamatreya,' which has a similar theme, it concludes with a gnomic or proverbial pronouncement which provides the only resolution Melville knew to a 'Conflict of Convictions':

YEA AND NAY –
EACH HATH HIS SAY;
BUT GOD HE KEEPS THE MIDDLE WAY.
NONE WAS BY
WHEN HE SPREAD THE SKY;
WISDOM IS VAIN, AND PROPHESY.

It is against this spirit of Ecclesiastes, echoed in 'The Stone Fleet' and many other poems, that the energy of the combatants is measured, and the product is a tragic irony peculiarly Melvillian in tone.

The irony of war is most predictable in those poems dealing with the fate of the young. It is in the harsh destiny of boys rushed into combat from school and farm that the conversion of hope and faith to cynicism and despair is most readily dramatized. Melville pondered that grim progress in three notable poems. It is some addition to their impact to read them together and in order. The first, 'The March into Virginia,' portrays the youth of the conflict itself as well as of the soldiers engaged in it. It tells the story of the Battle of Bull Run, the first important field engagement of the war, legendary among Civil War battles for the festive overconfidence with which the Union troops pranced toward their first stunning defeat, accompanied by sightseers of both sexes and all the accoutrements of a summer picnic. The theme of initiation receives a turn of the screw from the youth of the participants, but fundamentally the boys rollicking to their death are a collective metaphor for the mindless enthusiasm that forms the myth of righteous warfare in the popular mind: 'All wars are boyish.' Irony is implicit in the unsuspecting gaiety of 'Moloch's uninitiate,' and it becomes explicit in the pun which Melville sardonically permits himself in the concluding lines, in which these laughing boys 'die experienced' in a matter of days, 'enlightened by the vollied glare.'

This poem is followed by another on the same theme, dealing with the battle of Ball's Bluff, but here the angle of vision is significantly shifted to the 'Reverie,' as the subtitle indicates, of the poet-witness. The mood is reflective rather than bitter, and the irony grows out of a memory of sunlit laughter and cheering voices and marching feet recalled in the silence of the night. The final stanza culminates in one of Melville's most telling understatements:

> Wakeful I mused, while in the street
> Far footfalls died away till none were left.

Even more reflective, really historical in its perspective, is 'On the Slain Collegians,' requiem for the youthful flower of both North and South, who came from their common study of the liberal arts,

> With golden mottoes in the mouth,
> To lie down midway on a bloody bed.

Here the irony moves from personal to philosophical grounds, expressing the tension between the cultural ideals of higher education and the mutual slaughter of the exemplars of those ideals. Beneath its pathos, Melville's theme is that of all writers who have given their testimony on the futility of war: that military honor is a self-canceling concept.

> Warred one for Right, and one for Wrong?
> So be it; but they both were young.

The tragic irony Melville extracts from the fate of the young touches a deeper and more somber note when he turns to the fate of older participants in the struggle. In two remarkable poems, 'The College Colonel' and 'Commemorative of a Naval Victory,' there is a direct reversal of the ironic poles of innocence and experience. In place of the cheerful, high-minded boys striding off in confidence toward disaster, Melville pictured in these poems the scarred veteran returning through cheering crowds, victorious but silent, weighed down by an accumulated knowledge of horror. These leaders in battle have seen the heart of darkness and, like Benito Cereno, are beyond cheer. 'The College Colonel,' despite irregularities of form, is probably the better poem, sharper in imagery, more focussed and controlled in effect. It is a dramatic poem, opening abruptly with character and action; cinematic in pictorial immediacy and continuity; pausing just once for a strong, almost epic simile drawn from the life of the sea; and culminating in a penetrating glimpse of the buried life of the central figure. His deep, brooding sorrow, unlike Ahab's in a similar predicament, is 'not that a leg is lost,' but that in the spiritual fires of war has come, 'Ah heaven! – what *truth* to him.' The tact of that muted close shows Melville's poetic judgment at its best.

It is the conclusion of the companion poem, too, that is so memorable. The returning hero stands strangely depressed among the heady expressions of an adoring public, like a pensive Keats for whom 'love and fame to nothingness do sink.'

139

>There's a light and a shadow on every man
>Who at last attains his lifted mark.

The lines are almost a generic elegy for the Melvillian hero. The poem might appropriately have been ended there. But in the final line a stunning shift of rhetoric catapults the reader from elegiac generality to a marine image at once elemental and metaphysical:

>The shark
>Glides white through the phosphorus sea.

In its radically different way, the image of the shark in the glittering water is profoundly related to the 'truth' revealed at last to the College Colonel. All Melville's thoughtful men, at bottom, are Ishmael contemplating the fiery try-works.

Three more pairs of related poems conclude this survey of *Battle-Pieces*. One of these pairs, explicitly connected by overt reference to the first armored naval encounter, are 'The Temeraire,' in which the battle of the *Monitor* and the *Merrimac* is alluded to in an explanatory subtitle, and 'A Utilitarian View of the Monitor's Fight.' The first is largely nostalgic, a sentimental paean to the wooden battleships of the heroic age, inspired by J. M. W. Turner's famous painting of a once-noble participant in the battle of Trafalgar being towed to the scrapyard by (in Melville's words) 'a pigmy steam-tug.' A prophetic dread of the mechanization of warfare, which is only an undercurrent here, becomes thematic in the second poem. Instead of emphasizing the romance of a lost glory, in these lines Melville sardonically praises the new-style 'blacksmith's fray' in which victory is achieved 'by crank, Pivot, and screw.' He foresees, not an end to war, but the reduction of warfare to its proper place 'Among the trades and artisans,' and the dwindling of the soldier to the engineer. Again, Melville achieves a memorable concluding image in which the fires of technology consume the gentlemanly trappings of a dying military ethos –

>And a singe runs through lace and feather.

Given Melville's philosophic bent, it is not surprising that many of the battle-pieces have a reflective quality far transcending their occasional character. One such poem is 'The House-top,' subtitled 'A Night Piece.' The occasion is the New York draft riot of July, 1863, precipitated by the enactment of a measure enabling conscripted men to purchase immunity from service. To Melville this anarchy in the streets was a frightening parable of human depravity unleashed. Like Conrad, he saw society with a Hobbesian eye, and contemplated with horror the sudden release of men from the normal constraints of law and morality.

> All civil charms
> And priestly spells which late held hearts in awe –
> Fear-bound, subjected to a better sway
> Than sway of self; these like a dream dissolve,
> And man rebounds whole aeons back in nature.

This is precisely the fate of the infamous 'Mistuh Kurtz' at his lonely outpost up the Congo River in *Heart of Darkness*. But, unlike Conrad's festering jungle, Melville's New York is 'redeemed' by the force of military suppression. What emerges with such clarity from this short poem is Melville's fundamental religious stance. Listening to 'the Atheist roar of riot,' he wrote these lines 'corroborating Calvin's creed' and denying, as he always had denied, 'that Man is naturally good.' But 'The House-top' is not merely a case study in Melville's religious thought; as its title and subtitle suggest, it is a lyric as well, evoking a scene and a mood before moralizing on them. The ominous sights and sounds of a city night in midsummer are felt like a weight, the roof-tops under the stars are perceived as a wasteland, and a sense of impending doom is conveyed in an opening sentence sharper and more impressionistic than any other in Melville's writings: 'No sleep.'

Another example of the extraction of philosophic substance from the mundane realities of war is the curious metaphor of 'Dupont's Round Fight.' As an old sailor Melville would naturally have admired the tactical neatness with which Samuel Francis Dupont reduced two rebel fortresses flanking Port Royal Sound, South Carolina, by the symmetrical expedient of steaming in a circle and firing at each fort in turn. What Melville the artist saw in this maneuver was a Platonic principle uniting warfare, mathematics, astronomy, and poetry. As in 'The House-top,' his deeper subject is law. Here, however, he refers to its most cosmic sense, making the 'victory of LAW,' with which the poem ends, virtually a pun. The ultimate subject of the poem is not even law, really, even in that expanded sense, so much as it is art itself. 'Rules' and 'Unity' and 'geometric beauty' are the values extolled in these lines, as in that later poem, 'Greek Architecture,' seemingly so remote from the matters of war. 'Dupont's Round Fight' is in this sense the strangest of Melville's battle-pieces, and the one most important to understand if one is not to fall into the ancient error of judging Melville a merely primitive poet, or – more commonly – a merely romantic one.

141

On the other hand, Melville was undeniably a poet of feeling above all: 'I stand for the heart,' he had written to Hawthorne. 'To the dogs with the head!' And perhaps his final claim to eminence among American poets of the Civil War lies in the depth of sympathy communicated in the best of the battle-pieces. 'Shiloh' and 'Malvern Hill' are two brief elegies in which grief and hope are reconciled through the healing agency of nature. Both poems draw their power from an implicit contrast between human carnage and the still persistence of birds and trees. Both poems form closed circuits of imagery, 'Malvern Hill' framed by its waving elms, 'Shiloh' bounded by the recurring flight of swallows. Almost none of Melville's characteristic awkwardness creeps in to mar the nineteen spare lines of 'Shiloh,' which he fittingly called 'A Requiem.' The wheeling swallows control the poem with natural grace, carrying the mind across the now silent field of violence and death, and performing a kind of benediction in their flight. The neutrality of birds, too, hovers over the memory of combat, lending a perspective in which

> dying foemen mingled there –
> Foemen at morn, but friends at eve –
>> Fame or country least their care:
> (What like a bullet can undeceive!)

The sardonic parenthesis is just a passing touch of the old Ishmael, like a birthmark on the poem, and then the quiet music of the closing lines covers the bitterness:

> But now they lie low,
> While over them the swallows skim,
>> And all is hushed at Shiloh.

III

The last forty years of Melville's life, once regarded as a desert of silence, have gradually been filled in by the industrious scholarship of the mid-twentieth century; but the decade following the publication of *Battle-Pieces* remains *terra incognita*. At the end of that time, and nearly twenty years after the experience it reflects, *Clarel: a Poem and Pilgrimage to the Holy Land* appeared. The length of its gestation is scarcely to be wondered at, since it is one of the longest poems in English, nearly twice as long as *Paradise Lost*.

Clarel is in some ways the mystery among Melville's works. It is his 'lost' book, dropped almost stillborn from the press, quietly dismissed by

142

the author himself, and buried in nearly total neglect until exhumed in a masterful modern edition by Walter Bezanson in 1960. From a practical point of view this massive artifact is what, if it had been an architectural edifice, might have been called a 'folly': it is a monumental oddity, built at incredible pains in an inaccessible place for private and self-justifying reasons. Apart from a neurotic compulsion to self-expression, however, its resemblance to the Bavarian dream-castles of Ludwig is quickly exhausted; the romantic excesses of aesthetic debauch have nothing in common with Melville's Faustian drive to penetrate and master the ethical nature of his world. *Clarel* is in every line the product of the restless and elevated spirit who, in Hawthorne's memorable phrase, could 'neither believe nor be comfortable in his unbelief.' If it is in one sense a masterpiece of eccentricity, it is in another and equally valid sense the most plausible of Melville's productions. Given his life-long, agonized concern with religious and philosophical questions; given his wish from earliest days to write as he pleased, without regard to expectation or gain; given his personal pilgrimage to the Holy Land, still untapped in the well of experience; given the turn from prose to poetry thereafter; given, finally, the leisure after routine working hours to undertake a writing project as interminable as Penelope's web; given all these conditions, *Clarel* has an almost classic inevitability.

The book it most resembles among Melville's prior writings is *Mardi*, which shares its conception, its bulk, and its besetting faults. Both works recount the strenuous pursuit of spiritual resources, a search for nothing less than bedrock Truth. The persons portrayed in both are dramatized attitudes, aspects of the author's own nature, participants in an interior dialogue. The common narrative is a running critique of the times, Melville's dialectical views of past, present, and future, of faith, materialism, and progress. There are of course just as many points of difference, chief of them being the inescapable marks of a ripened sensibility. *Clarel* has none of *Mardi*'s variety and humor; in place of those ingratiating qualities stands a merciless and unwavering intensity of analysis that exposes the raw bones of nineteenth-century civilization. *Clarel*, as every critic – every reader – remarks, is Melville's ultimate wasteland, making of the arid and stony Palestinian landscape a perfect natural symbol of the sterility confronting modern man at what ought to be the life-giving fountain-head of his human hopes.

Like *Mardi*, too, *Clarel* runs upon a thin story line defined by the episodic adventures of a questing hero. The 'Taji' of *Clarel* is the title character, a nearly faceless figure, curiously devoid of dramatic interest.

143

This youthful American student is clearly an *alter ego*, yet he is not made the narrator, as Taji had been in *Mardi*, and he serves as a focal point more by default than by virtue of any sympathy generated by his personality or any concern raised by his vicissitudes. Among the manifold weaknesses of the poem, the vapidity of its central figure is the most damaging, allowing an already attenuated narrative to go slack at its very heart. But Clarel is at least, and at most, a type of the sensitive searcher for truth, and as such he reminds the reader, through his periodic reappearances, what the poem at large is about. It is about 'the growth of a poet's mind,' as Wordsworth said of *The Prelude*. But Melville entered the ranks of the Victorian poets at the end of his growth, and his great verse autobiography is an attempt to describe ends rather than beginnings. *Clarel* is not Prelude but Epilogue.

To the extent that the poem has life as philosophical reminiscence, it is not in the title character that it lives, but in a variety of more fully realized personages with whom Clarel travels and talks. In a helpful appendix to his uniformly helpful edition, Bezanson identifies thirty-two significant characters, counting Nehemiah's ass, of whom ten are 'major.' Most of these important figures group themselves, again with Bezanson's editorial assistance (lxx–lxxii), into three 'clusters' which illuminate both their relationships and the center around which they have their planetary existence.

Closest to young Clarel are two older Americans, Rolfe and Vine, by all odds the most interesting creations in the poem. Although Melville projected some part of himself into all the central characters, it is Rolfe who became his self-portrait as ex-sailor, world traveler, seeker and skeptic. One autobiographical passage may stand for many scattered through Rolfe's scenes: exploring the precipitous hills about Mar Saba (III. xxix), he recalls experiences essentially those of Melville in Typee, which the aging Melville was still later to recall in two short poems, 'The Enviable Isles' and 'To Ned.' Internally, the portrait of Rolfe reflects the deepest grounds of his creator's self-respect: the manly balance of head and heart, the unflinching penetration of mysteries, the outspoken earnestness which Hawthorne's reserve had taught him to recognize as a perhaps excessive virtue.

It is in fact precisely that remembered relationship which he portrayed in the interaction between Rolfe and Vine. Against Rolfe's bluff wish to have everything out is set Vine's reticence and unwillingness to open himself to others, his instinct to observe rather than participate. More than once on the long journey Vine's friends are repelled by some impalpable barrier of aloofness, of disengagement on his part, nowhere more tellingly than when he permits himself a flicker of wry amusement at a tourist in the garden of Christ's passion, and Clarel wonders at the brief glimpse into Vine's hidden nature: 'Paul Pry? and in Gethsemane?' (I.xxx.113). Melville could hardly have forgotten that 'a spiritualized Paul Pry' was the personal and artistic ideal Hawthorne had set for himself in 'Sights from a Steeple.' At any rate, Vine is pictured as a potential source of much solace and inspiration, who subtly frustrates his companions by withholding more from them than they withhold from him. The full expression of Melville's personal frustration in his strangely withered relationship with Hawthorne emerged only in the last year of his life when, in *Timoleon*, he published the little elegiac 'Monody' which opens his heart and also reveals the source of the curious name given the Hawthorne figure in *Clarel*:

> To have known him, to have loved him
> > After loneness long;
> And then to be estranged in life,
> > And neither in the wrong;
> And now for death to set his seal –
> > Ease me, a little ease, my song!
>
> By wintry hills his hermit-mound
> > The sheeted snow-drifts drape,
> And houseless there the snow-bird flits
> > Beneath the fir-trees' crape:
> Glazed now with ice the cloistral vine
> > That hid the shyest grape.

Flanking the central cluster of skeptical humanists are two contrasting clusters of lesser figures, almost foils, whose opposing views on questions of faith form the principal dialectic of the poem. Representing acceptance, either on naïve and mystical grounds or on grounds of good form and expediency, are Nehemiah and Derwent respectively. The former has a certain saintly unreality, but Derwent, an Anglican clergyman, is a complex and convincing portrait of a sophisticated Man of God, sincere and likeable but incapacitated for the deepest levels of human intercourse by a philosophy rooted in taste and optimism rather than conviction. He is a lineal development of the Reverend Mr Falsgrave in *Pierre*.

More to Melville's mind were the 'no-sayers' who resolutely resisted the easy answers of confidence men – men of confidence – even to the

145

self-destructive extreme of cynicism. A cluster of these bleak but intensely active spirits occupies a prominent place in the pilgrimage. Two in particular, Mortmain and Ungar, express and perhaps exorcise the demons of doubt and despair that colored the most characteristic thoughts of Melville's mature years. Another way of saying this is that they precipitated the Ahab qualities out of Rolfe and thus enabled Melville to confront the implications of his own darker impulses in dramatically discrete form without diminishing his essential sympathy with them. To carry the point a step farther, Mortmain himself may be seen as a precipitate of Ungar, subtracting from the character of the life-challenger the suicidal excesses of negation which remove him from the action before it has run its course. In diametrical contrast to Derwent, who blinds himself to all but the brightest views of things, Mortmain, whose very name means 'dead hand,' is never more in character than when he stoops to drink of the bitter waters of the Dead Sea (II.xxxiv).

It is Ungar, after the death of Mortmain, who dominates the fourth and final stage of the pilgrimage. A 'wandering Ishmael from the West,' he speaks for all who, like Melville, are 'by the adverse wind / of harder fortunes . . . / Kindled from ember into coal' (IV.x.189–93). This kindling effect is obvious in page after page where the quality of the verse rises in response to Melville's intimate relish in the tough-mindedness of his most disillusioned character. Witness Ungar on English and American materialism, an indictment of undiminished relevance:

'The Anglo-Saxons – lacking grace
To win the love of any race;
Hated by myriads dispossessed
Of rights – the Indians East and West.
These pirates of the sphere! grave looters –
Grave, canting, Mammonite freebooters,
Who in the name of Christ and Trade . . .
Deflower the world's last sylvan glade!' (IV.ix.118–26)

Or this prophecy of 'an Anglo-Saxon China . . . / In the Dark Ages of Democracy':

'Whatever happen in the end,
Be sure 'twill yield to one and all
New confirmation of the fall
Of Adam. Sequel may ensue,
Indeed, whose germs one now may view:

Myriads playing pygmy parts –
Debased into equality:
In glut of all material arts
A civil barbarism may be:
Man disennobled – brutalized
By popular science – Atheized
Into a smatterer – ' (IV.xxi.130–40)

Even before the advent of Ungar in book IV, Melville's most exciting verse is written in his spirit, as in the high-Victorian canto on Science and Religion, where the author in his own voice questions

Bright visions of the times to be – . . .
Before the march in league avowed
Of Mammon and Democracy?
          In one result whereto we tend
Shall Science disappoint the hope,
Yea, to confound us in the end,
New doors to superstition ope? (III.v.155–62)

In the end, it is not even the liveliest of the characters, and certainly not anything resembling a plot, that commends *Clarel* to a modern reader. It is as one man's spiritual epic that it must be read. Despite the concreteness, often quite vivid, of its landscape, the Palestine in which its slow events unroll is, like *Mardi*, a 'world of mind.' Its essential story springs from an intolerable yet inescapable skepticism, like that of the crippled Celio, who complains to his Christian God that 'the shark thou mad'st, yet claim'st the dove' (I.xiii.71), or the unflinching Rolfe, who sees his world as it is and asks:

          'They who freeze
On earth here, under want or wrong;
The Sermon on the Mount shall these
Find verified? is love so strong?' (III.iii.21–4)

The heart of the poem is not at all a statement, though the lyric affirmation of the Epilogue is commonly cited to the contrary, but rather a question, most poignantly posed by Clarel at David's Well, thirsting for the 'sweet water' of peace and certitude which he may never taste:

'But whither now, my heart? wouldst fly
Each thing that keepeth not the pace
Of common uninquiring life?

147

What! fall back on clay commonplace?
Yearnest for peace so? sick of strife?'

And then, though it is a rhetorical question, Clarel concludes his soliloquy with the query that may stand as the theme of the poem: 'how live / At all, if once a fugitive / From thy own nobler part?' (IV.xxviii.80–6).

The real trouble with *Clarel* is that it has gross defects as a poem. Defend it as we may, the tedium of its length, combined with the truncation of its octosyllabic line, produces a deadly conflict of aesthetic means. Reading it through, one finds continual support for the doctrinaire contention of Poe that there is no such thing as a long poem. *Clarel* contains passages of high intensity and great lyric beauty, but perhaps one canto only of the one hundred and fifty is a true, self-contained poem: the short (40-line) canto entitled 'Prelusive' (II.xxxv), in which the surrealistic prison prints of Piranesi are used as a metaphor for the involuted dungeons of the human heart. Taken in its vast and rather barren totality, *Clarel* is likely to betray the reader into the ludicrous error of the traveler who looked into the crater of Vesuvius and could see nothing in it. *Clarel* does not exist apart from the fires beneath its surface. It was composed by the Herman Melville who had written *Moby-Dick* and had yet to produce *Billy Budd*, and it is important if only because it is there. The reader who is willing to give enough of himself to it may be unexpectedly rewarded, if not by the whole of the work, then by glimpses of transcendent brilliance, such as Rolfe's insight concerning the door in the rock at Petra – a 'poem' to add to Melville's other great verses on art, and to set in the field of American poetry beside Wallace Stevens's 'Anecdote of the Jar.'

Mid such a scene
Of Nature's terror, how serene
That ordered form. Nor less 'tis cut
Out of that terror – does abut
Thereon: there's Art.' (II.xxx.41–5)

IV

In view of the tremendous productivity to which Melville was excited by his early public acceptance as a novelist, one wonders what prodigies he might have produced in verse in his later years had he been given the faintest encouragement. Since he received none, he wrote for himself – and perhaps for a discriminating posterity. What he liked best he preserved ultimately in the two privately printed volumes that complete the canon of his published work; the rest he 'immolated' or left aside in manuscript.

John Marr and Other Sailors (1888) is a tiny collection of eighteen titles and seven small 'Pebbles,' as he called them, all devoted to maritime subjects. Most of them, naturally enough, are heavily nostalgic, although the latent sentimentality of the best of them is offset by the hard wisdom that characterizes Melville's backward glances. Among his unpublished poems is one that exactly expresses this retrospective ambivalence:

> Time's Long Ago! Nor coral isles
> In the blue South Sea more serene
> When the lagoons unruffled show.
> There, Fates and Furies change their mien.
> Though strewn with wreckage be the shore,
> The halcyon haunts it; all is green,
> And wins the heart that hope can lure no more.

Two of the *John Marr* poems, 'To Ned' and 'The Enviable Isles,' recall these very scenes in uneven but compelling lines. The latter, especially, articulates an irony reminiscent of the double vision engendered by the title of 'The Encantadas.' Taken together, these late poems have been seen to unlock the deepest meanings of *Typee* amd *Omoo*.

Other poems, notably the first four in the collection, recall the world of *Redburn* and *White-Jacket*, or anticipate the world of *Billy Budd*. Their common subject is the portrayal of retired and remembered sailors, such as Jack Chase or Melville's cousin Guert Gansevoort. Anyone who has read the ballad which concludes *Billy Budd*, 'Billy in the Darbies,' has read the best thing Melville composed in that vein.

Two major 'Sea-Pieces,' so called, in *John Marr* are both skillful and profound. The better of the two, 'The Aeolian Harp,' has already been discussed. 'The Haglets' is at once a more ambitious and a less accessible poem than its companion piece; but it tells well a story of triumph and tragedy, and it uses to fine effect the symbolic value implicit in the 'haglets' themselves – three following gulls, three following fates. In the end, the density of its long sequence of eighteen-line stanzas gives way to the sudden simplicity of two final eight-line stanzas in trimeter. Thus stripped down, the essential imagery of the poem focusses on the wreck at the bottom of the sea and the refracted light upon the surface, producing at night

     The rays that blend in dream
     The abysm and the star.

These two sea-pieces, flawed though they may be in details, repay close
reading by anyone pondering the question of whether Melville ever
passed the primitive stage of development as a poet.

     Several of what Melville called his 'Minor Sea-Pieces' bear similar
marks of the thematic imagery of his sea novels. 'The Tuft of Kelp' and
'The Maldive Shark,' widely anthologized, fairly represent the pessimistic cast of mind that dwells on the bitterness of the weed and the
insensate malice of the predator. Or perhaps the irony of these poems is
even more characteristic: the co-consequence of bitterness and purity,
the co-existence of friendly pilot-fish and 'Pale ravener of horrible meat.'
Less familiar, 'The Berg,' subtitled 'A Dream,' recalls one of the most
memorable images of *Moby-Dick*: the blank forehead of the white whale,
which contained force sufficient to sink ships but yielded no hint of
intelligible expression. Part of Melville's problem in *Moby-Dick* was to
elevate the antagonism of Ahab and the whale above the level of personal
hostility to a point where it might plausibly assume the lineaments of a
cosmic struggle. In conveying the sense of that impersonal confrontation
the iceberg is an ideal natural symbol, standing somewhere between the
moving bulk of the sperm whale and the brick canyon of Bartleby's Wall
Street. Melville makes the most of its 'heartless immensities' (*Moby-
Dick*, ch. 42), emphasizing in every line the simple inertia of its mass,
which sends down 'the impetuous ship in bafflement' but shows no jar
or tremor along its 'dead indifference of walls.' The theme is fundamentally identical with that of 'The Aeolian Harp' and of those segments of
Clarel relating to the desert, the Dead Sea, and the 'blank, blank towers
[of] Jerusalem' (I.i.61).

     The philosophical concerns in poems like these link *John Marr* and
Clarel with the forty-odd poems gathered together and published in the
last year of Melville's life under the title *Timoleon*. About half of the
pieces in this final collection are grouped under the subtitle 'Fruit of
Travel Long Ago.' These poems are as retrospective as the sea-pieces of
John Marr, but they deal with memories and impressions of the 1857
trip to Europe and the Middle East. The best of them rise above their
merely historical and geographical interest and reflect the deepest
impulses of Melville's creative mind. At least two are of remarkable brilliance. 'In a Church of Padua' describes a confessional booth observed in
the church of St Anthony, the shape and use of which struck a stunning
analogy in his imagination:

> Dread diving-bell! In thee inurned
> What hollows the priest must sound,
> Descending into consciences
> Where more is hid than found.

At the opposite extreme from this imagery of darkness and submergence is the language of 'In the Desert,' which is really a hymn to light. The emphasis is quite properly on language in speaking of this poem, because perhaps nowhere in Melville's verse is his diction more sharply selected and compressed than in these lines. One image betrays his customary sailor's eye – 'Like blank ocean in blue calm' – but elsewhere predominates the imagery of flame, a word repeatedly suggested by rhyme or parallel but never actually employed. Most striking is the ironic force achieved by the juxtaposition of Napoleon's transitory triumph in Egypt and his inexorable defeat by the power of nature: 'bayonetted by this sun / His gunners drop beneath the gun.' In its prevailingly incantory quality, 'In the Desert' is unlike anything else in Melville's writings.

Not surprisingly, the poems that have attracted most critical attention in *Timoleon* are two which deal overtly with sex. The shorter and simpler of these, 'In a Bye-Canal,' transposes to Venice an experience Melville actually had in Cairo, according to his journal. Perhaps it was not so much an experience as what Joyce would have called an 'epiphany,' a sudden, full-blown sense of significance in the casual circumstances of a fleeting moment. As Melville dramatized it in this poem, the moment is a meeting of his glance from a passing gondola with that of a 'siren,' one of the city's 'deadly misses,' at a latticed window. It is an idle encounter – not even an encounter – but full of portent for the man who has taken the measure of all other evils and temptations in life:

> I have swum – I have been
> Twixt the whale's black flukes and the white shark's fin.

The poem has a light, almost jaunty, ending, as he stirs up the gondolier and congratulates himself on his Ulysses-like escape; but these lines midway in it are incontestably somber and speak emphatically of the power of sex, and perhaps of its repression, in Melville's emotional life.

Reflecting the same impulse and counter-impulse, but through a much more elaborate structure, is 'After the Pleasure Party.' Much has been made of the difficulties of this poem, but most of them have been generated by gratuitous psychoanalytical attempts to construe it as autobiography. There are no hints of a personal source for this poem in

151

Melville's journals, and the rhetoric of it establishes it clearly enough as the soliloquy of a female intellectual who has discovered too late that the austere pleasures of science, even the consolations of art and religion, are inadequate substitutes for the instinctual joys of young love. One approach to the poem that may minimize its apparent perplexities is to read it as one might read Milton's 'L'Allegro' and 'Il Penseroso' or Anne Bradstreet's 'The Flesh and the Spirit.' It is simply an inner dialogue between the heavenly and earthly parts of human nature, only in Melville's version 'Amor incensed' has the last word. No doubt he was wise to locate this debate in the heart of a woman and to make the woman an astronomer (Urania). Contrasting her, or having her contrast herself, with a barefoot peasant girl ('some radiant ninny') was easy; the psychic frustration which is the theme of the poem emerges with unlabored inevitability from that natural tension. In order to appreciate Melville's reversal of the Puritan dialectic, it may be helpful to glance in comparison from Milton and Bradstreet to Marvell and Herrick. The concluding couplet of 'After the Pleasure Party' echoes 'To the Virgins to Make Much of Time,' and the most remarkable section of the poem, complaining of the sexual division of nature, could hardly have been written unmindful of 'To His Coy Mistress':

> What Cosmic jest or Anarch blunder
> The human integral clove asunder
> And shied the fractions through life's gate?

But the most telling comparisons may be made with T. S Eliot's 'The Love Song of J. Alfred Prufrock,' one of the seminal poems of the twentieth century. Melville's poetry is not uniformly up to Eliot's, but its psychological theme and its bold associational logic place it far ahead of its time.

No other poems in *Timoleon*, no other poems that survive from Melville's pen, are of greater poetic power than 'After the Pleasure Party.' A few more deserve mention for the unabated rigor of their skeptical thought and the frequent felicity of their form and language. 'The Age of the Antonines,' though hardly a masterpiece of verse, is interesting as the final expression of Melville's political thought, looking back to a golden age of Roman history and drawing melancholy contrasts with the Gilded Age of America. Lovers of Hardy's bitter verses will take pleasure in 'The Margrave's Birthnight,' a Christmas poem similar in theme and tone to Hardy's 'The Oxen.' Two other poems are worth reading together for what they show of the unresolved tension in

152

Melville's mind between the constructive and destructive aspects of his life-long search for truth. On the one hand, the pair of corrosively cynical quatrains labeled 'Fragments of a Lost Gnostic Poem of the 12th Century' claim not only the inevitable triumph of brutality in the world but even the inevitable subversion of the good. On the other hand, 'The Enthusiast,' which appropriately extracts a line from *Job* for an epigraph, voices a ringing appeal, quite devoid of irony, for fixed ideals and steadfastness of purpose. As in so many of Melville's poems, occasional descents into mediocrity along the way are stunningly compensated in the closing lines:

> Walk through the cloud to meet the pall,
> Though light forsake thee, never fall
From fealty to light.

V

Scores of poems remain, many left in manuscript at Melville's death, all now available in print to the adventurous reader. The present survey must conclude by looking at two more specimens which have been widely admired in the twentieth century. Both possess a valedictory quality which makes its quiet commentary on the spirit of *Billy Budd* and offers the most balanced statement Melville left us of what his life had made him as man and poet.

'Pontoosuce' or 'The Lake' – the manuscript ponders both titles – paints a passionately loved moment of autumn in the Berkshire countryside near Pittsfield, Massachusetts. It is Melville's most Keatsian poem, both in its imagery and in its theme of natural mutability. The self-enforced comparison with Keats is necessarily to Melville's disadvantage, and may give us a final measure of how far short he fell of greatness among the chief romantic poets. But it reaffirms at the same time the company in which his sensibility lived and deserves to be judged. As in most of his poems, there are lines that rise ('And orchards ripe in languorous charm') and lines that sink ('A thought as old as thought itself, / And who shall lay it on the shelf!'). The thought referred to, being as old as thought itself, is not of remarkable originality; yet there is a warmth and breadth in the elderly Melville's quiet acquiescence in a state of nature which he had spent most of his life protesting: 'The workman dies, and after him, the work'; and the end of his brief reflection on death and renewal is the wisdom of age in its most pristine form: 'Let go, let go!'

The understanding that Melville had wrung from a strenuous and largely unappreciated life of creative thought is expressed finally in *Billy Budd* – where it is commonly misunderstood – but also in the nine lines of 'Lone Founts,' where it cannot possibly be misunderstood. These lines echo a philosophy touched on earlier, as in ' ' 'The Coming Storm,' ' ' or 'Jimmy Rose,' but distilled here in its most unalloyed essence:

> Though fast youth's glorious fable flies,
> View not the world with worldling's eyes;
> Nor turn with weather of the time.
> Foreclose the coming of surprise:
> Stand where Posterity shall stand;
> Stand where the Ancients stood before,
> And, dipping in lone founts thy hand,
> Drink of the never-varying lore:
> Wise once, and wise thence evermore.

The critical question of Melville's standing among the poets in English will not easily be settled, but a score or so of poems attest to the powers of imagination and language that produced *Moby-Dick*. In this small poem from his last year Melville affirmed both his dream and his capacity to

> Stand where Posterity shall stand;
> Stand where the Ancients stood before.

Bibliographical Notes

Chapter 1   The Time of Melville

The most comprehensive and digestible single-volume work on American history, and the one on which I have drawn most heavily, is Samuel Eliot Morison, *The Oxford History of the American People* (New York, 1965). An excellent short interpretive account is Henry Bamford Parkes, *The American Experience* (New York, 1947). Indispensable for the central period of Melville's life is Arthur M. Schlesinger, Jr, *The Age of Jackson* (Boston, 1945). A valuable study which focusses more narrowly on the events of the crucial year 1850 and their relevance to Melville's most significant work is Alan Heimert, '*Moby-Dick* and American Political Symbolism,' *American Quarterly*, 15 (1963), 498–534. For background on Melville's New York, Bayrd Still's *A Mirror for Gotham* (New York, 1956) offers a well-edited compilation of contemporary descriptions. Perry Miller, *The Raven and the Whale* (New York, 1956) deals directly with the literary life of New York 'in the era of Poe and Melville.'

Three books are especially useful on the maritime history and technology so important for an understanding of Melville's milieu: Samuel Eliot Morison, *The Maritime History of Massachusetts, 1783–1860* (Boston, 1921); Robert G. Albion and others, *New England and the Sea* (Middletown, Conn., 1972); and Alexander Laing, *The American Heritage History of Seafaring America* (New York, 1974). The most substantial book on whaling in particular is Eduard A. Stackpole, *The Sea-Hunters* (Philadelphia, 1953).

The intellectual and cultural life of Melville's times, especially of the formative years between the War of 1812 and the Civil War, has received classic treatment in Vernon L. Parrington, *Main Currents of American Thought*, vol. II: *The Romantic Revolution, 1800–1860* (New York, 1927). However, it is necessary to supplment Parrington with more recent and specialized scholarship. A good survey of the major stages in the history of American ideas is Richard D. Mosier, *The American Temper: Patterns of our Intellectual Heritage* (Berkeley, 1952). Two helpful books on the background of ideas are Perry Miller, *The Life of the Mind in America: from the Revolution to the Civil War* (New York, 1965); and Richard Hofstadter, *Anti-intellectualism in American Life* (New York, 1964), Two works of great value on the foreground of thought and taste are Carl Bode, *The Anatomy of American Popular*

155

Culture, 1840–1861 (Berkeley, 1959), reprinted under the title *Antebellum Culture* (Carbondale, Ill., 1970); and James D. Hart, *The Popular Book: a History of America's Literary Taste* (New York, 1950). Both of these studies contain extensive bibliographies. The usefulness of two contemporary novels, *Home As Found* by James Fenimore Cooper (1838), and *The Gilded Age* by Mark Twain and Charles Dudley Warner (1873), has been stressed in the text.

Fundamental to all historical studies of American authors is the *Literary History of the United States*, edited by Robert E. Spiller and others (New York, 1948), 2 vols and bibliography; bibliographical supplements, 1959 and 1972.

Chapter 2 Melville in His Time

Brief and fragmentary accounts of Melville's life by those who knew him or were contemporary with him have been collected by Merton M. Sealts, Jr, *The Early Lives of Melville: Nineteenth Century Biographical Sketches and Their Authors* (Madison, Wis., 1974). Full-scale biography began with Raymond Weaver, *Herman Melville, Mariner and Mystic* (New York, 1921). It was brought to something like a definitive state when the fruits of several decades of research were gathered by Jay Leyda in *The Melville Log: a Documentary Life of Herman Melville, 1819–1891*, 2 vols (New York, 1951, suppl. 1969). The standard narrative biography, based on the material of the *Log*, is Leon Howard, *Herman Melville* (Berkeley, 1951). The most recent life, Edwin Haviland Miller's *Melville* (New York, 1975), offers a coherent but overdramatized Freudian portrait. Other book-length works having the appearance of biographies (Mumford, Arvin, Mason, *et al.*) are more properly critical and interpretive studies and are listed in the General Bibliography.

The chief task of biographical research has been to discover historical information to replace conjecture based on an autobiographical reading of Melville's books. The two studies which have made the most important contributions to this effort are Charles R. Anderson, *Melville in the South Seas* (New York, 1939, 1966); and William H. Gilman, *Melville's Early Life and Redburn* (New York, 1951). Between them, these works make possible an authoritative reconstruction of the formative quarter century of Melville's life preceding his career of professional authorship.

Melville's letters have been collected and annotated by Merrell R. Davis and William H. Gilman in *The Letters of Herman Melville* (New Haven, 1960), and many documents and family traditions were assembled by Melville's granddaughter, Eleanor Melville Metcalf, in *Herman Melville: Cycle and Epicycle* (Cambridge, Mass., 1953). The notebooks are available as follows: *Journal of a Visit to London and the Continent by Herman Melville, 1849–1850*, ed. Eleanor Melville Metcalf (Cambridge, Mass., 1948); and *Journal of a Visit to Europe and the Levant, October 11, 1856–May 6, 1857*, ed. Howard C. Horsford (Princeton, 1955). Melville's essay 'Hawthorne and His Mosses' was first collected in *The Apple-Tree Table and Other Sketches* (Princeton, 1922), and has since been reprinted in many places, including *Herman Melville: Representative Selections*, ed. Willard Thorp (New York, 1938); and Edmund Wilson, *The Shock of Recognition* (New York, 1943, 1955), an anthology which takes its title from Melville's essay.

Most of the facts and quotations in this chapter may be found in the *Log* or the *Letters*, with some assistance from Alice Kenney, *The Gansevoorts of Albany* (Syracuse, 1969); and R. H. Stoddard, *Recollections, Personal and Literary* (New York, 1903).

Chapter 3   Travel Romance: *Typee* and *Omoo*

The vogue for travel and its literature in nineteenth-century America is treated by Foster Rhea Dulles, *Americans Abroad* (Ann Arbor, 1964); Carl Bode, *Antebellum Culture*, chapter 15; and Nathalia Wright, 'The Influence of Their Travels on the Writers of the American Renaissance,' *Emerson Society Quarterly*, 42 (1966), 12–17. The relationship between Melville's experiences in Polynesia and his uses of them in *Typee* and *Omoo* is documented by Charles R. Anderson, *Melville in the South Seas,* books 2 and 3.

The reception of Melville's books is detailed by Hugh W. Hetherington, *Melville's Reviewers* (Chapel Hill, 1961); and sampled by Hershel Parker, *The Recognition of Herman Melville* (Ann Arbor, 1967). Representative responses are also included in *The Melville Log.*

The fundamental simplicities of *Typee* and *Omoo* resist elaborate interpretation, but the views of them expressed here owe something to the following commentators: D. H. Lawrence, *Studies in Classic American Literature* (New York, 1923), chapter 10; R. W. B. Lewis, *The American Adam* (Chicago, 1955), 134–6; A. N. Kaul, *The American Vision* (New Haven, 1963), 214–38; Lillian Beatty, 'Typee and Blithedale – Rejected Ideal Communities,' *Personalist*, 37 (1956), 367–78; Richard Ruland, 'Melville and the Fortunate Fall: Typee as Eden,' *Nineteenth Century Fiction*, 23 (1968), 312–23.

Chapter 4   Philosophical Allegory: *Mardi* and *The Confidence-Man*

The artistic importance of *Mardi* was recognized by F. O. Matthiessen, *American Renaissance* (London and New York, 1941). Its genesis was charted by Merrell R. Davis, *Melville's Mardi: a Chartless Voyage* (New Haven, 1952). Davis also expounded a characteristic device of the allegory in 'The Flower Symbolism in *Mardi*,' *Modern Language Quarterly*, 2 (1942), 625–38. The allusive and cabalistic quality of *Mardi*, though judiciously handled by Davis, is a standing invitation to esoteric readings, such as the intricate horoscopic cryptogram proposed by Maxine Moore, *That Lonely Game: Melville, Mardi, and the Almanac* (Columbia, Missouri, 1975). Relevant traditions of sea literature are treated by Thomas Philbrick, *James Fenimore Cooper and the Development of American Sea Fiction* (Cambridge, Mass., 1961); the quotation in the text is on pages 228–9.

Scholarship has taken two approaches to *The Confidence-Man*. Historical research has reconstructed much of the public matrix of opportunism and charlatanry that forms the thematic background of the satire. A specific historical model for the title character is proposed by J. D Bergmann, 'The Original Confidence Man,' *American Quarterly*, 21 (1969), 560–77. Also helpful are

Carl Bode, *Antebellum Culture*, 133–5; parts of Arthur M. Schlesinger, Jr, *The Age of Jackson*; and two books by Van Wyck Brooks, *The World of Washington Irving* (New York, 1944), and *The Times of Melville and Whitman* (New York, 1947).

A second approach to *The Confidence-Man* has been through textual analysis, mostly symbolic, and the effort to find illuminating antecedents or analogues in literary history. Representative studies are E. H. Rosenberry, 'Melville's Ship of Fools,' *PMLA*, 75 (1960), 604–8, and Helen P. Trimpi, 'Harlequin-Confidence-Man: the Satirical Tradition of Commedia Dell'Arte and Pantomime in Melville's *The Confidence-Man*,' *Texas Studies in Language and Literature*, 16 (1974), 147–93. The effort to deduce how Melville constructed the book, and hence what he intended it to say, has been made by Watson G. Branch, 'The Genesis, Composition, and Structure of *The Confidence-Man*,' *Nineteenth Century Fiction*, 27 (1973), 424–48; but the conclusions, apart from a structural model similar to the one outlined here, should be weighed in the light of Hershel Parker's cautionary rejoinder, '*The Confidence-Man* and the Use of Evidence in Compositional Studies,' *ibid.*, 28 (1973), 119–24. See the note on *Moby-Dick*, below, for a parallel case. The best comprehensive analysis of *The Confidence-Man* remains that of Elizabeth S. Foster in the Introduction to her edition of the text (New York, 1954).

A specific interpretive problem alluded to in the text is the question of Melville's intention in ending his story with a statement seeming to indicate that it was to be continued. Melville's own justification of this truncation is implicit in *Pierre*, VII.8, where he argues the superiority of books that 'never unravel their own intricacies, and have no proper endings.' It no longer seems sensible to argue, as was once done, that *The Confidence-Man* is an unfinished work, simply dropped in exhaustion or disgust. Rather it may be regarded as a very precocious work. Recent studies of the modern novel and its development make the point that precisely the kind of openness or indeterminateness which has so disturbed critics of *The Confidence-Man* is a distinguishing mark of the novel in the twentieth century, as opposed to that of the nineteenth and before, in which the task of the novelist was to clear up all mysteries and bring events to a stand by the final page. In the words of Frank Kermode, *The Sense of an Ending* (New York, 1967), 64: 'We no longer live in a world with an historical *tick* which will certainly be consummated by a definitive *tock*.' See also Robert M. Adams, *Strains of Discord: Studies in Literary Openness* (Ithaca, NY, 1958); and Alan Friedman, *The Turn of the Novel: the Transition to Modern Fiction* (New York, 1966).

Chapter 5 Novel of Character and Initiation: *Redburn* and *White-Jacket*

The major problem in the proper understanding of *Redburn* and *White-Jacket* is the degree and manner of Melville's use of his own experiences in composing them as works of fiction. There is no reason to suppose that he himself thought of them as anything more than a loose form of journalism, but his clear effort to achieve a certain level of imaginative generalization in both books makes it important to locate with as much accuracy as possible the line of demarcation between report and invention. The most valuable studies of this question, already cited in chapter 2, are Gilman's *Melville's Early Life and Redburn* and Anderson's *Melville in the South Seas.* To these authorities must be added Howard P. Vincent, *The Tailoring of White-Jacket* (Evanston, Ill., 1970), a systematic investigation of the sources of that book as well as of the process of its composition.

The resultant literary character of *Redburn* and *White-Jacket* is a matter of ongoing critical discussion. The present account places them in the general tradition of the initiation novel or *bildungsroman*, but that classification is intended to be suggestive rather than definitive. The term *bildungsroman* was originally applied in German criticism to certain large-scale biographical novels of a heavily romantic cast by Goethe, Jean Paul Richter, and others, then adopted to describe the derivative English tradition starting with the novelistic portion of Carlyle's *Sartor Resartus* and extending into similar fictions by most of the major Victorian novelists. The works of Melville under discussion in this chapter are much lighter in texture and more modest in scope than such models, although Melville's interest in them at precisely this point in his career is attested by the record of his reading in 1850, which included all three of the authors mentioned above. But allowing for differences in tone and scale, *Redburn* and *White-Jacket* taken together, as here proposed, constitute an essential *bildungsroman* in their cumulative exploration of the spiritual education of a sensitive youth. My object is not to place Melville in the German tradition extending from Goethe and Jean Paul to Mann and Hesse, but to focus attention on the springs and trials of personal growth which give fullest meaning to the books in question. The reader who wishes to investigate the history of the term and the characteristics of the literature it designates will find a convenient overview in G. B. Tennyson, 'The *Bildungsroman* in Nineteenth Century English Literature,' *University of Southern California Studies in Comparative Literature*, 1 (1968), 135–46; and a fuller treatment in Susanne Howe, *Wilhelm Meister and His English Kinsmen: Apprentices to Life* (New York, 1930). A broader and more recent treatment is Jerome H. Buckley, *Season of Youth: The Bildungsroman from Dickens to Golding* (Cambridge, Mass., 1974). Buckley's introductory chapter is an excellent overview of the field, and its concluding pages are especially helpful in defining the shadow area between autobiography and fiction. None of these sources consider American literature. A relevant but limited study is Heinz Kosok, 'A sadder and a wiser boy: Herman Melville's *Redburn als Novel of Initiation*,' *Jahrbuch für Amerikastudien* (1965). William B. Dillingham, *An Artist in the Rigging: the Early Work of Herman Melville* (Athens, Ga, 1972), examines themes of initiation and development in these books from a different point of view.

Chapter 6   Epic Romance: *Moby-Dick*

The voluminous research and critical writing on *Moby-Dick* is surveyed historically and sampled by Hershel Parker in *The Recognition of Herman Melville* and in two collections which he edited in collaboration with Harrison Hayford:

Moby-Dick, Norton Critical Edition (New York, 1967), and *Moby-Dick as Doubloon: Essays and Extracts (1857–1970)* (New York, 1970). The latter work contains a definitive annotated bibliography from the year 1921, when the 'Melville revival' began. Melville's sources and his uses of them are exhaustively studied by Howard P. Vincent, *The Trying-out of Moby-Dick* (Boston, 1949). Among historic assessments and reassessments of the art of *Moby-Dick* two that have attained classic status are D. H. Lawrence, *Studies in Classic American Literature* and F. O. Matthiessen, *American Renaissance*.

The classification of *Moby-Dick* as a type of prose fiction is a difficult and unresolved question. Forster's proposal is symptomatic of the special effort required, and is quite compatible with the description of the work in this chapter. Northrop Frye's classification in *Anatomy of Criticism* (Princeton, 1957), p. 313, is also helpful, but the characteristics signaled by his term 'romance-anatomy' are more readily assimilated by the uninitiated reader through the traditional concepts of epic and romance. The kind of book Melville thought he was writing is described by Helen P. Trimpi, 'Conventions of Romance in *Moby-Dick*,' *Southern Review*, 7 (1971), 115–29.

Much of the mystery of Melville's intention in *Moby-Dick* might be dispelled if the process of its composition were understood. Most perplexing is the extent and nature of the Hawthorne influence, about which more is conjectured than known. A tradition of radical revision under that impetus takes its rationale from George R. Stewart, 'The Two *Moby-Dicks*,' *American Literature*, 25 (1954), 417–48. This hypothesis has been challenged on one side by James Barbour, 'The Composition of *Moby-Dick*,' *ibid*., 47 (1975), 343–60, who argues a three-stage process; and on the other by Jerome M. Loving, 'Melville's Pardonable Sin,' *New England Quarterly*, 47 (1974), 262–78, who favors a unitary process and calls into question the fundamental character of the Hawthorne connection. Unfortunately, no manuscript survives to settle the matter.

The influence of Emerson has also received much attention. Charles Feidelson, *Symbolism and American Literature* (Chicago, 1953) demonstrates Melville's debt to Emerson in his literary method, while Milton R. Stern, *The Fine Hammered Steel of Herman Melville* (Urbana, Ill., 1957) makes the case against Emersonianism in Melville's thought. Other notable treatments have been William Braswell, 'Melville as a Critic of Emerson,' *American Literature* 9 (1937), 317–34; E. J. Rose, 'Melville, Emerson, and the Sphinx,' *New England Quarterly* 36 (1963), 249–58; Perry Miller, 'Melville and Transcendentalism,' *Nature's Nation* (Cambridge, Mass., 1967), 184–96; and dissertations by B. R. N. Blansett (University of Texas, 1963) and J. B. Williams (University of Southern California, 1965). The general assumption, based on context, that Melville's praise of 'men who dive' was directed at Emerson has been challenged by Heyward Ehrlich, *Bulletin of the New York Public Library*, 69 (1965), 661–4, but his argument is not convincing.

On the question of point of view and narrative consistency, two of the latest critical works devoted to *Moby-Dick* are representative of the contemporary shift of attention from Ahab to Ishmael and of the concomitant interpretation of the story in terms of the narrative consciousness of Ishmael. Paul Brodtkorb, Jr, *Ishmael's White World: a Phenomenological Reading of Moby-Dick* (New

Haven, 1965), and Robert Zoellner, *The Salt-Sea Mastodon: a Reading of Moby-Dick* (Berkeley, 1973) both argue that the story cannot exist outside the mind of the narrator, a view which perhaps unnecessarily restricts the perspective of criticism. See Wayne Booth, *The Rhetoric of Fiction* (Chicago, 1961), 160. 'In dealing with the types of narration,' Booth remarks, 'the critic must always limp behind, referring constantly to the varied practice which alone can correct his temptations to overgeneralize' (page 165). See also Louis D. Rubin, Jr, *The Teller in the Tale* (Seattle, Wash., 1967), 212.

Chapter 7   Social Novel: *Pierre*

The commercial aspects of Melville's career have been studied by William Charvat, 'Melville's Income,' *American Literature*, 15 (1943), 251–61, reprinted in *The Profession of Authorship in America, 1800–1870* (Columbus, Ohio, 1968); and by G. Thomas Tanselle, 'The Sales of Melville's Books,' *Harvard Library Bulletin*, 17 (1969), 190–215. The detailed story of Melville's struggle to become a professional novelist, culminating in the disastrous hybrid *Pierre*, is told by Charvat in an extended essay left unfinished at his death and published in the 1968 volume as chapter XII.

The American popular novel in the mid-nineteenth century has attracted a number of good historians. My treatment of it here quotes James D. Hart, *The Popular Book*, 91, and Herbert Ross Brown, *The Sentimental Novel in America, 1789–1860* (New York, 1959), 360, 362. Other sources of general assistance are Carl Bode, *Antebellum Culture*; Alexander Cowie, *The Rise of the American Novel* (New York, 1951); Helen W. Papashvily, *All the Happy Endings: a study of the domestic novel in America, the women who wrote it, the women who read it, in the nineteenth century* (New York, 1956), with good bibliography; and Fred L. Pattee, *The Feminine Fifties* (New York, 1940).

Much of the philosophical speculation about *Pierre* is of little use to the general reader. Henry A. Murray's credentials as a psychologist give weight to his interpretive insights in the introduction and notes to the Hendricks House edition (1949) of the novel. My suggestion of a resemblance between Pierre and Hawthorne's Hollingsworth (*The Blithedale Romance*, written the same year) is taken from Murray's discussion of that relationship, pages lxxvi–lxxvii. For Melville's expressed interest in the character of Clifford Pyncheon, see his letter to Hawthorne, April 16, 1851. The comic and satiric aspects of *Pierre*, including what I have alluded to as the 'Hyena syndrome,' are treated in my *Melville and the Comic Spirit* (Cambridge, Mass., 1955), and expanded in useful directions by Richard B. Hauck, *A Cheerful Nihilism: Confidence and 'the Absurd' in American Humorous Fiction* (Bloomington, Ind., 1971).

Chapter 8   Historical Romance: *Israel Potter* and *Billy Budd*

The scholarship on *Israel Potter* is almost too slight, as that on *Billy Budd* is almost too voluminous, for useful notice here. My own studies of these works are reflected in the text: 'Israel Potter, Benjamin Franklin, and the Doctrine of

Self-Reliance,' *Emerson Society Quarterly*, 28, part 3, (1962), 27–9; and 'The Problem of *Billy Budd*,' *PMLA*, 80 (1965), 489–98. The relationship between Melville's and Whitman's uses of the John Paul Jones story is examined by Jack Russell, '*Israel Potter* and "Song of Myself"', *American Literature*, 40 (1968), 72–7. Research and criticism on *Billy Budd* through 1962 is listed by Harrison Hayford and Merton M. Sealts, Jr, in their definitive edition of the novel (Chicago, 1962). Bibliography and selected criticism are also to be found in William T. Stafford, ed., *Melville's Billy Budd and the Critics* (San Francisco, 1961); and Howard P. Vincent, ed., *Twentieth Century Interpretations of Billy Budd* (Englewood Cliffs, New Jersey, 1971).

Chapter 9   Short Stories and Sketches

Until recently Melville's short fiction attracted little sustained study. The first and still valuable collection of essays on the stories is Richard H. Fogle, *Melville's Shorter Tales* (Norman, Okla, 1960). A more systematic view of Melville as a short-story writer, focussing on sources and techniques, is R. Bruce Bickley, *The Method of Melville's Short Fiction* (Durham, NC, 1975). Two more books have been published too recently to be described here: William B. Dillingham, *Melville's Short Fiction, 1853–1856* (Athens, Ga, 1977), and Marvin Fisher, *Going Under: Melville's Short Fiction and the American 1850s* (Baton Rouge, La, 1977).

Periodical studies abound, particularly on the major tales. *Bartleby the Scrivener, a Symposium* (Kent, Ohio, 1966) contains research, criticism, and annotated bibliography. Two collections of essays, both with bibliography, have been published on 'Benito Cereno': *Melville's Benito Cereno*, ed. John P. Runden (Boston, 1965); and *A Benito Cereno Handbook*, ed. Seymour L. Gross (Belmont, Cal., 1965). Concerning the lesser tales there is wide critical divergence, both on the value of the stories as art and on the fundamental question of their meaning. The search for hidden meanings began with the demonstration of sexual symbolism in 'The Tartarus of Maids' by E. H. Eby, *Modern Language Quarterly*, 1 (1940), 95–100, and has proceeded with less justification to stories like 'The 'Gees,' where Bickley (56–8) and others now find twentieth-century liberal themes which might or might not have been shared by Melville; see Carolyn L. Karcher, 'Melville's "The 'Gees"': a Forgotten Satire on Scientific Racism,' *American Quarterly*, 27 (1975), 421–42.

Manuscript material mentioned in this chapter may be located as follows: Elizabeth Melville's private memoir of her husband is quoted extensively by Raymond Weaver in his biography and his edition of Melville's *Journal Up the Straits* (New York, 1935), and is printed in its entirety by Merton M. Sealts, Jr, in *The Early Lives of Melville*; Melville's story, 'The Two Temples,' is included with other fugitive prose in vol. 13 of the Constable edition of the complete works; Melville's outline of a story about a widow named Agatha will be found in his letters to Hawthorne dated August 13 and October 25, 1852.

Chapter 10   Poetry

In addition to the four volumes of poetry discussed in Chapter 10, Melville projected but did not live to publish a collection of reminiscent verses to be dedicated to Elizabeth under the title of 'Weeds and Wildings, with a Rose or Two,' and a group of sketches in prose and verse dealing with an imaginary 'Burgundy Club' and its guiding spirits the Marquis de Grandvin and Jack Gentian. All of these fragments are printed in vol. 16 of the Constable edition of Melville's works, and the versified portions in the Hendricks House edition of the *Collected Poems* (see General Bibliography). With the exception of *Battle-Pieces* and *Clarel*, Melville's poetry awaits definitive editing. Inadequacies and errata in the *Collected Poems* (1947) are damaging in themselves and misleading to critics whose judgments may be invalidated by corrupt texts: e.g. William B. Stein, *The Poetry of Melville's Late Years* (Albany, NY, 1970). A reliable critical survey is William H. Shurr, *The Mystery of Iniquity: Melville as Poet, 1857–1891* (Lexington, Ky, 1972). Readers who wish to supplement Bezanson's commentary in the Hendricks House edition of *Clarel* (1960) may consult Vincent Kenny, *Herman Melville's Clarel: a Spiritual Autobiography* (Hamden, Conn., 1973).

Several editors of selections from Melville's poetry have commented on it illuminatingly: F. O. Matthiessen, *Selected Poems of Herman Melville* (Norfolk, Conn., [1944]); Hennig Cohen, *Selected Poems of Herman Melville* (Garden City, NY, 1964); and Robert Penn Warren, *Selected Poems of Herman Melville* (New York, 1970). Critics and literary historians who treat Melville's verse as part of the larger field of American poetry are inclined to hold it in low esteem: Edmund Wilson, *Patriotic Gore* (New York, 1962); Denis Donoghue, *Connoisseurs of Chaos* (New York, 1965); Hyatt H. Waggoner, *American Poets* (Boston, 1968). Authors of comprehensive critical studies of Melville (see General Bibliography) invariably value the poems according to the thematic continuities or autobiographical revelations they discover in them.

General Bibliography

The major historical and biographical sources, together with textual and critical authorities on individual works, have been cited in the Bibliographical Notes to the chapters. The supplementary listing which follows consists of, 1, editions of Melville's works, 2, bibliographies, and, 3, major books of criticism.

1 Editions of Melville's works

There are three collected editions. The first, the Constable edition (C), edited by Raymond Weaver in 16 volumes, London, 1922–4 (reprinted 1963), is outmoded but still the only complete edition. The second, the Hendricks House edition (HH), produced seven volumes by various hands between 1947 and 1969. The third, the Northwestern-Newberry edition (NN), was begun in 1968 at Evanston, Illinois, the Northwestern University Press, under the general editorial direction of Harrison Hayford, and has produced to date seven volumes in chronological sequence. In addition, all of Melville's novels and many of the poems and short stories are now available in inexpensive, well-edited reprints. The following list indicates the original date of publication and the collected edition, if any, in which it has been reprinted. As a rule, the latest text establishes the standard.

Typee, 1846; C, NN.
Omoo, 1847; C, HH (1969), NN.
Mardi, 1849; C, NN.
Redburn, 1849; C, NN.
White-Jacket, 1850; C, NN.
Moby-Dick, 1851; C, HH (1952), NN.
Pierre, 1852; C, HH (1949), NN.
Israel Potter, 1855; C.
The Piazza Tales, 1856; C, HH (1948).
   'Bartleby the Scrivener,' 1853
   'The Encantadas,' 1854
   'The Lightning-Rod Man,' 1854
   'The Bell-Tower,' 1855
   'Benito Cereno,' 1855

'The Piazza,' 1856

The Confidence-Man, 1857; C, HH (1954).

Battle-Pieces and Aspects of the War, 1866; C (vol. 16, *Poems*), HH (1947, *Collected Poems*); and scholarly editions by Sidney Kaplan, 1960, and Hennig Cohen, 1963.

Clarel, 1876; C, HH (1960).

John Marr and Other Sailors, 1888; C (vol. 16, *Poems*), HH (1947, *Collected Poems*).

Timoleon, 1891; C (vol. 16, *Poems*), HH (1947, *Collected Poems*).

The Apple-Tree Table and Other Sketches [uncollected periodical publications not included in *Piazza Tales*], Princeton, 1922; C (vol. 13, *Billy Budd and Other Prose Pieces*).

'Hawthorne and His Mosses,' 1850

'Cock-a-doodle-doo!' 1853

'The Fiddler,' 1854

'Poor Man's Pudding and Rich Man's Crumbs,' 1854

'The Happy Failure,' 1854

'The Paradise of Bachelors and the Tartarus of Maids,' 1855

'Jimmy Rose,' 1855

'The 'Gees,' 1856

'I and My Chimney,' 1856

'The Apple-Tree Table,' 1856

Billy Budd, [1924]; C. Pending publication in NN the standard edition is *Billy Budd, Sailor*, ed. Harrison Hayford and Merton M. Sealts, Jr, Chicago, 1962.

2 Bibliography

Descriptive listings of the published writings of Melville may be found in Meade Minnegerode, *Some Personal Letters of Herman Melville and a Bibliography* (New York, 1922), in vol. 12 of the Constable edition of the collected works, and in an appendix to Raymond Weaver's biography.

The best reference bibliography to date is that of Stanley T. Williams, revised by Nathalia Wright, in *Eight American Authors, a Review of Research and Criticism*, ed. James Woodress (New York, 1956, rev. 1971). This is supplemented by the Melville chapter under various hands in *American Literary Scholarship: an Annual*, ed. J. Albert Robbins (1965-72) and James Woodress (Durham, NC, 1973 to date), and by listings compiled quarterly in *American Literature* and annually in *PMLA*. An indexed listing by Beatrice Ricks and J. D. Adams, *Herman Melville: a Reference Bibliography, 1900-1972* (Boston, 1973), is comprehensive but undependable. An indispensable key to the author's literary background is Merton M. Sealts, Jr, *Melville's Reading: a Checklist of Books Owned and Borrowed* (Madison, Wis., 1966).

3 Criticism

The history of Melville's reception is set forth with generous documentation by Hershel Parker, *The Recognition of Herman Melville* (Ann Arbor, 1967); and by Watson G. Branch, *Melville: the Critical Heritage* (London, 1974).

Most of the major studies of American literature produced in this century give prominent attention to Melville, starting with Carl Van Doren's *The American Novel* (New York, 1921) and D. H. Lawrence's *Studies in Classic American Literature* (New York, 1923). Among the most important critical studies in which Melville figures significantly are: W. H. Auden, *The Enchafèd Flood* (New York, 1950); Richard Chase, *The American Novel and Its Tradition* (Garden City, NY, 1957); Charles Feidelson, *Symbolism and American Literature* (Chicago, 1953); Harry Levin, *The Power of Blackness* (New York, 1958); R. W. B. Lewis, *The American Adam* (Chicago, 1955); F. O. Matthiessen, *American Renaissance* (London and New York, 1941); and Joel Porte, *The Romance in America* (Middletown, Conn., 1969).

General critical studies devoted to Melville are numerous and uneven in value. Near the head of any list must stand Newton Arvin, *Herman Melville* (New York, 1950); Ronald Mason, *The Spirit Above the Dust* (London, 1951); and William E. Sedgwick, *Herman Melville: The Tragedy of Mind* (Cambridge, Mass., 1944). Most provocative from a psychological point of view is Richard Chase, *Herman Melville: A Critical Study* (New York, 1949); from a literary point of view, Warner Berthoff, *The Example of Melville* (Princeton, 1962). It is a tendency of critical studies to adopt a method or an interpretive thesis which may create distortion in the service of coherence. Among those which can be recommended with that *caveat* are Lewis Mumford, *Herman Melville* (New York, 1929, rev. 1962); Lawrance Thompson, *Melville's Quarrel with God* (Princeton, 1952); Milton R. Stern, *The Fine Hammered Steel of Herman Melville* (Urbana, Ill., 1957); Merlin Bowen, *The Long Encounter: Self and Experience in the Writings of Herman Melville* (Chicago, 1960); James E. Miller, *A Reader's Guide to Herman Melville* (New York, 1962); Edgar A. Dryden, *Melville's Thematics of Form* (Baltimore, 1968); and John Seelye, *Melville: the Ironic Diagram* (Evanston, Ill., 1970).

Certain other studies are partial in the sense that they deal with special topics or limited aspects of the subject: William Braswell, *Melville's Religious Thought* (Durham, NC, 1943); Nathalia Wright, *Melville's Use of the Bible* (Durham, NC, 1949); Henry F. Pommer, *Milton and Melville* (Pittsburgh, Pa, 1950); Edward H. Rosenberry, *Melville and the Comic Spirit* (Cambridge, Mass., 1955); Dorothee M. Finkelstein, *Melville's Orienda* (New Haven, 1961); H. Bruce Franklin, *The Wake of the Gods: Melville's Mythology* (Stanford, 1963); and Richard H. Brodhead, *Hawthorne, Melville, and the Novel* (Chicago, 1976).

Index

167

Index

Eliot, T. S., 'The Love Song of J.
Alfred Prufrock,' 152
Emerson, Ralph Waldo, 10, 12,
13, 16, 18, 32, 52, 75, 84;
'The American Scholar,' 74;
'Hamatreya,' 138

Fern, Fanny [Sara P. Willis], 88
Fielding, Henry, *Tom Jones*, 55
Fly, Eli, 22, 118
Forster, E. M., *Aspects of the
Novel*, 73
Franklin, Benjamin, 5, 53, 103–8
Fuller, Thomas, 60

Gansevoort, Guert (cousin), 33,
112, 149
Gansevoort, Gen. Peter
(grandfather), 20
Gansevoort, Peter (uncle), 32
Gifford, Sanford R., 137
Goethe, J. W. von, 90
Greene, Richard Tobias ('Toby'),
23, 25, 36, 42

Hardy, Thomas, 'The Oxen,' 152
Harper and Brothers, 29
Harper's New Monthly Magazine,
29, 114, 121, 123
Hawthorne, Nathaniel, 1, 5–6,
12, 14, 15, 18, 19, 25, 26,
27–30, 32, 36, 41, 42, 50, 71,
84, 87, 88, 96, 121, 126, 127,
129, 130, 137, 142, 143,
144–5; 'The Artist of the
Beautiful,' 130; 'The
Birthmark,' 130; *The
Blithedale Romance*, 41, 93;
The English Notebooks, 30;
'Ethan Brand,' 130; *The House
of the Seven Gables*, 14, 35,
93; *Mosses from an Old Manse*,
27, 57, 114; 'Rappaccini's
Daughter,' 130; *The Scarlet
Letter*, 32, 71–2, 87; 'Sights
from a Steeple,' 145
Hawthorne, Sophia, 29
Herrick, Robert, 'To the Virgins

to Make Much of Time,' 152
Holmes, Oliver Wendell, 29; 'The
Last Leaf,' 20
Homer, 74

Irving, Washington, 13, 15, 25,
66, 87, 123; *Bracebridge Hall*,
36; 'Rip Van Winkle,' 104;
The Sketch Book, 132

Jackson, Andrew, 11, 13
James, Henry, 55
James, William, *Naval History of
Great Britain*, 111
Jefferson, Thomas, 15
Johnson, Samuel, *Rasselas*, 40
Jones, John Paul, 103, 105–8
Joyce, James, 100

Keats, John, 27, 153

Lincoln, Abraham, 15, 16, 134,
137
Literary World, The, 12, 25, 27,
36, 59
Locke, John, 123
Longfellow, Henry W., 17, 37
Lowell, James Russell, 15, 17,
126

Mackenzie, Alexander Slidell, 112
Martineau, Harriet, 6, 16
Marvell, Andrew, 'To His Coy
Mistress,' 152
Mather, Cotton, *Magnalia Christi
Americana*, 130
Mathews, Cornelius, 25
Matthiessen, F. O., 44
Melvill, Allan (father), 4, 20
Melvill, Maj. Thomas
(grandfather), 20
Melvill, Thomas, Jr (uncle), 21,
22
Melville, Elizabeth Shaw (wife),
25, 32, 109, 115
Melville, Gansevoort (brother), 21,
22, 25, 62
Melville, Herman, works by: 'The

168